Packaged Vacations

UNIVERSITY PRESS OF FLORIDA

Florida A&M University, Tallahassee
Florida Atlantic University, Boca Raton
Florida Gulf Coast University, Ft. Myers
Florida International University, Miami
Florida State University, Tallahassee
New College of Florida, Sarasota
University of Central Florida, Orlando
University of Florida, Gainesville
University of North Florida, Jacksonville
University of South Florida, Tampa
University of West Florida, Pensacola

University Press of Florida

Gainesville

Tallahassee

Tampa

Boca Raton

Pensacola

Orlando

Miami

Jacksonville

Ft. Myers

Sarasota

PACKAGED

Vacations

Tourism Development
in the Spanish Caribbean

Evan R. Ward

13 12 11 10 09 08   6 5 4 3 2 1

Library of Congress Cataloging-in-Publication Data
Ward, Evan R.
Packaged vacations: tourism development in the Spanish Caribbean/
Evan R. Ward.
p. cm.
Includes bibliographical references and index.
ISBN 978-0-8130-3229-0 (alk. paper)
1. Tourism—Caribbean Area. I. Title.
G155.C35W37 2008
338.4'79172900917561—dc22
2007047541

The University Press of Florida is the scholarly publishing agency
for the State University System of Florida, comprising Florida A&M
University, Florida Atlantic University, Florida Gulf Coast University,
Florida International University, Florida State University, New
College of Florida, University of Central Florida, University of
Florida, University of North Florida, University of South Florida,
and University of West Florida.

University Press of Florida
15 Northwest 15th Street
Gainesville, FL 32611–2079
http://www.upf.com

$14.50

*Dedicated to Jennie and Sydney, my travel companions,
and David Pearson, a Caribbean visionary*

Contents

List of Illustrations

Acknowledgments

This book would not have been possible without the assistance of many individuals and organizations. While space does not allow me to mention everyone who assisted along the way, I would like to name a few individuals, including Patricia Holley, Daniel G. Heimmermann, Robert Adler, Dean Vagn Hansen, Vice President G. Daniel Howard, Provost Roosevelt Newson, President William G. Cale, former interim president Garry Warren, and former president Robert Potts, all from the University of North Alabama (UNA). Sue Nazworth patiently processed my interlibrary loan requests. The College of Arts and Sciences and the University Research Office at UNA provided research grants at various stages of the project. Jennifer A. Rodgers, an undergraduate in the Department of Geography, created a beautiful map for the book, and Rebecca Green, an undergraduate in the Department of History and Political Science, ably compiled the bibliography.

Several important conferences and research grants also laid the foundations for this book. The Rockefeller Archive Center (Pocantico, New York), and the incomparable assistance of Amy Fitch, served as a launching ground for this project during a funded archival visit in 2003. The Hagley Museum (Wilmington, Delaware) provided an opportunity to share my ideas on Cuban tourism development at a conference in 2004. Philip Scranton and Janet F. Davidson subsequently offered helpful feedback on my project in conjunction with publishing the proceedings from that conference. Larry Clayton, University of Alabama, offered critical insight and opened his Latin American seminar to a presentation on Mexican tourism. The William Clements Center (Southern Methodist University) funded a symposium in 2005 and 2006 on border consumer culture that allowed me to create a paradigm for

Mexican tourism development. Alexis McCrossen ably coordinated the conference and encouraged me with my project at all stages. Bradley Coleman, command historian, U.S. Southern Command (Miami, Florida), graciously offered me an opportunity to share a paper on Cuban tourism development at the 2006 American Historical Association meetings.

In the field, David Pearson, of David Pearson and Associates (Miami, Florida), and Frank Rainieri Sr., of Grupo Puntacana, facilitated a research trip to the Dominican Republic, where the Rainieri family, including Frank Elías Rainieri and Francesca Rainieri, along with Grupo Puntacana management figures such as Adolfo Ramírez, Patricia Salazar, Carlos de Freitas, Jake Kheel, Walter Zemialkowski, and Francisco Alba, patiently answered questions. Administrative assistant Yajira Sosa brought everything together there. The perspicacious Wilson Andujar gave me an insightful guided tour of Punta Cana and Bávaro on that trip. Paola Rainieri offered helpful suggestions in revising the section on Punta Cana. In Mexico, Rodrigo Villagomez, director of marketing for Fondo Nacional de Fomento al Turismo (FONATUR), and his office staff (Mexico City), including Mariana Sánchez Gómez, prepared documents and arranged interviews for my research visit. The FONATUR staff in Ixtapa (Mexico), especially Manuel Arce Rodea, Gloria Angélica Hernández Peña, and Alejandra Guzman Nuricumbo, gave me an overview of a planned Mexican tourist community. FONATUR's Cancún director, Ricardo Gabriel Alvarado Guerrero, offered early insight into the evolution of Mexico's most famous planned resort. Finally, in Cuba, executives and employees of Cubanacán, Sol Meliá, and Iberostar consented to be interviewed. Ramón Martín Fernández, at the University of Havana's Centro de Estudios Turisticos, explained the uniqueness of Cuban tourism. Christina Molina (Sol Meliá Corporate Headquarters, Palma de Mallorca, Spain) and Ron Roy (Sol Meliá North America) provided significant insight on the expansion of Sol Meliá into the Americas. Gabriel Cánaves of Sol Meliá in Havana also answered important queries.

For my research on Puerto Rico, Dwayne Cox, at the Auburn University Archives (Auburn, Alabama), facilitated my research on Floyd Hall and Dorado Beach Resort. Near-centenarian Floyd Hall patiently answered my questions over the telephone about his career with Eastern Airlines and Caribbean tourism. Cathleen Baird, former archivist and librarian of the Conrad N. Hilton Library and Archives at the Conrad N. Hilton College of Hotel and Restaurant Management (University of Houston, Texas), provided important help on Hilton's developments in the Caribbean and the Habana Hilton in particular. In Washington, D.C., Stella Villagran, at the Columbus Library of the Organization of American States, prepared essential documents for the project. The resourceful used booksellers on Donceles Street in Mexico City once again delivered remarkable primary sources from their daunting stacks. Finally, the Archives staff at UNESCO in Paris scanned and provided vital documents.

Farther afield, a Rotary International Group Study Exchange Fellowship in 2005 allowed me to study Mediterranean tourism in Turkey, a helpful counterpoint to my studies of the Caribbean. Saudi architect Muhammed Abu Ablar (Fethiye, Turkey) graciously illustrated the viability of Spanish and Mexican architecture in the Eastern Mediterranean. Celebrated Spanish architect Alvaro Sans also provided information on resort design in the Americas.

Gillian Hillis, Jacqueline Kinghorn Brown, Eli Bortz, and Heather Romans made work with the University Press of Florida a pleasure. Former acquisitions editor Derek Krissoff took a chance on a unique project. Paul Wilkinson and an anonymous reviewer offered helpful suggestions to improve the manuscript. Robert Burchfield immeasurably improved the manuscript with helpful suggestions during copyediting.

Finally, I would like to thank God, my family, and my parents for their support throughout this project.

Two chapters of this book include material used with the permission of previous publishers. Chapter 8, "A Means of Last Resort," and the portion of the epilogue dealing with Havana and Varadero have been used with the permission of the University of Pennsylvania Press. They were originally published as part of a single essay by the author, "A Means of Last Resort: The European Transformation of the Cuban Hotel Industry and the American Response," in *The Business of Tourism: Place, Faith, and History*, edited by Philip Scranton and Janet F. Davidson (Philadelphia: University of Pennsylvania Press, 2007), and are reprinted by permission of the University of Pennsylvania Press. A small portion of chapter 1 has been adapted from my "International Basic Economy Corporation and the Transformation of Consumer Culture in the Americas 1946–1980," in *Rockefeller Archives Center Research Reports, 2004*, Rockefeller Archives Center, Pocantico, New York, and is reprinted with permission of the Rockefeller Archive Center.

Introduction

On July 27, 1961, after giving his blessing to sixty-four tourist cabanas, three shelters, and a club at the Playa Larga Tourist Center, Fidel Castro made his way to the Playa Girón Tourist Center some nine miles away. While Playa Girón (Bay of Pigs) held great political importance for Cuba, the tourist center—whose construction had been delayed by the American attack—was one of the Castro regime's boldest efforts to address chronic regional underdevelopment. Thousands of peasants joined three hundred national and foreign dignitaries to commemorate the triumph of the Revolution and inaugurate the two tourism centers. A visual and aural cacophony of revolutionary brigades led a parade before the reviewing stand. As one media report observed:

> The parade was headed by a group of peasant troubadours from various provinces wearing typical *sombreros* of palm straw, short peasant jackets and red kerchiefs. The native singers, who improvised revolutionary verses to the accompaniment of their trumpets, guitars, gourds and Maracas, won a resounding ovation. As the parade advanced, three planes flying in formation dropped flowers, pencils attached by little parachutes, [and] Conrado Benitez Brigade leaflets and decorative pennants. Then came a 73-piece Conrado Benitez literacy army rhythm band, followed by thousands of brigade members carrying pencils and notebooks. . . . Flowers decorated all the flag standards. Units with color guards, women's platoons, and groups of Young Rebels and Pioneers completed the brilliant but brief parade.

An awards ceremony for literacy efforts at Playa Girón and Playa Larga during the construction of the tourism infrastructure followed the parade.

As Castro addressed his audience, he used the platform to demonstrate the developmental role that the creation of the recreation centers could provide for the nation's workers. He reiterated the lack of accessibility to the Cienega de Zapata (where the two complexes were located) prior to execution of the project: "There were places in this [swamp] from which it took families three days to get out. . . . This was a zone which was completely cut off." Castro then hailed the transformation that had taken place during construction of the tourism centers. Draining marshes opened land for cultivation, literary brigades raised the general levels of education of local residents, and health care teams combated diseases such as typhoid, tetanus, and tuberculosis that had plagued the region. In sum, Castro emphasized the economic benefits of tourism development as he declared: "This is the part of our island which could be regarded as the most abandoned of all, the most forgotten, the poorest. Here, currently a change which has transformed it completely has been made. Family income is vastly higher . . . thousands of workers have been employed, . . . and currently there is also a large number of workers in housing construction."[1]

A third recreation center built near the Zapata National Park, at Guamá, celebrated Castro's appreciation of Cuban landscapes. Built on the Laguna de Tesoro, an inland lake that had gained international renown during the 1950s for its excellent trout fishing, Guamá foreshadowed the rise of exotic ecotourism resorts. In the wake of the Revolution, Castro commissioned architect Mario Girona and designer Gonzalo Córdoba to design fifty-nine geometric cabanas of differing configurations, including triangular, circular, octagonal, and two-floor structures, which would be distributed throughout the island. Boats and walkways connected the wooden structures, which were outfitted with wood and leather furnishings. To reinforce local identity, Cuban sculptor Rita Longa designed a museum at Guamá to celebrate native life on the island.[2] Subsequently, Cuban tourism retained vestiges of its unique natural packaging at the outset of the Cuban Revolution. Likewise, the strong relationship between decentralized tourism, economic development, and local culture and landscapes would be manifest elsewhere throughout the Caribbean basin in the post–World War II era. This was merely one variant of the "packaged vacation" shaped by unique political, economic, and cultural conditions in Cuba at the dawn of the age of mass tourism.

By the 1950s, the majority of Latin American nations, like Cuba, recognized the role of tourism as a tool for economic development, and as a product to be marketed to tourists from the developed world.[3] While European nations, such as Spain, played an indispensable role in the democratization and decentralization of the tourism experience on its beaches and islands, Caribbean nations contributed to the evolution of mass tourism as well.[4] By the late 1940s, for example, Puerto Rico had targeted upscale tourism as a means of promoting economic development through its much-publicized Operation Bootstrap.[5] The Mexican, Cuban, and Dominican governments soon followed suit, constructing tourism poles on the geographic peripheries of their nations to generate revenue and feature unique aspects of their cultures.[6] The purpose of this book is to examine the political, economic, and cultural forces that collided during the second half of the twentieth century to uniquely "package" some of the most important tourist poles in the Western Hemisphere, including Dorado Beach (Puerto Rico), Cancún (Mexico), Varadero (Cuba), and Punta Cana (Dominican Republic). The discipline of history offers important insights for understanding why these island destinations developed along distinctive economic, political, and social trajectories, despite sharing a common geographical region and language. An understanding of initial political, economic, social, and cultural conditions, as well as the global forces that shaped the creation of these tourist destinations, helps us better grasp why each of these localities is unique.[7]

This study also attempts to overcome a general weakness in the literature of tourism. Like many business-driven sectors, the tourism industry has often neglected to see the relevance of its past to its present and future. As R. G. Healy has observed:

> A key need [for tourism studies] is for retrospective studies of tourism development over relatively long periods of time. . . . Such studies should identify key policy choices at national, regional, and local levels, both within the tourism sector (e.g. policies to subsidize investment) and outside it (transportation systems). Particular attention should be paid to how policy choices have affected environmental impacts and the three classes of economic impacts . . . —linkages, locations, and beneficiaries.[8]

Accordingly, this book considers the short- and long-term effects of linkages between the political economies of Spanish-speaking nations in the Caribbean and their impact on the transformation of tourism under the import-substitution model. Each chapter explicitly or implicitly explores connections between state promotion of tourism and the behavior of the private sector in the industry.[9] In some locations, such as Mexico and Puerto Rico, state cooperation with the private sector was the modus operandi in tourism development. In Cuba, state tourism development under the Castro regime only took place with the retreat or expulsion of private hoteliers,

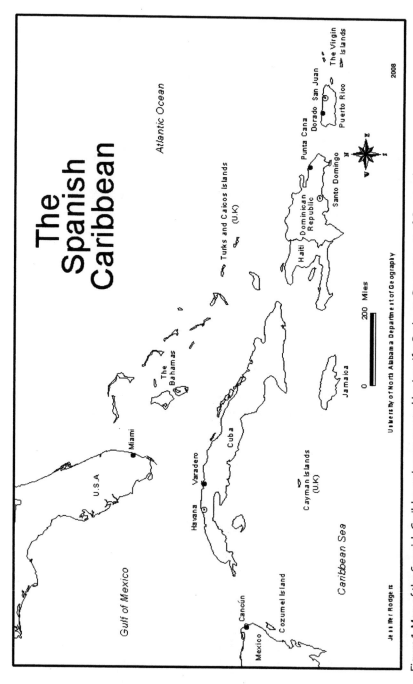

Figure 1. Map of the Spanish Caribbean. Image created by Jennifer Rodgers, Department of Geography, University of North Alabama (2008).

including Conrad Hilton and mob leader Meyer Lansky. The Cuban model has since retained linkages to capitalist tourism as a model for funding the socialist state. In the Dominican Republic, authoritarian ineptitude in the field of tourism development during the Rafael Trujillo dictatorship made private tourism development a more palatable option for private planners and developers interested in creating a world-class tourism infrastructure and superstructure.

This study examines the ramifications of national and private models of tourism development in rural areas throughout the Latin Caribbean in the post–World War II era. While tourism during the first half of the twentieth century was concentrated in and around metropolitan areas in the Caribbean, the mandate of using tourism for economic development pushed the frontiers of Caribbean tourism toward the edges of Latin American countries in the region after 1945. First, state governments exploited the myth that "sun and sand" tourism was eternally sustainable, anointing beach tourism as the preferred mode of tourism development. Second, the linkages between peripheral tourism poles and economic development also gave rise to creative ways of packaging tourism destinations that reflected their natural surroundings. At Dorado Beach, for example, the primary setting for guests at the RockResorts-run hotel was a former coconut plantation. At Cancún, state planners highlighted Mayan culture and the surrounding lowlands in the packaged environment on the Mexican periphery. In Cuba, tourism theorist Armando Maribona enjoined private groups in Trinidad to restore the colonial city so that tourists could experience the built environment of Cuba's best-preserved colonial city.

By the turn of the twenty-first century, however, efficient transportation linkages and/or vertical business organizations specializing in mass tourism transformed some of these tourism poles, which were initially decentralized, into "peripheral cores." Cancún morphed into the urban metropolis for a growing tourism corridor along the Riviera Maya, and the growth of the Punta Cana International Airport has contributed to the densification of tourism along the Punta Cana–Bávaro corridor on the eastern coast of the Dominican Republic.[10]

Ultimately, the linkages between political economy, spatial location, and culture provide the title and main theme of this book, as well as the questions it attempts to answer: How did the political, economic, social, and cultural conditions that accompanied the decentralization of tourism in the Latin Caribbean transform the packaging and presentation of international tourism there? And who were the creative individuals or agencies that had the vision to create these decentralized tourism zones, fraught as they were with the potential successes and challenges that each would face in its evolving social, political, economic, and cultural contexts?

This book is organized chronologically. The prologue briefly examines the aesthetics of air travel during the 1950s and 1960s. It metaphorically transports readers to Latin America, while also recognizing the art of catering to the cultural contexts of those nations serviced by various U.S. air carriers.

Part 1, "The American Caribbean," explores the urban and decentralized models of hotel and resort development in the Caribbean championed by U.S. investors during the 1940s and 1950s. Chapter 1 relies largely on documents from the Rockefeller Archive Center to reconstruct Nelson Rockefeller's involvement in the establishment of the Hotel Avila in Caracas, Venezuela, as well as Laurance Rockefeller's decentralized resorts (RockResorts) in Puerto Rico and the Virgin Islands. As part of his position as coordinator for Inter-American Affairs under President Franklin Roosevelt, Nelson Rockefeller helped to lay the foundation for American partnerships with local Latin businesspeople and their governments prior to the end of World War II in an effort to stave off European domination of the market after the war. Laurance Rockefeller's Caribbean resorts, operated under the RockResorts chain, offered a different aspect of American ingenuity in the region. Laurance Rockefeller's attention to the aesthetics of natural surroundings in the design of luxury resorts throughout the Caribbean created a model for self-contained resort communities that integrated hotels, residential communities, and golf courses, among other amenities. This chapter also explores the built environment of Rockefeller's resorts at Caneel Bay, St. John, American Virgin Islands, and Dorado Beach/Cerromar Beach outside of San Juan, Puerto Rico.

In a similar vein, chapters 2 and 3 explore Conrad Hilton's establishment of urban resorts in the Caribbean, drawing on materials from the Hospitality Industry Archives at the University of Houston's Conrad N. Hilton College of Hotel and Restaurant Management. Chapter 2 looks at Hilton's unique formula for crafting hotels that catered to both local and international clientele through the use of technological advancements in design and a globally trained staff. Chapter 3, in contrast, examines the place of Hilton International hotels within the social and cultural context of their host cities throughout the Caribbean. While Hilton's hotels often reconfigured the cultural focus of the elite in the host cities away from colonial centers, they also felt the effects of social and political upheaval in their new Latin American homes, particularly in the case of the Habana Hilton in 1960. In a changing political context, the Habana Hilton, which had anchored middle-class culture for a short year in the trendy Havana suburb of Vedado, became the centerpiece of an ideological struggle over the direction of Cuba's future. Ultimately, all three chapters illustrate that despite the high-minded efforts of the Rockefellers and Hilton to establish goodwill in Latin America through tourism development, political and social winds of change in the late 1950s and early 1960s gradually curtailed the interest of many American hoteliers from pursuing expansion in Latin America. At the same time, Europe and Asia were once again in a position to receive tourists, and companies such as Hilton International refocused their hotel-building energies to the east and west.

With the decline of American interest in private tourism development in the region, Latin American governments undertook their own developmental prerogatives in the field of tourism. Part 2, "The Latin Caribbean," examines three distinctive national models of tourism development in the region, including Puerto Rico, Cuba, and Mexico. Chapter 4 examines Puerto Rico's model for tourism development from the 1940s until the 1960s, which featured close relationships with American hotel developers, namely Conrad Hilton and Laurance Rockefeller. Hilton's arrangement with the Puerto Rican Industrial Development Company (PRIDCO), and its head, Teodoro Moscoso, is the most famous of these agreements, under which the Puerto Rican government built the Caribé Hilton in San Juan and gave Hilton International one-third of the revenue to manage the luxury hotel. To this point, however, very little has been written about the state's involvement in the evolution of Laurance Rockefeller's Dorado Beach Resort, twenty miles to the west of San Juan on the Atlantic Ocean. Documents from the Rockefeller Archive Center reveal the rigorous process of negotiation between PRIDCO and Laurance Rockefeller in the early 1950s to establish the resort. These documents ultimately highlight the shared negotiation of risk involved in developing peripheral resorts that required significant capital not only to build hotels but also to create a satisfactory number of leisure activities, including golf courses, to attract tourists away from urban hotels throughout the Caribbean. Chapter 5 examines a relationship of another sort in the expansion of the Dorado Beach Resort during the 1960s and 1970s. By studying former Eastern Airlines president Floyd Hall's papers, it is possible to examine what happened when Eastern Airlines purchased an 80 percent share in Dorado Beach and a 40 percent stake in RockResorts. Ill-fitted for tourism management, Eastern Airlines hoped to fund tourism development and route expansion throughout the Caribbean under Hall's direction by adding a large hotel, the Cerromar Beach Hotel, to the existing property at Dorado, Puerto Rico. The partnership provided the capital that Laurance Rockefeller desired to expand the resort, but laid the foundation for failure given the glut of hotel rooms in the nearby San Juan hotel market, as well as the declining image of the Puerto Rican tourism market.

Chapter 6 examines the reformist origins of revolutionary tourism in Cuba during the 1950s and 1960s. Through the writings of journalist, novelist, educator, artist, and Cuban tourism theorist Armando Maribona, we are able to understand linkages between competing models of Cuban tourism in the 1950s and their possible adaptation by the Castro government in the early 1960s. Maribona's writings explore the spatial diffusion of Cuban tourism away from Havana and its nefarious activities, focusing tourism instead on the natural beauty and cultural exoticism of the entire Cuban island. In doing so, Maribona offers a cultural, more so than an economic, justification for the decentralization of tourism. Basing his conclusions on the successful adaptation of "sun and sand" tourism on other Caribbean islands, Maribona exhibits a cosmopolitan understanding of Cuba's need to systematically innovate, or the country will continue to lose market share to other Caribbean tourism poles. The chapter concludes by suggesting possible links between Castro's interests in nature tourism and Maribona's earlier plans.

Chapter 7 offers a focused spatial analysis through historical documents of the evolution of Cancún's infrastructure and hotel superstructure. Utilizing memoirs, diagnostic reports from Mexico's Fondo Nacional de Fomento al Turismo (FONATUR) and other state agencies, government documents in the wake of Hurricane Wilma, and recent reflections on the changing nature of Cancún, the chapter explores the historical contingencies that have created Mexico's most important tourism pole, as well as the challenges Cancún has faced in confronting the reality of mass tourism as a revenue generator.

Part 3, "The Global Caribbean," examines the contemporary Caribbean, focusing on state and private projects in Cuba and the Dominican Republic. The use of the term "Global Caribbean" assumes the insertion of national tourism development projects or private projects into the global consumer economy.

Chapter 8 examines Cuba's turn to Europe in the late 1980s and 1990s in an effort to modernize its hotel infrastructure, examining in depth the case of Sol Meliá, one of several Mallorcan-based hotel corporations active in the Caribbean. Perhaps more important, the chapter also explores the ramifications of Cuba's political peripheralization in the global arena by the United States as a component of decentralized tourism development in places like Varadero. The chapter draws attention to the flagging American presence not only in Cuba but also throughout the rest of the Caribbean as national companies and Europeans have filled the void left by American firms in Caribbean tourism after the 1960s. Utilizing Castro's own observations on tourism development and political documents from the United States and Europe, this chapter illustrates that tourism development can be packaged with political conflict, as well as with distinctive built environments.

Finally, chapter 9 explores the impact of private resort development by American investors, including labor lawyer Theodore Kheel, and Dominican management, namely Frank Rainieri, on the western shores of the Mona Straits. Plagued with poor infrastructure and little interest from the Dominican government for developing tourism, Kheel and Rainieri created a sustainable tourism community there beginning in the 1970s. Isolation reinforced the importance of air travel, as well as underscored an identity based on local flora and fauna that attracted cosmopolitan tourists. By the 1980s, Spanish hoteliers arrived some twenty miles north of Punta Cana, at Bávaro, and initiated a series of mass tourism resort communities. Through oral histories, this chapter examines the emergence of Punta Cana in Caribbean tourism, with an analysis of its intense isolation and subsequent cooperation with mass tourism operators to the north.

While the present study is largely analytical and episodic in nature, there are at least three underlying themes that offer a dramatic, narrative element to the overall history of the transformation of tourism in the Latin Caribbean since World War II. These three themes have had a significant impact on the packaging of tourism poles in the region and intersect with the analysis of the individual decentralized tourism poles.

The first of these narrative threads involves the gradual decline of U.S. domination of tourism industries in the Caribbean, particularly after 1960 with the outbreak of social unrest and revolutionary politics throughout the region. U.S. economic interests by no means evaporated in the tourism sector (ITT Sheraton, for example, pushed ahead with expansion in the region in the late 1960s), yet social, political, and economic instability in the Caribbean made it harder for U.S. corporations to justify the assumption of additional risk there. Furthermore, declining U.S. interest in international hotel development in Latin America went hand in hand with the meltdown of vertically aligned hotel/airline partnerships in the U.S. air carrier sector. The difficulties of decentralized tourism development in the Caribbean best illustrate why U.S. air carriers linked to hotel corporations were not able to maintain their simultaneous dominance throughout the second half of the twentieth century. During the 1950s and 1960s, led by the example of Pan American Airways and its subsidiary, Intercontinental Hotels, U.S. air carriers focused on tourism in Latin American capitals.[11] Hoteliers like Hilton International also understood their dependence on reliable air carriers and built hotels in Caribbean destinations like San Juan and Havana. However, as

Caribbean tourism (following the Mediterranean lead) became increasingly decentralized, charter operations offered service where legacy carriers were hesitant to schedule regular flights. In contrast, vertically organized European tourism conglomerates, like Spain's Iberostar, employed charter flights that could be routed and rerouted to new locales with much less difficulty than regularly scheduled flights, the most common method of air travel in the United States. The greater degree of flexibility that vertical organization provided compounded the rapid loss of the Caribbean tourism market for American hotels and air carriers to their European counterparts.

Similarly, the second narrative theme that winds its way through the analysis involves the growing influence of Spanish hoteliers and tourism companies in the Latin Caribbean, particularly those businesses based on the Balearic island of Mallorca. The return of the Europeans to the Caribbean tourism market, both as producers and consumers, should not be seen as a condition brought on solely by the structural inability of U.S. corporations to adjust to decentralized tourism. To the contrary, the most important global influence on tourism development in the Caribbean, outside of state-sponsored development, has been the vertical integration of Spanish hoteliers, airlines, and tour operators, largely based in Mallorca. In the 1950s and 1960s, the Balearic Islands became the vacation pole of preference for Europeans, particularly Britons.[12] By 1998, Mallorca received approximately ten million tourists a year.[13] As the tourism industry matured in the 1970s and 1980s, and the Spanish tourism market simultaneously suffered from saturation, a tiny band of ambitious hotel chains, linked to local transport and tour operators, looked for new opportunities in the Caribbean. In 1984, the Barceló chain opened its first international hotel in Latin America in Bávaro (Dominican Republic). Followed by Sol Meliá, Occidental, Riu, Fiesta, and Iberostar, these companies soon dominated the hotel superstructure in the Dominican Republic and Mexico's resort cities of Cancún, Ixtapa, Huatulco, Los Cabos, and Loreto. The most marked example of their dominance, largely for politico-economic reasons, is evident in Cuba, where Sol Meliá controls the lion's share of luxury hotels on the island. In fact, the emergence of modern Varadero began with construction of the Meliá Varadero, the Meliá las Americas, and the Sol Palmeras. These strategic investments, incurred largely by family-run businesses and paired with flexible charter airline companies, have allowed the Spaniards greater mobility in developing decentralized locations throughout the Caribbean than their North American counterparts. Furthermore, the saturation of the Spanish tourism market for tourism producers also coincided with a wave of economic prosperity throughout Germany and other parts of Europe, signaling the emergence of an increasing number of European tourists willing to take long-haul vacations to the Caribbean, where they could enjoy the same brands and services they had grown accustomed to in the Mediterranean. The best example of these links between European tourists, Mallorcan tourism firms, and Caribbean destinations is demonstrated by the Riu group, a Mallorcan company linked to the renowned German tour operator TUI.[14]

Finally, in an analytical framework that focuses so much attention on the evolution of mass tourism at peripheral tourism poles in the Latin Caribbean, it is critical to recognize the growing importance of the need for sustainable development in the Caribbean's tourism sector. According to environmental historian Samuel P. Hayes, the heightened desirability of visiting natural spaces in the 1950s was the product of twentieth-century industrialization and higher standards of living in the United States.[15] The validity of Hayes's thesis is reflected in part by Laurance Rockefeller's decision to found luxury resorts near national parks and secluded spaces in the Caribbean Sea and Pacific Ocean. If Rockefeller was not the first person to introduce the idea of decentralized, luxury tourism to the Caribbean, he was the most prominent, planting low-rise casitas and hotels in the Virgin Islands (Caneel Bay and Little Dix Bay) and at Dorado Beach in Puerto Rico.

Sustainable tourism in the Caribbean responded to two influences: first, the economic possibility of offering a discriminating segment of elite tourists quiet, intimate settings for vacations; second, the disturbing conditions brought on by mass tourism throughout the world. In its purest form, sustainable tourism attempted to maintain the biological integrity of Caribbean beaches and ecosystems. Grupo Puntacana played a leading role in this process in the eastern Dominican Republic. In some ways, the explosion of low-density tourism complexes in the Riviera Maya near Cancún is a reflection of developments in the Dominican Republic. The fact that Spanish architect Alvaro Sans designed properties in both locales reinforces the connection.[16]

Twenty-one years after inaugurating tourism centers at Playa Larga and Playa Girón, Fidel Castro found himself in a suburb of Santo Domingo, Gramna province, Cuba, trying to convince Cubans of the value of camping as a form of domestic tourism. Reflecting on his own childhood, he revealed: "I remember that one of the things I liked best [as a youth] was scouting. I could hardly see a hill without feeling the temptation to climb it, and I not only felt the temptation but decided to climb the hill. When I was a boy, one of the things I liked best was to cross rivers, climb mountains, and be in contact with nature."[17] Castro's appreciation of Cuban landscapes is indisputable, as evidenced by his own preference for Guamá as a leisure destination. Three and a half decades after the inauguration of the Playa Girón Tourist Center, Bhoendradatt Tewarie, executive director of the Institute of Business at the University of the West Indies, St. Augustine, Trinidad and Tobago, characterized Cuba's tourism marketing strategy: "Cuba markets itself in the context of natural landscapes for both ecotourists and beach tourists. It promotes culture, history, and heritage. . . . Natural landscapes reflecting all the splendor of the Caribbean beaches, mountains, rivers, and rich flora are what Cuba is marketing."[18] Castro's active input to Cuban tourism, beginning in the late 1950s, helps us understand the distance between the creation of tourist centers at Playa Girón, Playa Larga, and Guamá, and the emergence of global tourism in the region. While global tourism has transformed the content of national and private tourism plans created by innovative entrepreneurs and planners throughout the Caribbean, the following pages illustrate the importance of historical development patterns in the unique tourism poles throughout the Latin Caribbean. Perhaps history will be a useful discipline in helping us understand the evolution of the tourism industry past and present, for as Caribbean tourism expert Paul F. Wilkinson has observed, "With a better knowledge of the past, perhaps there is a greater opportunity to influence the future, not just of individual Caribbean states or the Caribbean region as a whole, but also of other societies that are part of the global tourism system."[19]

Prologue

Departures

As the tourism infrastructure throughout Latin America improved during the 1940s and 1950s, getting to Latin America became a more sophisticated—and packaged—cultural experience as well. In the 1940s, Braniff Airways put together an international route system focused on Latin America, including Havana, Bogotá, Sao Paulo, Rio de Janeiro, and Buenos Aires. Company logos featured the American hemisphere, and Braniff's motto was "linking the Americas." DC-4 and DC-6 Conquistador planes transported passengers to vacation and business opportunities south of the border. In the 1960s, the culture and color of Latin America also adorned Braniff planes. In 1965, new CEO Harding Lawrence injected a colorful Latin image into the conservative yet profitable South American and Caribbean routes serviced by Braniff. In addition to purchasing Panagra Airline routes in South America from Pan American Airways in 1967, Lawrence also hired publicity wunderkind Mary Wells—creator of the "plop plop fizz fizz" ad campaign for Alka-Seltzer—to remake the image of Braniff into a sophisticated, cosmopolitan airline renowned for its international service. As part of the "End of the Plain Plane" publicity campaign, Wells called on the design expertise of Alexander Girard to enliven Braniff's drab terminal waiting areas and airplane interiors. Girard's tastes blended modernism and folk art, with a preference for Latin American and Native American designs. He was best known at the time for designing La Fonda del Sol Mexican restaurant for the enormously successful Restaurant Associates consortium in New York City. His designs for La Fonda del Sol—from the chairs to the coffee mugs—reflected a fascination with bright colors and chic retro-modern combinations of size, color, and texture.[1] This attention to color, an attribute of pre-Colombian and contemporary modern Mexican architecture and folk art, was also evident in his design work for Braniff. He first chose seven bright colors for the airline's jets. Girard then put the finishing touches on this triumph of the imagination by transforming the interiors of the planes to match the culture and colors of the Latin American destinations to which they would be flying. As one Mexican tour guide noted, Girard "scoured the neighboring country [Mexico] for Mexican antiques and artifacts to keynote Braniff waiting rooms now decorated in colorful—and authentic—Hispanic style. More, he brought Mexican fabrics right into the planes—no longer plain planes—and you can find your seat upholstered in them."[2]

In 1972, Braniff management also hired artist Alexander Calder to further enliven the Braniff fleet. At the rate of $100,000 per plane, Braniff gave Calder the task of making its South American fleet as colorful as the destinations they serviced. The first of his abstract designs appeared in 1973. At the time of his death in 1976, Calder was completing a design entitled "A Salute to Mexico," which integrated the colors of the Mexican flag into his signature designs of swirling waves of color and form.[3]

The sheer growth of travel to Latin America during and after World War II made the airlines agents of change for the growth of tourism in indirect as well as direct ways. Mexican journalist and travel writer Pepe Romero noted a correlation between the increase in American travelers to Mexico and the need for new airports that could handle the growing number of gringos looking for pleasure south of the border. He observed that more than eighty landing fields were subsequently built, some by the airlines themselves (American Airlines built four airports throughout Mexico, including one at Monterrey). These facilities attracted increased air travel. Pan Am scheduled flights to Mexico as early as 1927, creating in the process the future Mexicana Airlines. American Airlines began servicing Mexico during World War II. Newer, faster, and bigger planes contributed to the evolution of aviation infrastructure, forcing Mexico City to open Central Airport in 1952. Central Airport not only boasted a main runway 6,875 feet long (to facilitate the landing of large planes) but also many of the consumer comforts Americans and Europeans expected of modern airports. Jewelry stores, magazine kiosks, bank branches, and a record shop all signaled a new level of sophistication in Mexico's aviation infrastructure. "At the Central Airport," Romero boasted, "you first feel Mexican hospitality. There you see beautiful peacocks strutting their stuff. You will be served some of Mexico's excellent coffee or, if you prefer, a shot of tequila or a daiquiri cocktail." Ultimately, the growth of aviation infrastructure necessitated sufficient luxury hotels to accommodate Americans flush with expendable income they had saved during the war.[4] The fact that architect Fernando Parra Hernandez designed both Mexico City's new Central Airport and the Continental Hilton further reinforces the link between commercial aviation infrastructure and the hotel industry.[5]

PART 1

The American Caribbean

1

The Rockefellers

During the early 1940s and in the aftermath of World War II, the third generation of Rockefellers, particularly Nelson and Laurance, played a critical role in establishing paradigms for decentralized tourism. Nevertheless, their primary interests generally did not center on tourism for tourism's sake. Nelson Rockefeller's experience working for the Franklin Roosevelt administration as coordinator of Inter-American Affairs in the late 1930s and early 1940s provided him with the opportunity to work out a theoretical model for simultaneously improving relations with Latin American nations and promoting private business there.

By 1943, Nelson Rockefeller was planning for the postwar economy and promoting partnerships between private interests in the United States and Latin America. Looking toward the end of the war, Rockefeller observed, "There is only one way in which we can maintain the unity of objective and action which exists today, and that is by developing a program which will bring about a steadily rising standard of living for the peoples of all countries and classes throughout the hemisphere." Rockefeller stressed that immediate action throughout Latin America would be the key to building solid relationships throughout the hemisphere. "It is no exaggeration to say," Rockefeller wrote, "that the extent of the future prosperity and welfare of the Hemisphere will depend largely on the plans which will be laid during the coming year. We have a unique opportunity today, an opportunity which the United States will probably never have again." In order to strengthen existing relations, he noted the need for stronger ties between American diplomacy and business activities in the region. These business partnerships would build a solid defense against the return of European business interests following the war. Not surprisingly, the stimulation of tourism in Latin America played a part in Rockefeller's vision of postwar Latin America. One of the objectives of the Inter-American Development Commission's transportation committee was to stimulate tourism and air travel between Latin America and the United States, including the construction of airports, passenger terminals, and "facilities including hotels." Rockefeller noted that tourists would not only stimulate the growth of hotels, airport infrastructure, and commerce in Latin America but also serve as cultural ambassadors between North and South America. Sensing a closing window of opportunity, he urged expedient action: "It is reasonable to believe that Congress is not going to continue to make large appropriations to carry on the work in these fields after the war, and therefore arrangements must be made now to broaden the base of support of these programs so that when the war is over the most important part of the work can be carried out."[1]

Hotels and Tourism

Encouraged by Venezuelan officials, the Rockefeller brothers contributed to the stimulation of tourism and business travel through their funding of the Hotel Avila, beginning in 1940. A feasibility study, carried out by Robert Bottome, an executive working with the Rockefeller brothers in Caracas, clarified the benefits and challenges of building a world-class hotel in a developing nation. It was noted, to no one's surprise, that many of the hotel's clients would be stateside employees of the petroleum companies doing business in Venezuela. With very little long-term tourism traffic in Venezuela, day tourists in Caracas, either from cruise ships or airlines, would serve as another source of revenue. Venezuelan public officials and local elites would provide a third source of income.

Bottome's report also supported the Rockefeller brothers' proposed hotel through its assessment of the local hotel market. At the time, there were no modern hotels in Caracas. The six hotels that did operate offered only a combined 220 rooms. In January 1939, the acting American commercial attaché for Caracas, Ralph H. Ackerman, observed: "What is known as first class accommodations in the United States cannot be secured in Venezuela." The report corroborated this claim. Among other things, it noted deficiencies in food availability and preparation posed potential problems, as food service would provide revenue for the hotel. Skilled cooks could not be found in Caracas and would have to be imported. High-quality meat was also scarce.

Lack of construction expertise and materials posed challenges to creating a modernist hotel in Caracas. In terms of construction of a modern structure, the report noted, "There is no such thing in Caracas as a firm of architects. There are two or three sons of wealthy families who have studied abroad and who have been slightly exposed to the main principles of architectural practice, but none of these operate as architects except in an extremely casual way." This was exacerbated by poor construction practices, including poorly laid building foundations. "A first class earthquake would probably flatten fairly extensive areas of the newly developed portions of Caracas," Bottome concluded. It was recommended that American architects and contractors tackle the project, if the hotel was approved.

Site selection also played a critical role in assessing the feasibility of the proposed hotel. At the time, most of the hotels in Caracas were congregated downtown, around the main plaza and business district. In contrast, the Rockefeller brothers chose a largely undeveloped part of Caracas, the Gamboa neighborhood of the San Bernardino suburb, as the location for the hotel. The advantages of the peripheral site also accommodated the Rockefellers' concern for selecting a beautiful natural setting. Bottome's list of justifications for the Gamboa site illuminates many of these advantages:

a. It is elevated, giving a view of the whole valley and the city of Caracas. The rear view includes lovely mountains, mule trails going high up to various points of interest. . . . Access to town and to the Country Club section is about as short as it possibly could be if the San Bernardino road were built. . . .

b. Many beautiful old trees and plantings of various kinds, including an attractive bamboo grove, already exist on the plot, cutting considerably the necessity of a large initial landscaping cost.

c. With the possibility of four to five hectares in view, the actual plateau of Gamboa for the hotel site would include about three hectares. The lower land in the back of about two hectares would be property on which tennis courts, swimming pool, garage, and garden could be built to a good advantage.[2]

The Rockefellers also believed that by locating the hotel in a peripheral location, it would help to spur development in that part of Caracas.

From the beginning, the Rockefellers faced numerous challenges in adapting an American institution, the modern hotel, to a developing country. The architectural style of the building raised cultural questions. While the building needed to provide modern comforts, local design preferences favored Spanish-style facades over modern architecture. The feasibility study warned: "A great many of the newer houses that are now going up are modern, even modernistic, and although many Venezuelans, as well as foreigners, seem to like the modern style, there are many others who do not. The safest style, externally at least, would be the Spanish colonial."[3] In response, architect Wallace Harrison and his associates crafted a building that was at once Spanish in appearance yet modern in its infrastructure.

The question of designing the hotel was less of a concern than building the structure to meet global standards. Although the principal architects for the project were American, every effort was made to accommodate Venezuelan workers and professionals in the building process. Despite these efforts, Max Abramovitz reported to his New York–based architectural partners, Wallace Harrison and André Fouilhoux, in March 1940: "I am getting to sense a feeling that the local people do not like the idea of a foreign contracting firm settling down here. They feel they can do it themselves and take care of Caracas' future prosperity themselves. For the good of the hotel and goodwill for everyone it would be best to create the feeling that it is their hotel and that they and their people built it." Abramovitz suggested that a Venezuelan contractor oversee the construction of the hotel, along the lines of an American construction job. The policy of using American technical expertise and as much local experience as possible became a hallmark for the Rockefeller brothers in their commercial architecture ventures in Latin America.[4] When a fourth floor was added in 1945, local architects collaborated with American architects in the Harrison-Fouilhoux office to carry out the addition.

Construction and furnishing of the hotel also presented unanticipated problems for outfitting a modern hotel on the periphery of the developed world. Most of the furnishings and many of the building materials had to be imported from the United States and Europe. Because of the high cost of import duties, the Rockefeller brothers successfully petitioned the Venezuelan government to allow building materials to enter Venezuela duty free. By July 1940, Nelson Rockefeller's Caracas assistant, Charles Lane, prepared orders for materials in anticipation of the hotel's construction. Imported items included bathroom lavatories, kitchen fixtures, tiles, air-conditioning units, plate glass, and iron staircases. Due to World War II, the prospect of actually receiving the orders in a timely fashion was an entirely different question. Lane noted, "With Great Britain in the condition she is now in, a condition surely to get worse in the near future instead of better, we are assuming a very serious risk in getting any materials from there in the time we need them." Such transatlantic difficulties led to even more innovation, as Lane advocated the use of as many local products as possible. Moreover, Lane doubted that many of the imports would actually work in the Venezuelan context: "I doubt very much," he tersely wrote, "if British kitchen equipment would meet these [local] requirements."[5] In 1945, when the hotel added a fourth floor, beds, mattresses, chairs, other furnishings, and linens had to be cleared from export duties with the Venezuelan minister of development. The opening date of the new floor actually depended on the arrival of these imports.[6] Ann Hatfield of New York City, the same designer who would furnish Laurance Rockefeller's RockResorts hotels in the Caribbean during the 1950s and 1960s, carried out interior decorating for the new floor.[7]

Overcoming these significant obstacles, the Hotel Avila was completed by the summer of 1942. On August 11, 1942, the Rockefellers sponsored an elaborate inauguration that was well attended by political figures and the local elite. William Coles, a member of the International Basic Economy Corporation (IBEC) Board of Directors, described the ways in which the hotel had "nationalized" itself culturally in his description of the hotel's opening ceremony:

> At five o'clock the hotel presented a pleasing sight. The Venezuelan and American flags were displayed from the flag-poles for the first time. . . . President Medina and the Ministers arrived punctually and were greeted and conducted to the main lobby where, in the absence of the Archbishop who was ill, the Dean of the Cathedral awaited. Before an altar equipped with burning candles and a Cristo, the Dean gave the benediction in Latin and proceeded to bless everything on the main floor. It was a colorful sight—the Dean and his assistants in their red and gold robes, blessing all of the rooms with holy water. . . . I then said a few words and thanked the Venezuelan government for their cooperation. A "cup of champagne" appeared; the president drank, and the hotel was officially inaugurated.

This symbolic event, linking an American hotel with the social preferences of the local elite, including high government officials, reflected the Rockefellers' efforts to localize the introduction of new methods of tourism promotion and hotel management.[8] Throughout the early postwar era of tourism in the Caribbean, Conrad Hilton would follow a similar pattern of inviting celebrities and local dignitaries to the opening of his Latin American hotels in order to "localize" them. Nelson and Laurance Rockefeller, however, appear to have cast the paradigm.

Legitimate "localization" of foreign hotel properties went beyond simply throwing a memorable party for local elites and global celebrities. One hotel employee, Edward Robbins, best communicated the effort made by hotel executives to culturally adapt their services in a March 1, 1940, letter to Nelson Rockefeller: "Our public relations objectives have as yet only scratched the surface of the upper society. The people are impressed because we either speak or try to speak Spanish (Carl studies from three to four hours a day, all the girls are hard at it and Bob's progress is phenomenal). This however, as per the above example, is the general small talk reaction the people seem to have. A deeper understanding will only come after we have proved ourselves to be more than pleasant Americans around cocktail hour."[9]

Operating a luxury hotel in an increasingly anti-American climate presented substantial challenges to the Hotel Avila's management. From the beginning, labor problems bit at the heels of the American management team. Overreliance on foreign expertise to run the hotel accounted for many of the problems. In August 1942, Venezuelan authorities accused the Hotel Avila of breaking a local labor law stipulating that at least 75 percent of the workers at a business had to be Venezuelan. Manager William Coles attempted to explain to the labor inspector that foreigners, especially the European employees in the kitchen, were critical to the success of the hotel. Foreigners filled nine of the fifteen management positions, and 37 of the 109 laborers were foreign as well. Coles contended that if he fired the twenty-five cooks and waiters in the restaurant, the Venezuelans would ruin the kitchen, a key moneymaker for the Avila. Coles requested that the hotel be granted time to replace the Europeans in the kitchen. In return, the hotel would expedite the firing of foreign workers and replace them with Venezuelans in other key areas of the hotel. To make matters worse, however, many of the foreigners who had signed contracts to work at the Avila were growing disenchanted with Caracas, "not only because they found out on arrival that their dollars are not worth much in Venezuela, but also because there are so many unexpected difficulties connected with their jobs and there is little for them to do during their off hours." Coles expected that many would leave the hotel, and that the hotel would not have sufficient prospects properly trained to replace them.[10]

More direct labor challenges from workers during the mid to late 1940s also tested the administrative and fiscal patience of the Avila staff and board of directors. During the spring of 1946, the local hotel workers syndicate organized a strike against the Avila, claiming that they were being underpaid and lacked basic benefits, including meal and transportation allowances. A bold handbill announced their strike to the "people of Caracas," and named their nemesis, "the Yankee Imperialist Nelson Rockefeller, owner of that hotel." Appealing to the general populace, the syndicate requested the solidarity of the city for those seeking adequate pay and benefits. Manager William Coles and the staff at the Avila had experienced similar strikes before, yet this strike followed the negotiation of a new contract by an arbitrator the previous December. Working through the Ministry of Labor, Coles negotiated anew with the workers after they walked off the job. Kitchen workers responded to Coles's appeals for moderation by taking over the kitchen. Subsequently, the Ministry of Labor sent fourteen plainclothes agents to the hotel to restore order after police efforts failed. These emissaries of the federal government reluctantly assisted the hotel management in gaining control of the kitchen. Coles later recalled, "They were not too efficient at the start but we offered them coffee and when they found out the strikers had dumped salt in it they became more diligent in our behalf." The strike earned workers a minor raise and added benefits. Coles was much less concerned about the strike than what he smelled in the air: revolution. "Last week at a meeting of the rightist party three people were killed and many more injured," he later wrote to one of Nelson Rockefeller advisers, Barton Turnbull. "It is the kind of situation which radical elements can take advantage of. Unless there is a change, the outlook for foreign capital does not look promising."[11]

William Coles wrote from experience. Only one year earlier, a leftist coup against the military and conservative government threw Caracas into a bloodbath, affecting every institution, including the Hotel Avila. In the middle of his letter to Turnbull, Coles abruptly stopped and announced: "I interrupt this letter to report that there is some very audible shooting going on in town. It seems that there are revolutionary uprisings in three of the local military barracks."[12] The gunfire was only the echo of a leftist revolution in the city of Caracas during October 18–20, 1945. Military barracks, the presidential palace, and the military school were the targets of the uprising, but collateral damage filled the streets of Caracas. The detonation of bombs dropped from planes flying over the city periodically drowned out the sound of guns in the streets. From the roof of the Avila, Coles and the staff watched the carnage unfold. The conflict, however, spilled into the hotel on Friday afternoon. "The bellboys of the hotel who had not been on duty and our office boy appeared with new high-powered Belgina rifles and about every ruffian in town, including young boys, seemed to be armed and roaming about shooting," Coles later recalled. He remembered that on Friday, around 2:30 a.m., an armed faction fired on the hotel "on all sides." One bullet ricocheted into an apartment room at the hotel, but the occupants were out of town. The glass facade of the hotel paid a heavy price. Coles noted, "This shooting was especially terrifying because most of the rooms and the apartments of the hotels are entirely open to the outside except for panes of glass so that there are few walls to get behind. The architecture of the hotel is not suitable for revolutions." The Avila fared better than its main competitor, the Majestic Hotel, located in downtown Caracas. Coles reported that the Majestic Hotel had a "machine gun nest on the roof and fighting up and downstairs." Over five hundred people died, and two thousand to three thousand Caracas citizens were wounded throughout the city. Rómulo Betancourt assumed leadership of a ruling junta and attempted to hold off suspected Communist radicals who commandeered armored cars and randomly shot people in the streets. Such was the cost of operating a transnational hotel in a politically unstable climate. Conrad Hilton would pay a higher price during the Cuban Revolution.[13]

The willingness to adapt to cultural and political differences, as well as the perseverance of the Avila management during labor conflicts and civil unrest, eventually paid off. The success of the hotel warranted the addition of a fourth floor in 1945. Although the Rockefeller brothers divested themselves of the hotel in 1948, the hotel's importance as a business and social center for Caracas endured. Two decades later, the hotel's ballroom was legendary for its carnival dances and parties. A quasi-journalistic advertisement in the *Caracas Daily Journal*, dated March 25, 1966, reflected on the world-class status of the hotel twenty years after its founding. Entitled "A Is for Avila," the advertisement boasted, "Once 'on its feet' the Avila quickly became the center of activity for social and business life of the rapidly growing capital. Big name bands such as Xavier Cugat, Perez Prado and Los Chavales de España became a by-word at the Avila and the demand for hotel space increased rapidly."[14] Locally, the Avila served as a "keystone" institution, encouraging local competitors to modernize their properties and offer guests a uniform experience at a competitive price.

*   *   *

Like his brother Nelson, Laurance Rockefeller was fascinated by the opportunities for making money in Latin America, as well as creating jobs there. Laurence made his first trip through Latin America in 1941 and considered, according to his biographer, Robin W. Winks, building a hotel in Colombia on the new Pan-American Highway. This would have been at the same time the Hotel Avila was being constructed in neighboring Venezuela. Following World War II, Laurance Rockefeller used his influence to promote Eastern Airlines routes throughout the Caribbean, especially in Puerto Rico (site of one of his resorts, Dorado Beach) and Mexico. As his biographer notes, Rockefeller's decision to build resorts in the Caribbean was based on significant study and investigation, for "Rockefeller was an astute observer of

the region . . . and he believed that his type of resort would do more for local employment while also doing less against the environment than anyone
else's."[15]

Accordingly, Laurance Rockefeller organized a company, RockResorts, to
carry out his new concept in decentralized, nature-centered resorts. Rockefeller constructed his first resort in the Teton Range in Wyoming. He had
worked with his father on conservation efforts in the West for some time,
and the family had made substantial contributions of land for national parks
there, including Grand Teton National Park. His foray into the Caribbean
reflected his business savvy in Latin America, as well as a new challenge
away from the landlocked national parks of the continental United States.
According to Winks, Rockefeller selected his RockResorts sites based on
four criteria: natural beauty, potential for economic growth of underdeveloped regions, long-term profitability, and potential for conservation.[16]
Rockefeller explained the philosophy for his hotels: "In building our resorts,
we go to the frontiers of natural beauty and keep them in harmony with the
locale. It takes time and money to achieve this accord between man and
nature. . . . Aside from investing risk capital, our resort approach also relates
to the conservation, the preservation of beauty and the creation of job opportunities in our areas."[17] In pursuit of the best beaches, Rockefeller outfitted his boat, *Dauntless*, and plied the cerulean waters of the Caribbean in
the late 1940s and early 1950s, looking for the ideal locations for his resorts.
His methodology for selecting resort sites matched his passion for finding
secluded, yet beautiful, locations: "He would stop at bays that attracted him,
walk the beaches, swim with an aqualung, check out the coral, and write
careful notes about each stop, always using his camera to record, frame,
change, and provide deeper perspective on a place."[18]

Laurance, his wife, and friends visited Caneel Bay on the island of St.
John for the first time in 1952. Reflecting on the discovery, he later wrote, "I
found the combination of mountains, beaches, and sea unique in the Caribbean. . . . The unspoiled nature of the area appealed to me and I wish[ed] to
preserve it against overdevelopment."[19] Taken by the beauty of the mountain
climbs and white sandy beaches, Rockefeller purchased the six hundred–
acre Caneel Bay Plantation, with plans to transform the hidden paradise
into RockResorts' first Caribbean resort. Once owned by Dutchman Peter
Durlieu, the eighteenth-century sugar plantation lay largely untouched by
human hands until Rockefeller's purchase. With a balmy climate that aver-
aged within six degrees of seventy-eight degrees Fahrenheit throughout the
year, St. John provided the perfect setting for an island getaway. Rockefeller
practically ensured that the tiny resort (of no more than one hundred beds)

would not fall prey to runaway growth, encircling the development with a national park, of which he donated five thousand acres. The Virgin Islands National Park and Caneel Bay Resort both opened in December 1956.

Rockefeller's foray to Puerto Rico, in search of a second resort site in the Caribbean, reaffirmed the family's abiding interest in assisting with the island's economic development. At the suggestion of Teodoro Moscoso, director of Operation Bootstrap, the developmental plan for Puerto Rico's modernization, Laurence made his first visit to Dorado Beach in February 1953. While urban hotels like the Caribé Hilton had improved city tourism on the island, there was a strong desire on the part of the government to develop rural areas as well. According to Moscoso, "Our goal has always been to eradicate poverty throughout the whole of Puerto Rico, not just in metropolitan areas. What success we have had so far has been in spite of a natural inclination of industry and tourist facilities to concentrate. The field of tourism presents an especially attractive inducement for diversification, since many of Puerto Rico's most beautiful and promising resort areas are distributed throughout the Commonwealth."[20] With the desire to diversify the island's tourist offerings, Moscoso led Rockefeller to the former estate of Alfred T. Livingston, a New York physician. Located twenty-five miles to the west of San Juan, the estate had already been chosen by Robert Trent Jones Sr. as the location for an eighteen-hole golf course. Impressed by the beauty of the setting, Rockefeller purchased 225 acres of beachfront property, as well as other lands that pertained to the Livingston estate, which would be used not only to develop a resort but also for residential purposes. RockResorts built the resort along the idyllic beachfront, which included a "two and one-half mile coconut lined shoreline with crescent beaches providing both surf and sheltered water bathing . . . and one of the few virgin timber stands in the San Juan area." A private airport also offered convenient access between San Juan and the new resort.[21] The territory of Puerto Rico provided $1.3 million worth of financing through the Puerto Rican Industrial Development Company (PRIDCO). The resort opened the first week of December 1958.

Caneel Bay and Dorado Beach were monumental in the evolution of low-density resort design. Laurance Rockefeller believed that nature was the central component of, and not simply the backdrop for, a relaxing vacation. During the 1950s, the growing trend in resort hotel design was to build a bulky modern hotel, much like the Caribé Hilton in San Juan. In contrast, Rockefeller designed his resorts within the context of the preexisting natural setting. At Caneel Bay, he used the existing structures from the colonial sugar plantation as the backdrop for the resort's design. Contemporary buildings, including cottages and beach houses, complemented the original Dutch- and Caribbean-inspired designs. Similarly, at Dorado Beach, RockResorts placed the modern cottages, beach houses, and auxiliary buildings around the plantation that had been owned by the Livingston family. In the 1950s, some thought Rockefeller's insistence on respecting nature and blending the resort into its surroundings was a risky venture. Unlike most beach resorts in the 1950s, which stressed their access to the world via communication and transportation, RockResorts took every step in design to obscure modern civilization, including electricity, from the visual palate of its guests. At Caneel Bay, for example, RockResorts installed an underground cable to bring electricity to the island from nearby St. Thomas. Finally, RockResorts properties promoted their limited access to the surrounding areas. Unlike modern hotel resorts that catered to hundreds of tourists at a time, Caneel Bay only accommodated one hundred guests at a time. Limited accessibility and limited accommodations, in addition to higher than normal room rates, made the RockResorts experience one of appreciating the natural surroundings without destroying them. By the end of the twentieth century, this approach to upscale, low-density resort design, which stressed horizontal versus vertical development as well as design patterns that complemented local customs and cultures, would be conventional wisdom in resort design.

The architecture and interior design of Caneel Bay and Dorado Beach followed a pattern set by the Hotel Avila in Caracas some fifteen years earlier. Laurence Rockefeller's design philosophy suggested an understated elegance that remained in touch with the natural surroundings. This did not mean, however, that guests would have a Waldenesque experience in Rockefeller's Caribbean outposts. As he once pointed out, "The whole idea is to keep its beauty simple and unspoiled. . . . But you know simplicity can be a very expensive thing."[22] In order to provide quality accommodations and amenities for guests, RockResorts either remodeled or built cottages from the ground up, stressing the use of modern materials adapted to the appearance of the respective resorts. At Caneel Bay, a promotional guide boasted, "The architectural design of the new buildings takes advantage of the ideal climate of St. John and features native materials—stone, stucco, and wood—and earth colors of the traditional island shades." In order to pull off the feat of disguising modern buildings in a local context, "color swatches were taken directly from buildings in the islands for this purpose." Furthermore, many of the cottages and beach houses were screened for outdoor enjoyment of the beaches and nearby mountains. This would "open the interiors to the verdant setting and turquoise seascapes." The comfortable accommodations of the interiors of Caneel Bay also stressed modern functionality and cultural symmetry with the island surroundings. According to an early description of the rooms, "contemporary Danish furniture of walnut and teak, covered in Danish fabrics, has been used in the guest lounge with rugs woven in Puerto Rico. Bamboo has been used for the furniture in the cocktail lounge terrace and oil rubbed walnut table[s] are provided for dining, accented by the Carib china from Puerto Rico."[23]

The Dorado Beach Hotel featured ten beach houses, each with ten rooms, and two groups of beach cabanas. In addition, a central building accommodated meetings, restaurants, and shops, and the plantation house on the property was converted into a clubhouse for the golf course. Mahogany from Central America and redwood from California accented the steel and masonry of the hotel buildings. Like the Hotel Avila, the balconies on the second floors took advantage of grille work that added a colonial Spanish flair to the structure's facade. Air circulation systems also reflected the marriage of modern comfort with conventional technology employed by most islanders. The rooms were air-conditioned, but guests were encouraged to enjoy the strong Caribbean breezes. Puerto Rican tile covered the floors of the guest rooms and cabanas. Overall, the architecture and interiors were designed to not overpower the original human structures and natural beauty of the resort's setting.

Rockefeller also transformed the colonial home on the former Livingston estate into the architectural centerpiece of the resort. In this case, the 1930s-era Spanish colonial home was turned into the clubhouse for the golf course. "The double entrance stairway to the second floor veranda is a landmark," promotional material noted, "and there is a landscaped walled patio enclosed by two wings of the mansion and focused on a tiled fountain." While not an original Spanish colonial mansion, efforts to conserve the Spanish-style accents added an element of Spanish charm to the clubhouse. Other accenting details provided more authentic Hispanic touches, including the use of tiles imported from a monastery near Barcelona. This pattern of using modern structures for hotel and resort buildings and then accenting them with local cultural motifs has become conventional wisdom in upscale hospitality properties, but Rockefeller was one of the innovators.[24]

Collaboration between Robert Trent Jones Sr. and Laurence Rockefeller began at Dorado Beach and extended to projects in Hawaii and St. Croix in the Virgin Islands. While the golf course is not an American invention, its spread throughout the world after World War II, including in the Caribbean, reflected the leisure preferences of Americans who were increasingly traveling the world. Jones respected Rockefeller's design preferences that complemented the natural surroundings. Jones himself was not new to the Caribbean and Latin America, having already designed courses in Jamaica, Brazil, Venezuela, and the Dominican Republic by the mid-1950s. At Dorado Beach, he used the natural surroundings to his advantage in constructing a challenging yet beautiful course. "The Dorado Beach Course is routed to provide a constantly changing vista of tropical jungle growth, citrus groves, open lagoon area, and ocean," an early fact sheet teased. The grass, a Gene Tift Bermuda strain, was "brought over in one plane load from the states." Despite the natural tendency for rain on a frequent basis, 250,000 cubic yards of water were brought in to create the lagoons.[25]

Activities at the RockResorts in the Caribbean generally mirrored Rockefeller's goal of creating an "informal tropical beach resort." Caneel Bay was probably closest to the ideal of getting away from civilization. Advertised activities included "swimming and skin diving in the unusually clear waters of ten outstanding beaches, horseback riding, fishing, boating, hiking and planned trips to famous Danish sugar plantation ruins and Carib Indian relics." Within the context of a modern infrastructure, these "primitive" activities allowed guests to relax, recuperate, and explore nature's healing powers without actually living in the jungle.[26] The ambience of Dorado Beach was similar to that of Caneel Bay; however, there were more organized activities available for guests at Dorado Beach. In addition to the obligatory beach activities, Dorado Beach also boasted three tennis courts, two saltwater swimming pools, an eighteen-hole golf course, "bicycling[,] beach parties[,] lawn games[,] . . . dancing[,] fiestas[,] films[,] [and] air tours to nearby Caribbean islands."[27] Like staff at the Club Med collection of enclave resorts, the staff at Dorado Beach encouraged a participatory spirit through organized activities on the resort property. A 1967 Fodor's travel guide observed, "Dorado Beach is almost an island within an island. . . . A daily bulletin lists the events of that day, and there are usually such items as a photographic tour, a ping pong tournament, feature movie, dancing, entertainment."[28] The difference in the activities of the two resorts can probably be ascribed to the fact that Puerto Rico was already emerging as a mass tourism destination for Americans (particularly after the beginning of the Cuban Revolution), and Rockefeller saw greater opportunities for added amenities at Dorado Beach. Furthermore, the distinctive resort offerings provided tourists with a choice within the same chain of resorts.

The success of Dorado Beach in the 1960s prompted Laurence Rockefeller to transform the former plantation site from a single resort, at Dorado Beach, into a pair of resorts. Rockefeller spearheaded the creation of the Cerromar Beach Hotel on the sprawling seventeen hundred–acre Dorado Beach resort and residential development near San Juan. The modern design of the new hotel heightened the appeal of the resort complex. Opened in January 1972, the Cerromar Beach Hotel, designed specifically for conferences, featured eight stories with 503 rooms and suites. It lacked the intimacy of the cottages and beach houses of the Caneel Bay and Dorado Beach hotels and was the closest of any of the RockResorts properties in the Caribbean to a hotel designed for "mass tourism."

The Rockefeller family sold off the RockResorts name and properties in 1986. Since that time, the properties and corporate name have been passed on to other companies. The resorts at Caneel Bay and Little Dix belong to Rosewood Hotels and Resorts, an exclusive group of boutique hotels and low-density resorts. Hyatt Regency operated the resorts and golf courses at Dorado Beach from 1985 until 2006. All three properties have preserved, to a certain degree, the design standards envisioned by their founder. In retrospect, the tourism development of the Rockefeller brothers in Venezuela, the Virgin Islands, and Puerto Rico illustrates the ways in which American capitalists attempted to profit from or enhance Caribbean economies through their investments in the aftermath of World War II. While the Rockefeller brothers had a notable influence on U.S.-Latin American relations, they also experienced the disconcerting reality of operating a business in a volatile politico-economic context. It is well known that the brothers' father, John D. Rockefeller Jr., disapproved of their hotel investment in Venezuela, but their liquidation of interest in the Hotel Avila probably also reflected the difficulties in adapting to labor conflict and political chaos. Such would be the experience of larger, more visible American multinational hotel chains, namely Intercontinental Hotels and Hilton International, which used Latin America in the 1940s and 1950s as a launching pad for global hotel empires. Their initial enthusiasm for hotel building in the wake of World War II was tempered in the late 1950s and early 1960s by cries of revolution and heightened sociopolitical instability.

2

Conrad Hilton

Like the Rockefeller brothers, Conrad Hilton viewed hotel development throughout the Caribbean as an undertaking that would generate profits for the parent corporation and at the same time stimulate economic development and cultivate international goodwill in the host nation. In 1956, at the height of the golden age of American tourism in Latin America, Hilton addressed a glittering crowd of Mexican and American cosmopolites at the opening of the Continental Hilton in Mexico City. Built on the Parisian-style Paseo de la Reforma, away from the traditional colonial center of the Mexican capital, the Continental Hilton towered over the wide boulevard as a modern cathedral of comfort beckoning everyone who was anyone to enjoy the trappings of a modern American lifestyle fused with motifs of ancient Mexico. Whereas Mexico City's elite had converged on the stone-faced Metropolitan Cathedral to see and be seen a century earlier, now they flocked to the glass-covered Continental on a nightly basis to mingle at Belvedere's nightclub on the hotel's rooftop.

Hilton's new hotel not only reoriented Mexico City's cultural geography but also served as a symbol of the growing economic nexus between the two nations. This was more than an extension of Hilton's effort to assist in the Cold War effort by building hotels in strategic cities. The Continental Hilton was a steel-and-glass metaphor for the future of U.S.-Mexican relations. Speaking in Spanish, Hilton addressed his guests at the hotel's grand opening in a speech entitled "A Continental Hotel for Continental Unity." He recounted his own multicultural upbringing in San Antonio, New Mexico, swimming in the river with his Hispanic playmates. In the intellectual tradition of Pan-American enthusiast Herbert Bolton, Hilton outlined the historical links between the two nations, as well as the cultural high points of Mexico's pre-Colombian and colonial periods. In his concluding remarks, Hilton stressed, "It is my greatest hope that the Continental Hilton will be for many years a symbol and beacon of the goodwill and true friendship that exists between the Mexican Republic and the United States of America. . . . Mexico and the United States should go forward, and go forward quickly, with a spirit of cooperation and harmony."[1]

Origins of the Cathedrals of Comfort

Global trends played a large role in setting the stage for Hilton's establishment of luxury hotels in Latin America. As Europe found itself embroiled in war in the late 1930s, more and more Americans traveled to Latin America for business or pleasure. American affluence in the postwar years, as well as longer vacations, made foreign travel a growing possibility for many Americans. As *Fortune* magazine editors opined in 1955, "the biggest promise of new leisure expenditure lies in foreign and domestic vacations." Americans spent approximately $600 million on foreign tourism in 1947, and that amount grew to over $1 billion by 1953.[2] More often than not, however, even Latin America's capital cities lacked quality hotels that catered to the "at home" comforts Americans craved, including warm water for baths, ice water to drink, and private, in-room bathrooms. In the early 1940s, for example, the Colombian government's hotel guide compared the Niza Hotel in Popayán, Colombia, with "the best in Europe and the United States." In contrast, travel writer Kathleen Romoli found a hotel comprised of numerous old homes (each centered around an inner patio) with two showers to be shared among all the guests. "My room has good clean sheets," she recalled, "a most unusual abundance of furniture, insufficiently screened glass sides, and a double door that left a crack by which passers-by commanded an excellent view of the best." The servants derived pleasure from announcing the comings and goings of guests from the bathrooms. With a hint of sarcasm, Romoli commented, "Incidentally, some of the more luxurious hotels might take a leaf from the Niza in the matter of obliging service."[3]

The initial impetus for building hotels abroad came from the U.S. government. Following the American victory in Japan in August 1945, the State Department and Department of Commerce approached Pan American Airways and the Hilton Hotels Corporation and asked them to consider building luxury hotels around the world. The federal government hoped that these modern hotels would serve as a boon for developing countries and generate revenues for foreign exchange. As Hilton International was the first corporation to open a string of the new international hotels in the wake of World War II, its experience served as valuable testimony in linking government aid to the promotion of American businesses abroad. On March 3, 1954, Hilton International executive vice president John Houser testified before the House of Representatives Committee on Foreign Affairs about the role that the Caribé Hilton played as a nexus for attracting American companies to the island and stimulating business there. "There have been over 280 industries established in Puerto Rico since the opening of the Caribé Hilton," he testified, "and the hotel which has added so greatly in bringing the tourist flow has been given credit for assisting the Government also in this way." Given the visual importance of these new cathedrals of comfort in Latin America, it is interesting that Houser noted, "The Americans are imaginative and as they see these other lands they apply their American background to realizing the industrials potentialities." In the case of Pan American Airways, the Import-Export Bank provided loans worth $25 million to underwrite the financing of the individual Intercontinental hotels. For Conrad Hilton, the government's vision of facilitating trade and development through Hilton hotels meshed with his philanthropic goal of transforming hotels into centers of international goodwill.[4]

There were also less direct forms of governmental support for the growth of American hotels in Latin America. In the late 1930s, Nelson Rockefeller took control of the State Department's new Office of Inter-American Affairs, hoping to generate goodwill between the United States and the Latin American republics during wartime. Rockefeller's office enlisted the creative efforts of Walt Disney in this hemispheric task of spreading goodwill. As a result, Disney produced two full-length films, *Saludos Amigos* (1943) and *The Three Caballeros* (1945). While the initial purpose of these films was to generate hemispheric goodwill, they also sent a message that no doubt encouraged tourism and travel to Latin America. Both films were travelogues of trips south of the border. *Saludos Amigos* meshed the travels of Goofy and Donald Duck in Latin America with film footage of one of Walt Disney's three trips to Latin America. In *The Three Caballeros*, Disney combined Carmen Miranda's beauty, the samba sounds of Brazil, and Acapulco's pristine beaches to promote goodwill and travel throughout the Americas. If the films themselves did not stimulate travel abroad, they reflected a growing wartime trend of Americans taking vacations to the lands to the south.

Donald Duck and his fetish for Brazilian samba dancers should not be given all the credit for opening the doors of Latin American countries to these hotels, which required significant capital input from the host country. Latin American governments accepted the premise set forth by the U.S. government that these hotels would encourage development in their countries and provide foreign exchange to offset excessive importation of foreign goods. As a result, Latin American governments offered significant inducements to Hilton International and Intercontinental Hotels to locate hotels in their primary cities. In Puerto Rico, for example, where the first Hilton International hotel was built in 1946, the commonwealth government paid for construction and furnishing of the hotel, leaving Hilton International with the task of managing the property. Intercontinental Hotels pursued a similar management strategy in the establishment of its hotels: depending either on foreign governments, organizations, or investors to pay for construction of the hotels and leave the hotel's operational expenses to the corporation. The Military Officers Pension Fund in Colombia, for example, owned the Hotel Tequendama in Bogotá, with financing for the structure handled by the Export-Import Bank.[5] Other indirect governmental inducements for these new hotels included exemption from import duties on materials used in construction and operation of the hotels.

If the State Department mandate was to build hotels around the world, then why did Hilton International and Intercontinental Hotels begin in Latin America? To answer this question, the war-torn condition of Europe must be taken into account. Although Hilton International had already contracted to build the Caribé Hilton in San Juan, Puerto Rico, Conrad Hilton's reflections on a trip to Europe in 1948 to survey the hotel industry there provides some insight as to why Latin America, as opposed to Europe, had been selected as the starting point for America's first global hotel chain. Hilton toured the continent looking for development opportunities with his son, Nick (the first of Elizabeth Taylor's husbands); his brother, Carl; and business associate Joe Binns. First and foremost, the plodding nature of business transactions in Europe made Hilton realize that it would take more time to develop hotels in Europe than elsewhere. "It was in England," he noted, "that the fact was brought home to me that American business methods are uniquely American. . . . I found that the time sense varied most definitely. Ours is a new land. Theirs is very old. It makes for a variance in perspective."[6] In contrast, Latin American governments and business interests were often able to move development schemes through bureaucratic channels very quickly, thus facilitating a swift transformation of hotel plans into the actual structures themselves.

Public opposition to international hotels also cooled Hilton's ambitions in Europe. The Communist Party in Italy stymied his efforts to open the

Cavalieri Hilton in Rome until 1964. When he visited Italy in the 1950s, the Communist Party continued its efforts to keep the hotel from being built, blocking access to the licenses needed to initiate construction. In Latin America, on the other hand, Hilton experienced little public opposition in establishing hotels in San Juan (1949), Mexico City (1956), and Havana (1958). While Europe was dealing with the aftermath of war, Latin American republics were interested in placing a modern face on their skylines in order to announce the "arrival" of modernity to their nation's principal cities. In the case of Puerto Rico, the government development division, PRIDCO, not only made sure that the hotel was built, but also assured that it commanded the best beach-front views on San Juan's Condado Beach. In Mexico City, former president Miguel Alemán Valdés served as the landlord of the Continental Hilton. Finally, Fulgencio Batista's regime opened the doors of Havana to Hilton by making state pension funds available for construction of the Habana Hilton. Hilton's debt to the Batista regime is reflected in the fact that Batista's wife served as the guest of honor at the hotel's dedication in April 1958. In the end, the feeble nature of democracy throughout Latin America contributed to the lack of opposition to hotel development there.

Popular magazines and industry experts also promoted the Caribbean at a time when travel to Europe was difficult. In a January 1950 *Mademoiselle* article entitled "'TenSHUN! Eyes South!" writer Mary Parker proclaimed, "Today all eyes are turning south, thanks to three interdependent factors. First, the campaign for so-called off-season travel. . . . Second, the airlines have made the Caribbean area accessible the year round to the person of average income. Third, the islands themselves have waked up to the fact that they are as charming in summer as they are in winter, are building new hotels to tempt people to spend whole vacations there."[7] Two months earlier, General J. Leslie Kincaid, president of American Hotels Corporation, "predicted wonderful opportunities for developing tourist trade among Caribbean nations . . . [and that] overtaxed European facilities would drive thousands of foreign tourists to this hemisphere."[8] While Kincaid's predictions were self-serving—his company managed seventy hotels throughout the Americas, including several for the Trujillo government in the Dominican Republic—they reinforced the reality that Caribbean hotels benefited from the destructive impact of World War II on Europe. From the management perspective, these trends meant that Latin America would serve as the training ground in the late 1940s and 1950s for the expansion of Hilton and Intercontinental into Europe and Asia. As former Hilton International president Curt Strand noted in a 1994 address to the Conrad N. Hilton College of Hotel and Restaurant Management, "Our goal was to get into Europe, because that was the place with the greatest demand for rooms both for business people and for tourists, particularly with the introduction of jet planes in the late 1950s."[9]

Hilton's International Formula

With support from the U.S. government, Latin American republics, and local investors, Conrad Hilton positioned himself to be the host of the Americas. Hilton emerged as one of the early pioneers in the field of globalization through the use of a management formula that created a reliable and highly visible brand identity throughout Latin America from 1946 until Trans World Airlines (TWA) purchased Hilton International in 1967. Hilton employed an innovative management strategy, world-class personnel, Hollywood star power, and modern design in adapting his cathedrals of comfort to Latin American cities in the post–World War II world.[10] When he approached the board of directors of Hilton Hotels Corporation to request support for an international subsidiary, the board expressed reluctance to expand globally, in part because of rising inflation in the postwar years as price controls were eased.[11] The recent experience of World War II, coupled with the threat of unrest and revolution in developing nations, also tempered the board's response to Hilton's proposal. In the end, the board offered Hilton a paltry $500,000 to begin his experiment and required that Hilton International be created as a separate entity from Hilton Hotels.

Given the lack of support from the board of directors of Hilton Hotels, Hilton utilized a management agreement that would become the industry standard for modern hotel management in the post–World War II era. As a rule, Hilton International and Intercontinental Hotels entered new nations with fiscal trepidation. With insufficient capital to purchase hotels outright, Hilton and Intercontinental looked to leverage foreign capital in host countries to build the hotels, which could be financed either by local or international financial institutions. As a result, instead of owning foreign real estate, Hilton and Intercontinental leased or managed these properties for their foreign owners, or both.[12] This approach, to limit investment of time and resources to the management of the hotel instead of pursuing hotel ownership, had been developed in the domestic market, but offered an even more attractive management approach abroad. Unfortunately, it also reinforced a long-standing image that many Latin Americans had of American corporations in their republics: corporations would come to extract profits, but leave as soon as reverses presented themselves. From the perspective of the hotel chains, however, this arrangement allowed them to focus on hotel management without getting involved in the potentially messy legal mine-field of foreign real estate ownership.

Conrad Hilton's innovative management contracts in the hotel industry were both a matter of necessity (lacking sufficient backing from Hilton Hotel Corporation's board of directors to engage in significant real estate invest-ment abroad) and a convenience (that is, there would less involved in exit-ing an unstable country). The success of Hilton International as a business entity, however, would not have been possible without the services of a very sophisticated, polyglot, and predominantly European group of executives to operate Hilton International. Howard B. Meek conducted an exhaustive study of the hotel industry in Latin America in the early 1950s and noted an apparent paradox in the hotel management at the Caribé Hilton in San Juan. "It is interesting to note," he wrote,

> that the great American hotel organization, Hilton Hotels, Inc., oper-ating an American type resort on an American island for an American clientele relies extensively on the professional skills of the Swiss hotel keeper. First in command at the Caribé is Arthur E. Elminger. Associ-ated with him is R. W. Basler, another Swiss who was first met by the author when he was operating the hotel Kawana . . . in Japan before the war. We have found Swiss hotelmen all over the world and we were to meet many in South America.[13]

A good number of the Hilton International executives and staff working in Latin America were either European or trained in European hotel schools. Frank G. Wangeman, first manager of the Caribé Hilton in San Juan, was a native of Frankfort-on-Main, Germany, who studied in schools in Germany, Switzerland, and England prior to receiving a Bachelor of Arts degree at the Sorbonne University in Paris. Having paid for school by working in Europe's finest hotels, Wangeman went to Zaragoza, Spain, where he completed post-graduate work prior to moving to the Caribbean. After working in Bermu-dan hotels for a short stint, he began working at the Waldorf-Astoria Hotel in New York City. He then moved into a management position with Hilton Hotels at New York's Plaza Hotel. While many believed that his subsequent transfer to the Caribé Hilton in San Juan was a demotion (given the number of Americans who did not want to live and work in Puerto Rico), Wangeman turned Hilton's first international venture into a success. He had studied at the famous Lausanne Hotel School in Switzerland, and he frequently hired its graduates to work at the Caribé Hilton. "I gave them preference not because

I had graduated from that school," he noted in an interview, "but because they, in a way, were internationalists, and it really took an understanding of the Spanish culture and a way of thinking that was different from what you found in the United States to run an international hotel." Wangeman's cosmopolitan experience also led to one of the great successes of his tenure at the hotel: the organization of a tennis and swimming club. "We intermixed the locals with the tourist[s] and the American businessmen who were established down there," he remembered. "Somehow, up until the opening of the Caribé Hilton there were two sets of society. The Puerto Rican society, which sort of kept to itself, and the American businessmen, which did not make the effort to learn Spanish or to mingle with the Puerto Ricans. The Caribé Hilton really got them together in the tennis and swimming club and did something that should have happened [in San Juan] long before."[14]

Arthur Elminger, assistant manager at the Caribé Hilton when it opened in 1949 and later the head of Hilton International's Latin American division, was born in Lucerne, Switzerland. Like Wangeman, Elminger studied at the Lausanne Hotel School. Following this formal training, he worked in every facet of the hospitality industry at hotels in London, Milan, Monte Carlo, Rome, Budapest, and Munich, among other European cities. During World War II, he sailed to South America and soon became general manager of the Gran Hotel Bolivar in Lima. Elminger quickly added the Country Club of Lima to the hotel's property holdings and was named a director of the parent company, A y F Wiese S.A. He traveled throughout South America during this period and served as an adviser to the state-owned Compañía Hotelera del Peru. Elminger joined Hilton after nine years in South America, where he was able to put the five languages he had learned to use with the international clientele. In addition to his impressive training and professional experience, Elminger had a flair for putting on a good show. His colleague Curt Strand recalled, "When somebody had a violin trio, Arthur would have twenty-two violins. And if somebody had three guitars, he would have twenty guitars. He was just tremendously showmanship oriented."[15] A man after Conrad Hilton's heart, Elminger brought European sophistication and training to Hilton International's Latin American division in the 1950s.

Strand, a Swiss native who immigrated to the United States at the age of seventeen, began working for Hilton at the Plaza Hotel in New York in 1947 and eventually became president of Hilton International in 1968 after TWA purchased the international subsidiary from the Hilton Hotel Corporation. Trained in Cornell University's prestigious hospitality program, Strand maintained an internationalist perspective in making personnel decisions in relation to Hilton International's efforts to cater to its cosmopolitan clientele. From the beginning, he noticed that Europeans were much more likely to leave home and learn languages than their American counterparts. As a result, foreigners staffed many of the positions in Hilton International. In reflecting on the evolution of Hilton International's personnel, Strand later observed:

> The language capabilities and development of pride, the idea of advancement was what created . . . [quality management]. In fact the key management people *became* multi-national. This was perfectly obvious when you think how poorly Americans travel. They travel well for pleasure but not for working abroad. You can send Americans abroad for a short time, then they want to come home, they want to get their kids educated here, etc., etc. We found that the best travelers that we had were Germans or Austrians. Because of the language abilities, and perhaps because there were fewer opportunities at home at this time, they had therefore greater impetus to go and stay abroad. . . . It was as though some nationalities were more keen to live abroad, and be transferred from one place to another. And we learned that as we went along.[16]

As a result, Strand established a training school for these "Hilton International gypsies," who were willing to move throughout the world for the sake of maintaining management excellence within the company.[17]

The gravitation of Europeans to Hilton International hotels was not merely a Latin American phenomenon, but one evident throughout the global organization of the company. Former Hilton executive Udo Schlentrich's observations in the 1970s relative to Hilton personnel corroborate this pattern: "Most of our general managers then were of Swiss, Austrian, and German background. As a result of their strong trait training, they were also . . . more fluent in several languages. They were generally more adaptable or willing to adapt to foreign working environments where it would be difficult to transfer a Frenchman to a foreign country than a German or an Austrian or a Swiss. It was more difficult in general to transfer an American away from an American environment."[18] Schlentrich also observed that in his estimation, not enough Americans worked for Hilton International. "Many young Americans were not willing to pay the apprenticeship fee of relatively low pay, learning of the language, learning new customs, and learning new cultures in order to develop an international career. . . . There were not many, but those who were willing to pay the price and look at it as personal challenges were very successful."[19]

There may also be another significant cultural reason why cosmopolitan

Europeans fared so well with Hilton International. For the Latin American elite, which comprised a significant number of the guests at Hilton's hotels, high culture, cuisine, and patterns of socializing had more to do with European traditions and culture than with American mass culture. As Meek points out:

> These capital cities [in Latin America] are cosmopolitan centers. A few American tourists, businessmen or technical experts may frequent their hotel lobbies, but they share the spotlight with local statesmen and officials and their ladies, with consular staffs representing all the world's nations, with businessmen from Europe or South Africa. Naturally, therefore, the hotels are run for Latin Americans and Europeans, as well as for North Americans. The design and operation of the [hotels], the menus, the staff organizations show Latin and European influence even more than they do North American.[20]

Star power was another cornerstone of Hilton Internationals' key to success in Latin America. Without the benefit of global television networks and satellite transmissions, Conrad Hilton ingeniously used his Hollywood connections and access to powerful national media networks in the United States to attract both North Americans and Latin Americans to patronize his hotels, which were considered to be among the most desirable options for nightlife and dining in many cities throughout the hemisphere. A fragmentary record of the home country of guests who stayed at the Caribé Hilton in San Juan in 1950 and 1951 suggests that approximately two-thirds were from the United States and one-third were either foreign nationals or Puerto Ricans.[21]

How did Hilton utilize an imperfect system of global communication to achieve this level of diversity? First, during hotel grand openings, Hilton flew in planeloads of dignitaries and Hollywood icons, whom he would "host" during a three-to-four-day inaugural extravaganza. While these proceedings were sent back to the United States and Europe as film shorts intended to precede feature films, the actual presence of the silver screen's finest in a Latin American city attracted the interest (and business) of local elites. The association of Hilton International hotels with the jet set lingered long after Conrad Hilton loaded up his several hundred friends and headed back to the United States on a charter flight. In the United States, Hilton utilized nationally syndicated radio and television programs to promote the Caribé Hilton and Habana Hilton. On January 19, 1950, for example, WOR radio station (New York City) host Bob Elson interviewed Ben Bauer, sales and service coordinator for the contract division for Marshall Field and Company, about his company's role in furnishing the Caribé Hilton. Bauer not only explained the technical aspects of outfitting the hotel but also emphasized the international appeal of the furnishings offered there. "It is a very beautiful hotel," he assured WOR listeners, "very modern. The design leans a little to Swedish modern. It's very interesting, and has been proclaimed by those who visited it as being one of the most beautiful hotels they have ever visited." Elson then emphasized one of the key features of these new hotels: their physical orientation in relation to the visual spectacles offered by each host city. "Mr. Bauer, is the hotel right on the water?" Elson asked. "The hotel," Bauer responded,

> the short side of the hotel, I should say, faces the ocean. Now on this short side are the presidential suite, the manager's suite, and a few choice suites. The other rooms, however, have the unique distinction of each of the rooms have a complete view of the ocean. This is done by a sort of slanted window effect, which, when you walk up to it, gives you a complete view of the ocean from either side of the building. Each room is completely air-conditioned, all furnished in a studio type of a room, which makes it a very livable thing by day and by night.[22]

Ultimately, Hilton knew how to use mass advertising to his advantage and exploited every medium to promote his international hotels.

Hilton International's corporate newsletters also kept track of the prominent entertainers, politicians, and businessmen who patronized or appeared at its hotels. In November 1960, Lucho Azcarraga and Clarence Martin entertained guests at the Panama Hilton. In December 1960, Jose Greco and Company, Anna Maria Allegretto, Xavier Cugat, Abbe Lane, Eartha Kitt, Tony Martin, Vic Damone, Jane Morgan, and Los Chavales de España lit up the winter nights at the Caribé Hilton. Abbe Lane and Xavier Cugat made return visits to the Caribé Hilton in March 1961. Hilton International's commitment to featuring local and Latin American stars underscored the sophisticated appeal of the company's hotels. In July 1961, for example, "among the recent hit headliners at the Club Caribé were Lucho Gatica, noted Chilean singer; Pepe Lara, well-known Mexican song stylist and Daniel Frilobos, Argentine entertainer." Hilton International hotels were also a place to see the stars in their "private" lives (perhaps Hilton's best form of advertising). The Las Brisas Resort in Acapulco, with its private cabanas and beachfront setting, attracted major celebrities and dignitaries from across the United States. In December 1961, Jack Lemmon, Dolores del Rio, Robert Cummings, and Robert Kennedy were guests at the resort. The previous month Miss Universe, Linda Bement, made an appearance at the Panama. But few of the Hilton International properties in Latin America could top the Caribé Hilton for star appeal. The Hilton bulletin for February 1961 calmly noted, "[Among] celebrities visiting the hotel in December were Bob Hope, Zsa Zsa Gabor, Jerry Colonna, and Janis Page." The highly regarded hotels also served as the backdrop for major films. Guests at the Caribé Hilton in September 1961 shared space with three movies being filmed on the property.[23]

Like the Rockefeller brothers, Conrad Hilton packaged American services to fit the needs of tourists within a Latin American context. This complex synthesis is best understood by looking at the architecture and design of Hilton's Latin American properties from the inside out. As architectural historian Annabel Wharton has illustrated in her study of Hilton International's modernist architecture, *Building the Cold War*, the concrete, glass, and steel hotels symbolically represented American geopolitical hegemony in the post–World War II era. It should not be forgotten, however, that these structures were also inspired by a modernist architectural tradition that originated in Europe and was adapted to the needs of the American business world in the modern era. In this sense, the exterior of these buildings was a reflection of American hegemony as well as a statement of global cultural taste. In effect, the exterior of a Hilton International hotel was a type of global packaging that reflected the cosmopolitan orientation of the corporation. It is significant that very few of the Hilton International hotels in Latin America, unlike the Intercontinental hotels, were refurbished properties. This dichotomy is nowhere more evident than in Havana, where Intercontinental leased the stately Hotel Nacional, an architectural paean to Cuba's Spanish heritage. A couple of miles away, in contrast, the Habana Hilton, an imposing tower of steel and glass, lorded over the Malecón (Havana's waterfront promenade) as a testament to the forward, modernist vision of Hilton International. Winning the Cold War may have been one of Conrad Hilton's goals, but expressing the cosmopolitan, internationalist flair for art, architecture, and culture was a significant priority as well.[24]

Hilton International hotels also reflected an eclectic mix of global cultures in the services that they provided to guests. For example, when Frank Wangeman opened the Caribé Hilton in San Juan, many of the methods used to welcome customers originated in Hawaii. He later noted:

Hawaii had a visitor's bureau which really knew how to make the tourist feel at home and indoctrinate him into Hawaiian law and atmosphere—songs, hula, and all that. It was in Hawaii that I learned about the welcome drink with the coconut, pineapples, the leis and all the accoutrements that the tourists from the United States welcomed and found as eye-openers to sub-tropical hospitality. I mentioned this because later on when I had to open the Caribé Hilton, an awful lot of what I saw and learned in Hawaii, which was way ahead of any other tourist-type of welcome, even in Southern Florida, I introduced from Hawaii into Puerto Rico.[25]

In addition to Wangeman's efforts to incorporate a Pacific-based tourist ritual into the welcome ceremony at the Caribé Hilton, Conrad Hilton featured dishes inspired by restaurant entrepreneur Victor J. Bergeron Jr., or "Trader Vic," at Hilton International hotels. Hilton sent Trader Vic to Puerto Rico to "transplant his recipes for tropical drinks to the Caribé Hilton."[26] These efforts at linking Pacific culture to the Caribbean were so successful that Hilton later added a Trader Vic's restaurant to the Caribé Hilton. Another Trader Vic's opened on the ground floor of the Habana Hilton in 1958. While Trader Vic's is no longer a part of the Habana Libre, the Pacific influence clearly remains in the wooden Polynesian sculpture outside of the restaurant, which has been renamed El Polineseo.

The great diversity of international cuisines, which was complemented by plenty of American food, reflected another global aspect of Hilton International hotels. In addition to featuring international restaurants at each hotel, local chefs coordinated recipe standardization throughout the chain. As culinary critic James Beard remarked in an advertisement in the May 26, 1958, *New York Times*, "When Hilton reached across the ocean [or down into Latin America] to establish hotels, a new food pattern had to be planned. It was a wise decision to staff the kitchens largely with native chefs and helpers and to plan menus that would appeal both to Americans who would travel there and to the native populations of the various cities. Great interest was taken in presenting the foods of the particular country, and tourists accepted the challenge to try them."[27] By the late 1960s, the sharing of international recipes was standardized at the training school in Montreal.[28] Even as writer George Bradshaw poked fun at the "average" Hilton customer, who "peered through his glasses at his native breakfast: fresh orange juice, wheat cakes and maple syrup, and plenty of good hot coffee," he also praised the excellence of Hilton restaurants around the globe. "In Tokyo," he noted, "the Grill Room is utterly French with a menu a mile long." In Hong Kong, Bradshaw watched the natives sitting around the bar, "having roast beef and Yorkshire pudding and trifle." Local cuts of beef could also be transformed into steaks for discriminating American tourists: "The beef may be from Kobe or Australia or Florence, but it is all marbled and tender."[29]

Hilton International's commitment to offering amenities that appealed primarily to an American clientele is evidenced in the improvements made to each Hilton hotel built in Latin America during the 1940s and 1950s. Marshall Field of Chicago provided at least 80 percent of the furnishings for the Caribé Hilton. In the largest peacetime airlift to that time, thirty large airplanes, including C-54 cargo planes, delivered three thousand chairs, six hundred beds, 654 tables, 335 floor lamps, silverware, pots, pans, and linens to the new hotel in November 1949.[30] In addition to luxury furniture, Hilton made sure that other technological conveniences were available for his discerning guests. A single cabinet featured radio and telephone facilities in each guest room at the Caribé Hilton, matching the understated elegance of the modern furnishings. The Carrier Corporation provided an extensive air-conditioning system for the hotel complex, including 337 Weathermaster units for the guest rooms. While the open-air architecture of the hotel allowed the ocean breezes to waft through public spaces, guests used to the more climate-controlled interior spaces of the United States enjoyed power over nature in their rooms. Six air-conditioning units were also provided for the public spaces, should conditions require their services.[31] A York plant icemaker and an ice-cutting machine were also installed to produce that most famous of American requests while traveling abroad: ice. The ice plant generated 104 cakes of ice, which could then be reduced to fifteen thousand ice cubes per hour by an ice-cutting machine. Carrier cooling equipment also made it possible for guests to enjoy ice water in their rooms.[32] Mexican journalist Pepe Romero noted in his review of the "ultramodern" Continental Hilton that all four hundred rooms enjoyed "private baths and showers and filtered ice water, radios with stations offering continuous music, telephone and television facilities." In addition to these in-room features, Romero continued, "the hotel also has a modern chemical dry cleaning and pressing plant, and a fully mechanized guest laundry." And for the most cautious of tourists, the Continental Hilton, like the Caribé Hilton and Habana Hilton, boasted "a continuous water supply and the finest of purifying equipment . . . installed to guarantee the tap water for drinking."[33] By the time the Habana Hilton was completed, Conrad Hilton had fully committed his resources to the age of television. In addition to providing guests with in-room televisions (an amenity not offered guests at the opening of the Caribé Hilton some nine years earlier), Hilton equipped his Havana hotel with a closed-circuit broadcasting system. "A television tower on the top level [of the hotel] makes possible direct telecasts of major events from the hotel," a reviewer noted. "A closed circuit channel enables guests to view programs taking place in the function rooms of the hotel on television sets in their rooms." Each of the 630 rooms was also equipped with three-channel radios and circulating ice water.[34] Finally, the location of these hotels—away from the traditional city centers of San Juan, Mexico City, and Havana—accommodated another technological innovation: the automobile. Brochures alerted tourists and locals to the ample amounts of parking surrounding or underneath the hotels. In the case of the Habana Hilton, "guests arriving by automobile drive into an elaborately decorated and planted front court where attendants take their cars down a unique spiral ramp to an underground garage." The pharonic size of the Habana Hilton's foundation easily accommodated a two-level parking deck for 450 cars.[35] These conveniences had a mesmerizing effect on some guests, including the Reverend Robert M. Hamilton, who stayed at the Caribé Hilton in August 1951. So impressed was Hamilton with the Americanized facilities that he wrote to Conrad Hilton, "The view from our room (1017) is beyond description and we truly feel 'at home' in the Caribé Hilton, our home in Puerto Rico."[36]

Set against the global infrastructure of the hotels, Hilton International integrated elements of local art and culture into each hotel. Conrad Hilton, in both his domestic and international hotels, discouraged the idea that his properties formed a "chain"; instead, they were stylized to the individual personalities and attractions of the city in question. Former Hilton International president and one-time planner for the company Curt Strand noted, "We had to build new hotels, mostly in places where there was little precedent. . . . We learned from each project and had to set standards which could, with lots of adjustments to local codes, ideals, prejudices, available materials, budgets, time schedules or lack of them, be fashioned into the prototype of the modern international hotel."[37] This is evident in the interior furnishings of the Caribé Hilton and Continental Hilton. Author J. Knight Willy noted in a review of the Continental Hilton for *Hotel Monthly* that designer David T. Williams "adapted and stylized Mexican arts and designs to create a hotel that is not only thoroughly modern, but also breathes the atmosphere and traditions of the cultural background that is Mexico's." Unlike the Caribé Hilton, most of the interior furnishings of the Continental Hilton were made in Mexico, "making use of native arts and crafts and styling their designs as adapted from ancient Mexican history." The furniture for the hotel was designed in Mexico under the direction of Williams and Morris T.

Bailey, a prominent California furniture designer. Although Marshall Field did not outfit the Continental Hilton, as it did the Caribé Hilton, David Williams formerly worked for Marshall Field for fourteen years as a decorator and designer.[38]

Sometimes, however, distinctions between local and global design elements blurred. If materials were not available locally or were not up to the quality needed for the hotel's image, they could be imported and stand side by side with local elements. For example, at the Continental Hilton, the circular staircase leading from the lobby to the arcade of shops on the mezzanine utilized Mexican white onyx extracted near Tehuantepec. The registration desk also incorporated Mexican white onyx, but the counter was covered with black Belgian marble. This contrast of imported and local materials continued throughout the hotel. J. Knight Willy observed, "To surface the walls on the bank of elevators on the lobby floor, a clear mottled greenish white onyx marble is used. It comes from the Valle de Bravo, State of Mexico. The entrances to the hotel and the large square columns that form a colonnade on the exterior of the hotel are all faced with black Belgian granite."[39] At other times, American artists might be asked to lend a hand in "localizing" the hotel. In the case of the Caribé Hilton, Mary Burger Studios in Los Angeles completed all of the paintings for the guest rooms. The 305 paintings included images of Puerto Rican landscapes and historical landmarks. Burger also made an oil painting of Puerto Rican governor Luís Muñoz Marín, which was placed in the presidential suite. Hilton's choice of a Los Angeles studio to complete the hotel's "Puerto Rican" paintings speaks less to ease of access to American art studios than to Burger's international reputation. "The portrait assignment was well placed," one publication noted, "as Miss Burger is the only artist to paint all the presidents of the Latin American countries." Ultimately, Hilton's access to international resources brought the top talent and materials together for packaging "glocal" hotels.[40]

The Habana Hilton exemplifies the intersection of a modern infrastructure with local cultural motifs. Conrad Hilton spared no expense in making the Habana Hilton a shrine to Cuban folk art and Cuban interpretations of modernism. Hilton International signed an agreement on September 9, 1952, with the Gastronomical Workers Retirement Fund of Cuba to build a "first class hotel" in Havana.[41] Hilton International awarded the architectural and design contract for the hotel to Welton Becket and Associates of Los Angeles. The original artwork, much of which remains well preserved in the Habana Libre Hotel today, betrays the fact that the hotel went over

Figure 2. The former Habana Hilton, Havana. In the post–World War II era of American tourism in the Caribbean, boxy, modernist hotels such as the Habana Hilton lorded over the landscapes of tropical destinations. This is now a Spanish-operated Sol Meliá hotel, the Habana Libre. (Author's photo)

budget and cost approximately $24 million. In April 1959, Welton Becket and Associates took inventory of the Cuban artists whose works adorned the hotel. The most stunning of the exterior works was the Venetian glass mosaic mural in soft blue, turquoise, white, and black that covered the entrance. Constructed in Italy and transported to Cuba, the mural "contained fifteen million separate pieces and weighed nine tons [and] represents an abstract pattern of Cuban fruits and flowers." Upon entering the hotel, one notices the hardwood staircase rising to the mezzanine and then the bronze fountain with fish and coral forms, designed by Roberto Estopinan. This artificial lagoon serves as the centerpiece of the lobby. Walking up the angular staircase and into the Antillas Bar, located between the mezzanine and the outdoor swimming pool, one encounters the juxtaposition of a black-and-white checkerboard marble floor and a bamboo-covered bar set in front of a stunning pastel stone mosaic next to the glass doors leading to the pool. Artist Rene Portocarrero designed the ten panels of seventy-five twelve-by-twelve-inch tiles that represented Cuban legends in abstract. Welton Beckett boasted, "This mural is possibly the first of its type done and was featured by colorings of beige, brown, gunmetal, pale yellow, orange, and 24-karat gold." The works of Cuban artists covered the public spaces of the hotel and adorned the rooms as well. Guest rooms featured serigraphs by Raul Milian, Augustín Fernández, Mirta Cerra, and Servando Morens. Those willing to pay for the suites at the Habana Hilton enjoyed paintings and tapestries designed and rendered by Cundo Bermudez, Lolo Solvida, Rene Portocarrero, Raul Milian, Servando Caberra Moreno, Lopez DiRube, and Luís Martínez Pedro. Fidel Castro, who made the Habana Hilton his home, apparently believed that the artistic significance of the hotel should be preserved. The murals on the exterior of the hotel and in the Antillas Bar have been preserved, and new works of abstract art dedicated to the Revolution have been added to the hotel, including one added in the early 1970s that looks like a firing tank rolling off the wall into the Antillas Bar.[42]

The use of local cultural motifs as a vehicle for promoting a global brand has become de rigueur in the world of international business and has been supplanted by brands that are simply global and not multicultural. Hilton's genius rests on the fact that his brand was at once global and multicultural. Furthermore, his contribution to the stimulation of folk art throughout Latin America, at least for the purposes of building his hotels, was significant. The art in the Habana Hilton is still worthy of praise as an example of fine art. Moreover, while Hilton imported many of the furnishings for his hotels from the United States, import restrictions, such as those imposed in

Mexico during the 1940s, forced Hilton International to work with local artisans to furnish the Continental Hilton. Sid Wilner, legal counsel for Hilton International from 1958 into the 1980s, remembered: "In Mexico we revived the pottery and lamp industries, which became very important exports, and some furniture. This was true in so many places where designs would be made, old crafts would be restored, orders would be given in building the hotel, which were of sufficient size as to warrant the renewal or the creation of factories to produce, in accordance with the designs they were given."[43]

Socially, Hilton International hotels in Latin America demonstrated unique functions as corridors of both American and global culture. What Conrad Hilton stated with regard to his domestic hotels in a 1954 speech at Cornell University might have been applied to his international hotels as well: "The very architecture of our buildings contributes to the city: Their interiors are generally authentic reproductions of period and contemporary art, décor and furnishing. Efficient equipment and facilities dramatically exemplify American life and its achievements. You know as well as I know modern American hotels typify and epitomize, even carry within themselves, a cross-section of American life."[44] The function of Hilton International hotels in Latin America and the rest of the world only magnified the American way of life for travelers who dared not venture out among the locals. Eleven years later, George Bradshaw elaborated on the idea of Hilton International hotels as American "spaces" for an article in *Vogue* magazine entitled "The View from a Tall Glass Oasis: The Subliminal Pleasures of Hilton Hotels." The design and placement of these buildings catered to the traveler who did not want to be in the middle of the city's action, but did want to have spectacular views of the city. "Wherever possible they are set a little apart from the city on a rise," Bradshaw observed. "In Istanbul or Teheran, in Rome or Hong Kong or Athens or Tokyo you can have from your room a panorama of the entire city. . . . I never really saw London until I looked out of eighteenth-story windows, and in Istanbul, the sweep of the Bosporus with Asia beyond is one of the most pleasing sights in the world." Inviting gardens and swimming pools, another American symbol of post–World War II affluence, embellished every property, allowing business guests and tourists the opportunity to "reconnect" with their own "native" culture. What Bradshaw wrote about Iran could easily have been written about the function of Hilton International hotels in Latin America: "Don't tell me it isn't a joy to set down in Iran and discover that you are living at a Waldorf in the wilderness. All you need is a shower in an imperial bathroom . . . for your shakes to disappear. In a couple of days you feel quite at home in the bazaars of Teheran or the ruins of Isfahan, and even that man in the dining room who seemed, the first night, . . . so exotic . . . now seems quite usual, part of Things as they Should Be." Furthermore, Hilton International negotiated the process of shopping for guests, providing ample area for shops. The ground floor of the Habana Libre is still one of the major shopping arcades in the Cuban capital. In effect, the imposing hotel is structurally sustained by the ample shop space on the ground floor. In Bradshaw's experience with Hilton hotels, "Unless you know a city well, it is at the very least time consuming to dig out the right shops. The Hiltons have solved that by bringing the shops to you."[45] In sum, Hilton International hotels sheltered the less adventurous traveler from the vicissitudes of foreign culture by offering the comforts of home and a negotiated cultural introduction to the host country.

At the same time, however, Hilton International also functioned as a corridor of global culture, business, and politics. Well before the Rockefellers had conceived the concept of the World Trade Center, Conrad Hilton styled his Hilton International hotels as "community centers." Apart from his efforts to help the United States win the Cold War, Hilton's hotels served a legitimate international ideal related to the exchange of ideas and culture and the transaction of business. "We all know that a hotel should be the center of the community," Hilton stated in 1954. "It now becomes even more than that. It becomes a focal point for the exchange of knowledge between millions of people, foreigners and natives, who have come there because they want to know each other better, trade with each other and live in peace. They become exposed to the best their history has produced: their art, their architecture, their religion, their philosophy, their natural beauty, their national personality—their very way of life."[46] Space for banquets, conventions, the fine arts, and restaurants provided the ideal climate for the exchange of business, political, and cultural ideas. John Houser reaffirmed this ideal as a very real function of international hotels: "The hotel has a vital role to play [in furthering international exchanges]. It is no longer merely a place where the creature needs of the guest are met. It has become the social and civic center of the city and country [and nowhere was this more true than in Latin America]." This not only pertained to the creation of a place where people could share ideas but also to the infrastructure and technical skills to facilitate exchange between foreigners. "The international hotel is the logical source of language needed for communication," Houser continued. "Multi-lingual switchboards, stenographic and translating services must be available so that the hotel can serve as a temporary office for the business traveler. The new international hotel must be all things to all men, as far as humanly possible."[47] In an advertisement in the *New York Times* in 1958, Richard Joseph similarly noted, "Next to absorbing local atmosphere, the average American traveler wants to get to know some of the people in the countries he is visiting." In addition to the hotels providing space for business meetings, socials, weddings, and banquets, "American visitors are likely to encounter many local English speaking residents in the lobbies, restaurants, and bars." Joseph also noted the growing social function of the public relations director at each Hilton International hotel. This individual promoted the hotel and also introduced American guests to local residents.[48] As mentioned, the ratio of lodging customers at the Caribé Hilton in 1951 was approximately one foreign visitor (including Puerto Ricans) for each two American customers.[49] The number of non-Americans who either ate in the restaurants, participating in social events there, or attended meetings at the hotel probably pushed the number of non-U.S. citizens visiting the hotel into closer balance with those from the United States.

Hilton International's Latin American properties functioned as significant global corridors in the region's major cities. The company kept close records of the international dignitaries and delegations that visited its properties and important events held at each hotel throughout the late 1950s and 1960s. At the Continental Hilton in December 1960, for example, the French Comite de Elegance planned to host a French Night, complete with a fashion show. The hotel's services also won the accolades of Angelina Acuna Castañeda of Guatemala, recently selected as the "Woman of the Americas." She praised the hotel, "its setting, its service, and its atmosphere." That same month, Hilton's Acapulco resort, Las Brisas, hosted Prince Albert and Princess Paola of Liege. Company publications also noted that the Panama Hilton served as a stopping point for numerous cruise ships sailing through the canal, including the SS *New Amsterdam*, SS *Mauretania*, SS *Rotterdam*, SS *Bianca C*, and SS *Cristoforo Colombo*. The busy month of December 1960 saw the Rotary Club hold a party attended by President Roberto Chiari. Pan American Airways also held a meeting at the Panama Hilton for "the inauguration of its new jet service to South America." During the fall of 1961, the Ford Motor Company brought three groups of employees, comprising fifteen hundred associates, through the hotel. The following year, Paul Anka entertained five hundred children from welfare institutions at the Caribé Hilton in January. During the same month, Sears Roebuck, the Mexican Supreme Court of Justice, the Germany embassy, and the Knights of Columbus held conventions at the Continental Hilton. The Panama Hilton reported at the same time that "the President of the Republic of Panama, Roberto F. Chiari, has . . . been a frequent guest."[50] Perhaps the biggest testament to Hilton hotels serving as community centers in Latin America occurred after the Habana Hilton had been taken over by Castro's regime in 1960. Shortly thereafter, the Soviet Union established its first Cuban embassy on two floors of the hotel. This also became the de facto meeting place for Cuba's allies. Castro held his important press conferences on the top floor of the hotel with its commanding view of the Malecón.

3

Cathedrals of Chaos

Hilton International's early history in Latin America was marked by numerous challenges, including adverse tropical weather, earthquakes, contract disputes, and the Cuban Revolution. Adverse weather, particularly during the hurricane season, negatively affected occupation rates at Hilton's seaside resorts. In September 1960, for example, Hurricane Donna kept occupancy rates low at the Caribé Hilton. The worst, however, happened elsewhere on the island, as floods and heavy rains claimed hundreds of lives in the region. Weather also impacted publicity for the tourist industry in the United States. At the Virgin Islands Hilton on Saint Thomas, Hurricane Donna did not inflict any damage on the property, but did affect occupancy rates for at least one weekend in September.[1] Two months later, bad weather, coupled with an airline disaster in the New York City area, drove the number of no-shows at the hotel as high as 65 percent.[2] A heavy cloudburst at the seaside Las Brisas Hilton on November 12, 1961, inflicted minimal damage on the hotel, but the hotel staff spent the day keeping guests calm, many of whom "contributed to relief funds for homeless and hungry people in Acapulco and the countryside who had suffered from the storm."[3]

Inland hotels were also subject to the capricious effects of natural disaster. During July 1957, a strong earthquake rumbled through the Valley of Mexico, causing hundreds of deaths and structurally damaging many buildings, including the Continental Hilton. As one reporter who was staying at the hotel remembered, "Plaster fell, lights went out. From a few blocks away there came a tremendous roar as a five-story apartment building collapsed on itself into a heap of . . . rubble. . . . Pure, blind uncontrollable terror resulted here as it would have anywhere." As guests made their way through the dark, the stairs and hallways filled with debris. Guests attributed the relative calm that prevailed in the hotel to the staff for their "complete, errorless, total efficiency."[4] Following the earthquake, Hilton International reinforced the hotel under the direction of earthquake specialists "to insure that this hotel would be completely structurally sound and safe under any foreseeable circumstance."[5] Unfortunately, the great Mexico City earthquake of 1985 helped seal the fate of the Continental Hilton, inflicting irreparable damage to the structure. The hotel was subsequently torn down.[6]

Contract disputes also plagued Hilton International's Latin American operations. Following the sale of Hilton International to TWA in 1967, the hotel chain continued to operate several hotels in Mexico, including the Continental Hilton in Mexico City, the Guadalajara Hilton, the Acapulco Hilton, and Las Brisas Resort, also located in Acapulco. In 1982, Hilton International encountered contract disputes with the Alemán family, owners of the Continental Hilton, the Acapulco Hilton, and Las Brisas. The Mexican constitution of 1917 strictly stipulated that leases in coastal Mexico expired after a ten-year period. The Alemán family decided not to renew the lease, hoping to sell off the property instead. Former Hilton International president Curt Strand remembers that the Hilton managers were threatened with bodily harm if they did not leave the hotel premises in Acapulco. In Strand's recollection, "One of the managers was driven to a country road and thrown out of a vehicle." Cooler heads prevailed, and the Mexican court system settled the dispute in the Alemán family's favor. Rodolfo Casparius, a former Hilton International executive and preeminent authority on the Mexican hotel industry in the twentieth century, remembers the event somewhat differently. According to Casparius, the Alemáns contended that the lease with Hilton generated higher revenues for the chain than for the owners and wanted the lease canceled. Casparius argues that Hilton brought suit against the former Mexican president. In Casparius's recollection, "negotiations deteriorated and the Hilton International management team was thrown out of the property by men carrying machine guns."[7] Whatever the case, this episode was a serious setback to Hilton in Mexico, not to mention a significant failure in negotiating the political landscape of the country.

The biggest challenge for Hilton International in Latin America during the 1950s was the Cuban Revolution. The Habana Hilton opened in 1958 against a backdrop of political and economic unrest. Less than a year later, on January 1, 1959, hotel employees crammed the three entrances to the hotel, fighting to keep mobs from overrunning the hotel. When the July

26th Movement's soldiers descended on Havana, the ultramodern, world-class Habana Hilton turned into a revolutionary enclave.[8] José Menendez, general manager of the hotel, remained optimistic that Hilton would benefit in the long term from its exemplary treatment of all parties concerned. "The good will that the Habana Hilton has gained for itself will not be forgotten," Menendez told workers in a special meeting on January 5, 1959, "as, in addition to taking care of its guests, who were fed hot food three times a day, troops of soldiers were lodged and fed during all hours of the night, as they would arrive, and the hotel has received nothing but praise for the able way in which they were handled." Menendez told workers that conditions would improve quickly, and "now that freedom has been restored in Cuba, tourism will again flourish and the hotel is to be readied for the influx of tourists when everything is completely back to normal again." Although Hilton executives remained optimistic, such conditions at the hotel would not prevail until over thirty years later, when the hotel was placed under the management of a Spanish hotel chain.[9]

When Fidel Castro rolled into Havana during the second week of January, he selected the Habana Hilton as his temporary home and base of operations. This offered Hilton International executives unusually easy access to Castro and his plans for tourism on the island. Hilton International legal counsel Sid Wilner remembered Castro as a likable fellow. He praised Castro for his moderation in private, but could not understand his revolutionary rhetoric in public. Wilner remembered: "The problem was that if you met him in the evening and he talked very calmly and rationally in a very friendly way, and then he'd get on the radio and start talking and he'd talk for hours and he'd work himself up and then go into all these tirades against American imperialism . . . and of course it negated all the tourism initiatives he had set in [trade]." As a result, most of the guests at the Habana Hilton during 1959 were "mostly scavengers, sharks, looking to see what advantage they could take in this situation."[10]

Castro's regime and Hilton International executives collaborated to try and head off fears that Cuba was not a safe place to vacation. Castro issued a statement on January 10, 1959, inviting American tourists and businessmen back to Cuba, "with the assurance that they will be welcomed by all citizens of our country." He assured tourists that Cuba was "back to normal." Hilton International published Castro's statement as a press release the following day. "This statement," the release asserted, "was borne out by the orderly removal of troops from the hotel's main ballroom."[11]

Meanwhile, in the United States, Henry Luce's press arsenal attempted to bury the Castro regime and discourage tourists from traveling to Cuba. To add insult to injury, however, not even articles in the American press that promoted Cuban tourism in early 1959 gave much confidence to travelers. On Monday, January 12, 1959, Phyllis Battelle, a syndicated writer for the Hearst Headline Service, recounted her "positive experiences" in Havana. "It is frightening to land at Havana's airport and see two dozen troops of these proud, grimy-bearded ones waiting," she wrote. After being herded into the customs area at the airport, she noted, one waited for some time before being authorized to travel into Havana. If you were cleared for not carrying weapons into the country, then it was off to the Habana Hilton. "Lounging [behind a rope around the entrance] are more of the same," she reported. "Dozens more beards, with the other paraphernalia of the rebel[s], the bland faces and the guns. They let you pass and you go to the desk where the assistant manager greets you cheerfully." To put one's mind totally at ease, Battelle noted, "For three days, you never get on an elevator without seeing a rifle—but the rebels are usually polite enough to point it at the ceiling." Such ringing endorsements of Cuba under siege had dire effects on tourism.[12]

Hilton International executive Robert Caverly returned several times to Havana to assess the status of the Habana Hilton as well as the social, economic, and political conditions in the Cuban capital. On February 1, 1959, Caverly wrote to Conrad Hilton while flying on an airplane headed out of Havana to Puerto Rico. "The situation at the Habana Hilton is nerve wracking," he opened. "However, every time I see the grandeur of the hotel and think of the volume of travel to Havana in normal times I am impressed with the fact that we should eventually have a fine, profitable operation—if we can just keep the hotel alive until the situation normalizes." Caverly's muted optimism reflected the corporation's continued commitment to the long-term success of the hotel and a willingness to operate under the dictates of the new regime. Despite dismal predictions for reservations and conference bookings, and rapidly declining summer vacation prospects, Caverly expressed a desire to press forward. Chronic labor issues and a government edict to close the casinos posed additional problems for the profitable operation of the hotel. Furthermore, nightclub business had virtually ground to a halt at the hotel. "There is [an] emphasis on quietness and unostentatiousness with the feeling that any extravagance might lead to questions about where the money came from," he reported. "This results in virtually no patronage in night clubs, etc., but local business is starting to come back to [quiet], dark restaurants such as our Trader [Vic's]." The Habana Hilton was not alone in its difficulties. During his stay in Havana, Caverly cased the properties of the Riviera, Nacional, and Capri hotels to assess their business prospects. At the Riviera, there were not more than 20 people in the lobby, bar, or restaurants at the normally lively hour of 9:30 p.m. on a Saturday night. At the Nacional, he found about a dozen people at 10:00 p.m. on the same night, and at the Capri, Caverly encountered only a couple of people in the public areas around 10:30 p.m. In contrast, when he returned to the Habana Hilton at 10:45 p.m., the approximately 150 people in the ample public areas must have overwhelmed him. "This is certainly not a conclusive survey," he continued, "but the number of people I saw in the various hotels bears out our feeling about the relative amount of business each is doing." Despite the clouds that loomed overhead, Caverly had some basis for his optimism.[13]

The political evolution of the new regime further hampered Hilton's efforts to attractively package tourism in Cuba's capital. Arthur Elminger visited the Habana Hilton in July 1959 to assess conditions there. Thousands of peasants from western Cuba had descended on the capital to support Castro's land reforms. The hotel, Castro's temporary headquarters, was besieged by the mass confusion. "They came from early in the morning till late at night," Elminger remembered, "some in shoes, some with hats, some without. Most of them had never seen a city, nor electricity, not to speak [of] the wonders of the [Habana] Hilton." As on many other occasions during 1959, the hotel staff worked to accommodate the masses of farmers and military men milling through the hotel. "At first we were requested to provide available accommodations and food," Elminger wrote, "but eventually succeeded to admit 400 [peasants] to sleep in the garage on improvised cots; they were fed in the employees cafeteria." Elminger left Cuba with doubts concerning the viability of the hotel's future there. "To what extreme this new trend of politic[s] will grow seems not yet tangible," he wrote to Conrad Hilton, "but in calm observation and in the spectrum of these past weeks, Cuba most certainly develops . . . [nationalism], at the price of capital and foreign interests."[14]

The Castro regime's failure to promote tourism, as much as the radicalization of the revolutionary movement in late 1959, turned the initial optimism of Hilton International's executives for working within the framework of Cuba's new governmental structure to pessimism in the fall of 1959. When television personality Jack Paar visited the Habana Hilton in October 1959, he reported that only about thirty-five other people were staying at the hotel. "Tourists have stopped going to Cuba in the most part," he told his national audience over WRCA-TV (New York) and NBC-TV on his October 12, 1959, show. "It's because of the [media] scare," he continued. "I can tell you that I saw nothing but friendship and a welcome out to all Americans, there are so few. But they need tourism very, very badly." Paar's appeals went unheeded, but they illustrated the dire business straits in which the hotel found itself.[15] While lack of customers made access to Castro easier—Paar told stories of the revolutionary being spotted in the hotel's restaurant frequently or micromanaging the casino—it did not ease the concerns of Hilton executives regarding the hotel's long-term profitability.

In fact, evidence from Conrad Hilton's papers suggests that Hilton International played a much more proactive role in its exit from Havana than previously thought. As early as February 1959, executive Robert Caverly suggested that one option Hilton retained for the Habana Hilton, should the new government continue to drag its feet on tourism promotion, would simply be to pull out of the hotel and let the government manage the property.[16] Caverly and other Hilton executives clearly understood that Hilton did not own the property, the company merely managed it. "I believe we will have to force the issue in whatever action we decide to take," he wrote to Hilton. "The Government is so disorganized that they do not have any intra-government communication or administrative procedure for reaching a major decision regarding [tourism labor issues]. It does not appear that any one Minister—and probably not Castro himself—would make such a decision on his own."[17] As occupancy rates at the property continued to fall and the Cuban government failed to attract tourists in sufficient numbers to fill the Habana Hilton or the other large luxury hotels of Vedado, including the Capri Hotel, the Hotel Riviera, and the Hotel Nacional, executive attitudes shifted toward pulling out of the venture.

Hilton International legal counsel Sid Wilner played a significant role in Hilton's exit from Havana. As credit lines made available by the new regime early in 1959 began to dry up in the fall of the same year, Wilner approached the new Cuban government about the possibility of extending more credit for hotel operations. Ernesto "Che" Guevara's appointment as head of the Bank of Cuba and the growing influence of Communism in the labor unions portended a gloomy day for the future of mass tourism in Cuba. As a result, Wilner, according to his own recollections, presented Fidel Castro with an ultimatum. "I wrote a letter to Castro, being quite bold," Wilner remembered several decades later, "telling him that we had tried cooperation with them to make this hotel a success . . . but we were now running out of working capital and I could see only two solutions. One was for the government to continue to pour in money or two, what might make more sense, was for the government to take over. *As a result of that, that was when they nationalized our company.*"[18]

In November 1959, Conrad Hilton wrote a brief letter to Arthur Elminger, who had served as the head of Latin American hotels for Hilton International. "It looks like Castro has destroyed all business," Hilton observed, "and is rapidly destroying all future business in the country. Here we are in Puerto Rico completely booked up and no one wants to go to Havana." After briefly discussing Wilner's options for Hilton International in Cuba, he asserted, "We are definitely not going to put another nickel down there so I am wondering what they [the government] are going to do."[19] Elminger concurred, noting that the new regime was growing increasingly more radical—and looking for new channels of revenue—as time went on. He also noted that the Cuban government had recently taken over operations of the Hotel Riviera. While Castro had previously been viewed as a friend (and guest) at the Hilton, such a move, in Elminger's eyes, meant that it was "not impossible for Fidel Castro to see fit to frown at [the possibility of taking over] the Habana Hilton." Elminger agreed with Conrad Hilton, noting, "Our recommendation is to continue to operate the Habana Hilton until the end of the year on a day to day basis, but we wholeheartedly concur with you that we should not put an additional nickel into the hotel."[20]

In light of these documents, two new conclusions regarding Hilton's presence in Havana during the early phases of the Revolution have come to light. First, Hilton International executives, including Conrad Hilton himself, displayed an unusual degree of flexibility in trying to find a viable way to operate and package the hotel within the political and economic context of the new Cuban government. Despite the presence of socialist and Communist tendencies, profitability—as much as ideology—determined the realist approach of the corporation to its difficult situation in the Cuban capital. Second, Hilton International played a far more proactive role in its exit from Havana than Fidel Castro later suggested.[21]

In the wake of Hilton International's expressed intent to leave Cuba if tourist-planning efforts did not improve, Castro made two separate speeches to the Hotel Workers Union and Food Workers Union on June 16, 1960. Almost identical in substance, Castro informed the tourist-sector employees that Cuban tourism would now cater to Cuban nationals and not to foreigners. The climax of the speeches came when he announced to the workers that the Habana Hilton would shortly be renamed the Habana Libre. Castro stressed the degree to which Cubans had been exploited in the building of these hotels, laying particular stress on the financing agreement reached with the Food Workers Union for construction of the Habana Hilton. "The Riviera was built with state financing, for the most part and then turned over to foreign interests," he remarked. "The National Hotel had been state property for many years, and then was turned over to foreign interests." "But the final straw," he emphatically noted, "was reached with one of the most immoral and shameful acts committed in our country in the case of the Hotel Hilton." Wild applause followed Castro's comments. Castro derided Conrad Hilton for owning a chain of hotels around the world and requiring Cubans to finance his hotel in Havana. With Castro having issued the definitive challenge to Hilton International's presence in Cuba, the company quickly exited the island.[22] On June 22, 1960, Robert Caverly, who initially believed Hilton International could work with the new regime, fired off a memo to all Hilton hotels, informing them that the hotel had been renamed and that any requests for reservations at the hotel should be "courteously declined with the simple statement that the Hotel has been [taken over] by the Cuban government and that the Hilton organization at the present time has no control over its management or any relation to its operation and is therefore not in a position to confirm the reservation." A month later, Hilton International executive John Joseph admonished all Hilton general managers to comb their hotels for "matches, tent cards, advertisement reproductions, etc." advertising the Habana Hilton and discard them. Hilton's short but storied history in Cuba had come to a close.[23]

The Hilton International Legacy

By 1963, the golden age of international travel in Latin America had passed. Jet travel brought Europe within closer reach of American tourists. Revolution and political instability had also cast a cloud over the romance of tropical tourism and high profits south of the border. With the stabilization of Europe and Japan, Conrad Hilton traded his predominantly north-south business patterns for east-west transactions. A video produced by Hilton International that same year, *Hilton: Innkeeper Extraordinaire*, featured the opening of various Hilton hotels, from London to Tokyo. Conrad Hilton's commitment to Latin America had not flickered out, as Hilton International would continue to expand in the region. Yet the region's role as a training ground in the postwar world had expired, and more profitable markets beckoned. By 1968, Conrad Hilton stepped down from the chairmanship of Hilton International, and the company had been sold to TWA. In the 1990s, Hilton International became an orphan once again, only to be acquired by the European corporation Ladbrooke.[24]

Yet the impact of Hilton International in Latin America would be longer lasting than its initial establishment of hotels in the region during the late 1940s and 1950s. Perhaps the Caribé Hilton had the greatest effect. Following its design by Puerto Rican architects Toro and Ferrer, a rash of modernist hotels sprang up across the island, not only in San Juan but also at Dorado

Beach and in the pearl of the Caribbean, Ponce, Puerto Rico. Latin American hotel expert Howard Meek noted as early as February 1953, "The impact of the Caribé Hilton on the other hotels of Puerto Rico has naturally been quite marked. In the capital city area the Condado Beach Hotel has come up with a new wing fully air-conditioned. La Rada, shortly to open, has apartments and individual suites and porches of ultra modern design. The Normandie has already greatly modernized one floor and has much further renovation planned, and the nearly complete Darlington is also most modern."[25] The impact of Hilton innovations was felt elsewhere throughout the region. The father of modern hotel management in Mexico, Rodolfo Casparius, credited Hilton International with transforming the hotel industry in his home country due to its innovative new management techniques and the high-quality services it provided for guests. "The success of Hilton created an interest in Mexico towards large investments in the hotel industry," he later observed. "The Hotel Alameda, the Camino Real hotels, Fiesta Palace, Plaza Internacional, Princess and many others that today form the nucleus of the five star hotels in Mexico . . . [and that] should be considered because of their construction, equipment, and service, among the best in the world."[26] Casparius, who was a valued Hilton International executive, would go on to apply many of the skills he had learned with Hilton to the Mexican state-owned Camino Real chain. He would be responsible for opening luxurious urban hotels, such as the Camino Real in Mexico City, and for one of the first luxury resorts in Cancún.

In fact, it might be said that Conrad Hilton's greatest legacy in Latin America had less to do with the direction that he charted for the turbulent history of Hilton International and more to do with the future of its competitors. Since the late 1960s, Hilton International began to lose market share in Latin America as competing American chains, namely Sheraton, recently purchased and infused with cash by telecommunications giant ITT, opened a string of hotels throughout the region. This continued when ITT sold the chain to Starwood, which reaffirmed its commitment to luxury hotels in Latin America, including refurbishment of an exquisitely located—and recently refurbished—Argentine property overlooking Iguazu Falls. More important, Hilton and Sheraton have lost ground in the market to national hotel chains, such as Camino Real in Mexico, and European chains, including Sol Meliá (see chapter 8). Terrorism directed at Hilton properties in countries such as Colombia during the 1980s further inhibited confidence in the region. As a result of instability in Bogotá, Hilton pulled out of the city in the late 1980s, leaving the Policemen's Pension Fund with an empty skyscraper that had been built as the new Bogotá Hilton. For the domestic

Hilton chain, Barron Hilton, Conrad's son, credits the Caribbean properties, particularly the Caribé Hilton, the chain's first casino, with steering Hilton's Hotels Corporation into the world of gaming.[27]

Ultimately, Conrad Hilton's legacy in Latin America transcends his avowed war on Communism. While this touched his corporation in an unforeseen way in Cuba, his initial interest in the region had as much to do with his childhood days playing with friends in the Rio Grande, where Spanish and English mingled with the laughter and the splashing water. Like Nelson Rockefeller, Conrad Hilton understood, as well as any American businessman could, the spirit, culture, and social nuances of Latin America's elite society. Furthermore, he offered efficiency and American management techniques to an industry that had previously relied on traditions dating back to the colonial era. Nevertheless, the social, political, and economic vicissitudes of the 1950s and 1960s challenged U.S.-based tourism development throughout the region and caused a shift toward national tourism development throughout the Caribbean.

PART 2

The Latin Caribbean

4
Dorado Beach

The Puerto Rican government, through PRIDCO, was not only the first Latin political entity to develop a strategy for state-directed tourism development in the mid-1940s but also the most likely to involve American hotel companies in its projects. While the Caribé Hilton was the first state-sponsored hotel, Laurance Rockefeller's decentralized Dorado Beach resort community, located some twenty-five miles to the west of San Juan and opened in 1958, represented the first Puerto Rican attempt to approach tourism development through a low-density approach. Nevertheless, in 1967 Rockefeller agreed to sell 80 percent of his Dorado Beach Resort to Eastern Airlines, along with a 40 percent stake in the RockResorts chain of decentralized, low-density hotels located in the continental United States, Hawaii, the Virgin Islands, and Puerto Rico. This decision placed Rockefeller in a close relationship with a corporation possessing the capital to expand the resort property, which already included two Robert Trent Jones Sr. golf courses, approximately thirty residential home lots, and a golf clubhouse, but it was also driven by the need for short-term profits. Additional investment capital could provide additional golf courses, condominiums, and a new convention hotel to complement the original Dorado Beach Hotel. For Eastern Airlines, under the leadership of Floyd Hall, Dorado Beach fit into the airline's plans to diversify revenue streams through tourism development in the Caribbean. The danger, however, lay in Eastern's inexperience with tourism development and its unrealistic expectations for quick returns on investments.

For Rockefeller and RockResorts, the danger in the alliance lay in the possibility of transforming a low-density project into a higher-density resort with a split personality.

Ironically, no one understood the implications of this merger—for either RockResorts or Eastern Airlines—better than outsider Paul S. Weber, president of Almar International, a construction equipment company based in Wyckoff, New Jersey. Weber had been a highly satisfied customer of the Dorado Beach Hotel, with no apparent professional connections to either Eastern or RockResorts. His correspondence with Floyd Hall, however, was almost prophetic in regard to the impact Eastern's merger would have on the resort property. Weber boldly wrote to Hall on September 29, 1967, in the wake of the merger announcement:

> It was with a certain amount of trepidation that I read in the *NY Times* yesterday of the purchase of 80% interest in the Dorado Beach Hotel by Eastern Airlines. I notice that no changes are planned, the present management [RockResorts] will continue to operate, etc. But somewhere along the line your board of directors will decide that the operation is not sufficiently profitable. The physical plant will have to be expanded, the services and facilities downgraded, package tours arranged—and the Dorado Beach becomes just another Miami or San Juan Beach Front. I can only hope my wife and I can go back one more time before these changes occur. Places with the charm and serenity of the Dorado Beach are fast disappearing, and just as good money is driven out by bad money, quality gives way to quantity.[1]

A week later, on October 3, 1967, Hall defended his company's acquisition with a cordially tepid reply. Perhaps missing the point of Weber's letter in regard to the resort's environmental sustainability, Hall noted, "I can assure you that it is profitable and that it has every expectation for continuing profitability in the future. Had this not been so, we at Eastern Airlines would not have invested in it." Hall also defended RockResorts' and Eastern's ability to preserve RockResorts' charm, but within the context of future profitability (something Weber had warned against in his initial letter). "It is our intention to preserve those qualities indefinitely," Hall concluded, "for we believe there is a growing number of people who appreciate the finer things and I see no reason why quantity must displace quality."[2] In a final response, Weber reiterated that the issue at stake had less to do with who managed the property than with the principles that governed a resort's management, be they either those of sustainable tourism or mass tourism:

> I am quite sure the Dorado Beach is a profitable operation (it was certainly doing a capacity business when I was there). My point was that when an operation is profitable there is a tendency to try to make it more profitable. I have not yet heard of any business venture immune to this. Almost the only way a resort doing capacity business can make more money is to expand. I hope this will not happen to the Dorado Beach for a long time, but I reserve decision until the effect of larger and larger capacity planes can be determined. For the present I can only hope that the Caribbean and Hawaiian Islands will not become Coney Islands.[3]

According to Hall's correspondence, the Eastern president did not engage the New Jersey advocate of sustainable tourism in another round of letters. Ironically, however, these brief exchanges at the beginning of Eastern's tenure as partner in RockResorts and majority owner of Dorado Beach Resort illustrated the central dilemma for Hall and Eastern Airlines as well as for Laurance J. Rockefeller and his vision for Dorado Beach's future.

This conundrum—profitability versus sustainability—took place in a certain politico-economic context of Puerto Rican tourism development. While chapter 1 briefly explored the architectural evolution of the Dorado Beach and Cerromar Beach hotels, this chapter examines the processes of negotiation for the privileges of tourism development, as well as the initial challenges of building the Dorado Beach Resort in the late 1950s as Puerto Rico's premiere planned resort community. Ultimately, RockResorts and Eastern Airlines were jointly responsible for the downward economic spiral of Dorado Beach as a result of the massive expansion plan that included the construction of the Cerromar Beach Hotel, an additional Robert Trent Jones Sr. golf course, and thirty-four condominiums. Eastern's demands for quick returns on sizable investments, and RockResorts' belief that cooperation with an airline company that knew very little about tourism or resort development would help to expand Dorado Beach with the same system of values, landed the resort community in the hands of creditors by 1976 and management for the two hotels in the hands of Regent Hotels International by 1977. Hyatt Regency would purchase the hotel properties in 1985. Ultimately, when the pendulum swung from sustainable tourism to larger-scale resort projects, the owners of the Dorado Beach Resort lost economic control of the property Weber so fondly remembered from his stay there.

Origins of a Decentralized Resort Community

The brief historiography of Puerto Rico tourism has generally privileged the contributions of Teodoro Moscoso, director of PRIDCO, during the 1940s and 1950s, particularly in relation to the development of the Caribé Hilton.[4] Moscoso would also be Laurance Rockefeller's key contact in developing Dorado Beach. However, Puerto Rican governor Luís Muñoz Marín provided philosophical inspiration for Rockefeller's decision to develop a decentralized resort on the island. On June 16, 1955, while delivering the commencement address at Harvard University, Muñoz Marín elaborated a new plan, entitled Operation Serenity, whose purpose was to match Puerto Rico's industrial development with an equally vigorous development of Puerto Rico's people through educational, cultural, and recreational programs. At the opening ceremony of the Dorado Beach Hotel on December 2, 1958, Rockefeller observed, "In regard to Operation Serenity, it is our hope that the concept of decentralization, which we have used in the development of Dorado, and the fact that we are seeking to bring people back into direct daily contact in their lives with Nature and its enjoyment and inspiration, will be, at least indirectly, a contribution in that area too."[5]

Creating Dorado Beach as an integrated hotel, residential, and golf course development required more, however, than a shared admiration of Operation Serenity. Geographically, the city of Dorado, Puerto Rico, is located approximately twenty-five miles to the west of San Juan. Established as a municipality under Spanish control in 1842, Dorado was built near the Tao River, an artery for the many sugarcane and cattle haciendas that drove the local economy.[6] The area developed by RockResorts from the 1950s through the 1970s originally belonged to hacienda owner Pablo Ubarri during the late nineteenth century, and was sold to New York physician Alfred Livingston in 1905 while the doctor was on a business trip in the Dorado area. Dispatched to the island in 1903 to verify an ultimately fraudulent land deal, Livingston ended up purchasing sixteen hundred acres of land adjoining Sardinera Bay, where he developed a coconut and pineapple plantation. Following her father's death in 1923, Clara Livingston maintained the estate. This included defending the bay from Puerto Rican law enforcement officers, who believed the family did not have clear title to the land. The U.S. Supreme Court eventually threw out the case against her. By the early 1950s, Clara Livingston wanted to pass the land to a responsible individual or entity. California-based investor Frederick Crocker Whitman, great-grandson of railroad baron Charles Crocker, considered the location ideal for a new hotel. Robert Trent Jones Sr. was also designing an oceanfront golf course in front of Sardinera Bay.

By early 1953, Fred Whitman had contacted Laurance Rockefeller to see if RockResorts would be interested in developing a hotel at the Livingston estate.[7] Laurence Rockefeller visited the estate with Teodoro Moscoso on February 14, 1953.[8] Rockefeller then found himself in the precarious position of entering a development project with Whitman's architect, Burton Schutt, who was already engaged on the design of the hotel. RockResorts initially worked with Schutt and Whitman to move the project forward in 1953, but soon found the projected hotel untenable due to exorbitant cost projections for the new structure. Schutt's proposed design included 152 rooms, two swimming pools, and thirty-four cabanas. Given the largely undeveloped nature of the local surroundings, an electric plant and sewage system would also be necessary. Schutt's hotel was projected to cost $2.16 million.[9] Moscoso intimated to Rockefeller that the initial development would only merit a $500,000 loan package, with options for enlargement should the project prove profitable. Rockefeller cited design differences and cost overruns as reasons to dismiss Schutt in June 1953, and he subsequently appoint Harmon Goldstone as project director later that year.[10]

At the end of July, Laurance Rockefeller and RockResorts began their own development plans for La Sardinera in earnest. Armed with a prominent New York City architect for the project, RockResorts planned to design the hotel around the existing Livingston estate, integrating the home as a restaurant in an effort to preserve and accent any modern installations on the property.[11] Subsequently, Guillermo Rodríguez, president and general manager of PRIDCO, opened the formal process of negotiations for resort development at Dorado Beach. PRIDCO initially pledged no more than $600,000 in loans (over eighteen years) for a seventy-five-room hotel with a cost expenditure of approximately $12,000 per room, much less than the projected $20,000 per room in Schutt's plans.[12]

Thus began a process of financial bargaining with PRIDCO that would last two years before construction of the Dorado Beach Hotel began in 1956. As with most commercial architecture and urban planning, design and architecture were simply handmaidens to whatever financial package investors wanted to offer. RockResorts executives initially bristled at PRIDCO's first offer of a $600,000 loan, leaving the company to invest $400,000 of its own money in the project, with the risk that if the hotel failed, ownership of the property would be transferred to PRIDCO.[13]

While RockResorts executives prepared new offers for PRIDCO, Laurance Rockefeller summoned his brother, Nelson; Eastern Airlines president, Eddie Rickenbacker; and architect Wallace Harrison to visit the proposed hotel site at La Sardinera. As a result of their visit, new design proposals began to mold the resort into its finished form. Instead of building the resort cottages around the Livingston estate, somewhat secluded from the beach, Nelson Rockefeller, Rickenbacker, and Harrison encouraged Laurance Rockefeller to move the hotel to where it would be exposed to the crescent-shaped beach.[14] RockResorts executive Allston Boyer elaborated on the new design of the hotel in a letter to Carlos M. Passalacqua, president and general manager of PRIDCO. In regards to the decision to move the hotel nearer to the sea, Boyer noted, "It was my feeling that the American tourists especially would wish to be nearer the swimming facilities." Boyer also observed that two swimming pools would be built "near the terrace of the hotel rather than try to provide sheltered swimming facilities by the construction of an enclosed rock pool." Citing the predilections of American tourists for safety, Allston commented, "Sea urchins, unfortunately favor sheltered places like rock pools." Ultimately, however, Allston's letter appears to have been a ploy to increase PRIDCO's financing offer. He notes that the golf course would perhaps only be constructed for nine holes, citing the potential financial overruns of completing an eighteen-hole course. Boyer also hinted that the hotel itself would also have to be reduced to between forty and fifty rooms in order to meet PRIDCO's current offer. Ironically, despite misgivings about Schutt's extravagant hotel designs, Goldstone had similarly estimated that the project would cost an average of $20,000 per room. Boyer's letter ended with a subtle hint of what type of agenda RockResorts desired during Laurance Rockefeller's mid-December visit, including discussion of a longer mortgage agreement, a higher price ceiling per room, "and all other matters in which we have a mutual interest."[15]

Following Laurance Rockefeller's visit to Puerto Rico, Passalacqua hammered out yet another PRIDCO offer, stopping short of soliciting PRIDCO's Industrial Investment Committee's approval for the new tender. While his letter to Rockefeller outlining the offer largely dealt with questions of financing, Passalacqua also expressed some concern over the decentralized nature of the project. For the approximately twenty-four-square-mile municipality of Dorado, the U.S. Census tallied 11,749 residents, most of whom had no experience working in the tourism industry.[16] Furthermore, the proposed resort found itself more than an hour away from the international airport in San Juan, a location Passalacqua considered "rather distant for the ordinary tourist, but reasonably accessible for the tourist that will come to Puerto

Rico to take a few days relaxation." On the plus side, however, the rural location presented new opportunities for Puerto Rican tourists. In order for
the project to work, according to Passalacqua, the resort needed to provide
ample recreational opportunities for tourists, including a golf course, golf
clubhouse, swimming pools, and tennis courts. Passalacqua expressed some
concern at the diminution of the hotel to sixty rooms, but commented, "In
spite of this, since we do not wish for a hotel to suffer in any way from lack
of enough amenities for visitors, and also since a golf course of this type is
of general advantage to the Commonwealth, we are willing to cooperate in
its financing as hereinafter explained."[17]

In an effort to make PRIDCO's first comprehensive offer more palatable to
RockResorts, Passalacqua suggested that several alterations be made to the
proposed design, including cutting the size of the proposed swimming pool
by 50 percent, for a savings of approximately $60,000. He also suggested
diminishing the size of the central building, the dining room, and terrace,
at a projected savings of $40,000. The refurbishing of the Livingston house
for a golf clubhouse could be reduced from $96,000 to $46,000. Passalacqua
also called for the addition of tennis courts ($15,000) and air-conditioning
of the hotel rooms ($40,000). In total, the alterations would reduce the cost
of the project, including the golf course, from approximately $1.7 million to
$1.5 million.

At the time, PRIDCO represented the cutting edge of tourism development services in the Caribbean for international chains attempting to locate
hotels on a foreign island. The purpose of agencies like PRIDCO was not
simply to attract promising clients to Puerto Rico but also to assist them
in navigating their way through Puerto Rico's legal and economic bureau-
cracies. In doing this, Passalacqua offered Rockefeller diagnostic services,
including "observations of the behavior of the beach in order to record anything that may be useful in the design[;] . . . observations of wind velocity
and direction, temperature and humidity[;] . . . investigation as to what type
of greens would best grow in the land to be used for the golf course[;] . . .
[and finding] out in more detail the requirements of the Planning Board,
Health Department, Aqueduct and Sewer Authority, Water Resources Authority, and other agencies which will have something to do with the project."[18] In addition to offering project financing, PRIDCO's promise of additional developmental services functioned as a competitive lure to chains
like RockResorts to induce site location in Puerto Rico. PRIDCO's model
of offering comprehensive tourism development services, as well as financing, would become standard in the industry by the end of the twentieth
century.

Passalacqua based PRIDCO's initial comprehensive offer on the basis of a 59 percent average occupancy rate for the hotel. The state agency would provide a $700,000 mortgage to RockResorts for development of a sixty-room resort at 5 percent interest over a period of eighteen years, with a three-year "breathing spell" during which RockResorts would only pay interest on the loan. PRIDCO's loan would also provide 50 percent of the cost of furniture and equipment at a 6 percent rate over a ten-year period, with no "breathing spell." In addition, Passalacqua offered a $200,000 loan for construction of the golf course at 5 percent interest over a period of eighteen years, with a three-year "breathing spell." Anticipating Rockefeller's plans to use land obtained from Clara Livingston to develop residential tourism, Passalacqua stopped short of offering development funds for the real estate portion of the project, and further required RockResorts to apply 15 percent of the revenues from the land sales to the amortization of the golf course.[19]

RockResorts associate Joseph Jennen analyzed the offer and concluded that the new package increased PRIDCO's loan ceiling to $900,000, but still left RockResorts with the burden of investing $500,000 to initiate the project.[20] A week later, Harmon Goldstone assessed Passalacqua's offer from the design perspective. At the projected cost of $1.5 million for the entire project, each of the sixty hotel rooms would cost an average of $25,313, almost double the rate of the original estimated offer from PRIDCO in early 1953. Goldstone had no problem with the reduction in the size of the swimming pool, but questioned changes to the central building, dining room, and terrace, as well as cost reductions to refurbish the Livingston house. According to Goldstone, in order to maintain project quality, the number of lockers for the golf clubhouse would have to be cut by 50 percent and "other furnishings to a bare minimum." Ultimately, Goldstone suggested that the requested reductions be determined after full plans for the project had been drawn up.[21]

On January 18, 1954, Laurance Rockefeller officially responded to Passalacqua's offer, observing that a $900,000 ceiling on the PRIDCO loan would expose him to undue financial risk in the neighborhood of $500,000. He underscored this difficult situation by reiterating that he had informed Teodoro Moscoso that he intended to invest only $300,000 to $350,000 in the initial development of the resort. He also detailed that he had spent around $75,000 on initial development expenses and that this would further complicate the availability of liquid capital for initiation of the project.[22]

Passalacqua continued PRIDCO's aggressive recruitment of RockResorts ten days after Rockefeller's letter, offering loan assistance for 75 percent of the hotel, as opposed to PRIDCO's previous offer of two-thirds support for the structure. He also offered to raise PRIDCO's land valuation allowance for the property that Rockefeller would obtain from Clara Livingston at greatly reduced prices. In all, the additions to the package raised PRIDCO's investment from $900,000 to $1,059,000. As a result, according to Passalacqua's calculations, Rockefeller's initial investment for the project would decrease from approximately $500,000 to $409,200 and the value of the land. Although the current loan offer carried a 6 percent interest rate, RockResorts would enjoy "a ten year tax exemption on profits and a six-year exemption on property tax." PRIDCO also offered assistance in finding appropriate financing for worker housing, given the resort's distance from Dorado and San Juan. Passalacqua unveiled a whole host of promises before Rockefeller, including assistance in gaining private beach status for the new resort, a casino concession, and assistance with grand opening publicity. Thus, in spite of Passalacqua's insistence that PRIDCO would not be able to bend further to attract RockResorts to Puerto Rico, obsequious offers only emboldened RockResorts to seek even better financing terms from PRIDCO.[23]

By March 4, 1954, Laurance Rockefeller had once again traveled to Puerto Rico to consult with PRIDCO on the Dorado Beach project. Passalacqua further amended the January 29, 1954, offer, promising a twenty-year, instead of an eighteen-year, loan period, and a drop in interest rates from 6 percent to 5.5 percent per year on the loan. Passalacqua also attempted to enhance the deal by following up on nonfinancial perks to the plan. On the topic of worker housing, he noted, "We have discussed this matter with the local director of the Federal Housing Administration. He showed a great deal of interest but could not give a definitive assurance as to use of regular F.H.A. financing to facilitate such housing. However, he promised that if we gave him data on what these employees would earn . . . they could make a decision in just a few days."[24]

Rockefeller's patience in dealing with PRIDCO rested on several factors. First, he had already demonstrated a commitment to using tourism as a tool for regional development in the American Virgin Islands at Caneel Bay. Second, he had also communicated a desire to not assume too much risk in a decentralized project at Dorado Beach. Finally, as tourism development projects at other locales throughout the Caribbean in the post–World War II era would illustrate, many times state governments were the only entities willing to attempt such risky projects that demanded a significant capital outlay both for hotel development and for provisioning of infrastructure in a remote location such as Dorado Beach. It was probably the combination of these motives that accounted for Rockefeller's polite rejection of Passalacqua's March 4, 1954, offer. Citing a "cash deficiency indicated by the terms of the loan," Rockefeller appeared to bow out of the running for PRIDCO assistance in developing La Sardinera for tourism.[25] On the same day, Passalacqua sent a cablegram proposing the extension of the loan from twenty to twenty-two years, with a "breathing spell" of five years and a reduction in interest to 5 percent.[26]

If Passalacqua appeared to be an overzealous courtier of RockResorts, Laurance Rockefeller could not put the idea to rest. One day after all but writing off PRIDCO, he once again engaged Passalacqua in plausible proposals. Prior to this point, Rockefeller had proposed to Moscoso that the two entities participate in the hotel through a joint-stock agreement, to which Moscoso responded that PRIDCO could not participate in a joint-stock arrangement unless it controlled the company.[27] Rockefeller replied to Passalacqua on March 12, 1954, expressing his regrets that the mortgage negotiations had not worked out, but signaling a new possibility for development at Dorado Beach:

> In light of the thorough study I have made of the Dorado project, I have come to the conclusion that the only practical way in which it could be handled, would be for the Puerto Rican government to build all the facilities, based on the plans we have worked out and to operate the hotel and golf course under a management contract, with an option to purchase all facilities on previously agreed terms. These would be about the same conditions as those applied to the Caribé Hilton, [which,] at the time it was conceived, was found to be too risky to attract private capital in a commercial and tourist hotel venture new for Puerto Rico, and which turned out to be a great success. Similarly Dorado is also a new step in the international resort business and the Caribé Hilton can, I think, be invoked as a precedent.[28]

Rockefeller's letter reveals his ultimate concern regarding the risk of developing the decentralized resort. While RockResorts would not assume too much risk, its leaders did believe the Puerto Rican government would be willing to share a significant amount of the risk in developing a decentralized resort community. Rockefeller's letter solicited a special delivery response from Passalacqua, who gracefully deflected Rockefeller's new proposal into a rehashing of PRIDCO's previous proposals. PRIDCO's manager gently rebuffed Rockefeller's new model of a completely state-financed resort, observing that PRIDCO desired a higher level of private participation because "an enterprise that fails, not only makes us lose money, but represents a very great set back [sic] in our effort for the economic development of Puerto Rico, because other firms become reluctant to take any risks. In short, we rate our success only by the successful enterprises that came to Puerto Rico with our program." Passalacqua largely attempted to minimize the financial risk that RockResorts would assume in developing its innovative resort. He also reassured Rockefeller that the property in question would not only hold one "but even . . . another hotel enterprise of considerable size." Furthermore, any residential developments would attract local as well an international clients. "As you know," Passalacqua tempted, "Puerto Ricans are so land conscious that to date all high grade real estate subdivisions have been perfect successes." The manager also reiterated the ease with which RockResorts would obtain a casino license, as well as an interest-free year on a loan, worth $52,960, from PRIDCO, which would be repaid "from funds used for special incentives to factories that need a very special help for some reason, like training for employees." This carrot at the end of the letter represented a particularly rare promotion package, as "no factory gets more than $25,000, and the average of those that qualify at all only get $10,000." Passalacqua confided, "This is the first time this fund is used for a hotel and it will probably be the last. This is an additional financial help that can be very useful to you in making the operation profitable."[29] Rockefeller graciously recognized the lengths to which PRIDCO had gone to make the project succeed, but ultimately concluded, "I am not only taking into consideration the financial aspect of the problem, but even more so the risk in failing to achieve our objectives, which would be detrimental to both of us."[30]

Despite these parting words, Rockefeller, Passalacqua, and Moscoso were back at the negotiating table by the end of May, working toward a quick resolution of the deal. Initially, Rockefeller wanted to explore the options of a business model along the lines of that constructed by Hilton International, when it built the Caribé Hilton in San Juan. Joseph Jennen had traveled to Puerto Rico to meet with Passalacqua on May 19, 1953, and discussed an equity-partnership between PRIDCO and RockResorts under which PRIDCO would purchase the land for the hotel from Rockefeller and then pay for and furnish the hotel, with RockResorts and PRIDCO receiving 50 percent of the profits. Rockefeller's architect, Harmon Goldstone, would be retained to "consult" with Puerto Rican architects on project design.[31] Subsequent to these discussions, Allston Boyer met with John Houser of Hilton International to discuss the financial relationship it had worked out for the Caribé Hilton. Given the risk that Hilton was willing to assume as the first luxury hotel chain on the island, the Puerto Rican government offered Hilton its best terms: one-third of annual operating profits with a 5 percent cost on furniture annually. PRIDCO also assumed all of the hotel's construction costs. After consultations with Hilton International on the hotel management versus hotel ownership options, RockResorts continued to pursue the hotel management approach, with PRIDCO building the hotel.[32]

On August 6, 1954, Rockefeller vacillated on his commitment to the integrated resort project, suggesting to Passalacqua that while the golf course was critical to the success of the development, "it may be to our mutual interest to sell the property to others who would operate it as a golf course." This approach would lower the shared risk of RockResorts and PRIDCO. Rockefeller also requested approximately $250,000 for the land needed for the hotel and golf course, a fee that included his development costs to date. Finally, the RockResorts chairman asserted that his company should only have to pay a 3 percent, instead of a 4 percent, rental fee for the properties in managing them, "because profits of the operation are to be shared equally, and also because I feel that if, contrary to our mutual belief, the operation, despite all our efforts, were not a financial success, it would not be reasonable to have the full burden carried by the management. Further, of course, my capital contribution to the project represents the primary risk portion of the financial situation."[33] At this point, Passalacqua revealed his negotiating limits to Rockefeller, responding to his August 6, 1954, proposals with some annoyance. "We are quite willing to continue negotiations," he announced, "if you are prepared in going ahead with this project more or less along the lines and within the spirit of the conditions embodied in our [May 19, 1954] notes to Mr. Jennen . . . but these conditions represent in my opinion the limit to which we can go in helping finance your project." At this point, Passalacqua began to demand Rockefeller's reciprocation of PRIDCO's assigned risk, as opposed to PRIDCO's previous accommodation of RockResorts' requests. "In other words," he continued, "if you are to insist on certain new conditions which you consider necessary to go on with the project from your organization's point of view, you should be ready to consider favorably offsetting clauses which we in turn might consider equally important in our behalf, so that the resulting transaction is, from the point of view of this company, more or less of the order of the financial risk embodied in my notes."[34] In later correspondence, Passalacqua stuck to his May 19, 1954, offer, enjoining Rockefeller to obtain an appraisal for the actual land cost, requiring 4 percent rent for the hotel facilities under the management contract, and refusing to have the golf course and hotel considered as separate entities.[35] Moscoso's intervention at the end of 1954 appears to have been decisive, as he promised, "The next time Carlos or I are in New York we are going to make a point to sit down with you and work something out which is acceptable both to you and to our Investment Committee."[36]

By the winter of 1955, RockResorts and PRIDCO returned to the bargaining table, disregarding the May 19 proposal under which PRIDCO would pay for complete construction of the hotel and RockResorts would participate solely as a management group. The new negotiations returned RockResorts to the role of potential owner and developer of the Dorado Beach Hotel. By the end of February 1955, PRIDCO offered RockResorts $1,059,000 worth of financing for the hotel, furnishings, and golf course construction—a far cry from the initial offer of $600,000—for a hotel that would eventually feature 136 rooms, as opposed to 60. PRIDCO also appears to have granted RockResorts a one-year interest-free loan during construction of the hotel, as well as 5 percent interest on the balance of the financing package.

Of greatest significance to the history of tourism development, however, is the assessorial role that PRIDCO continued to offer RockResorts in adapting to the Puerto Rican context of conducting business. With the status of employee availability in the area and employee housing still on the minds of RockResorts executives, Allston Boyer pointed out to Laurance Rockefeller, "Harmon [Goldstone] is under the impression that PRIDCO will gladly undertake a complete economic survey of the availability of personnel and housing in the environs of Dorado at no cost to us." Decentralization also influenced planning efforts for transportation routes to the hotel from San Juan. Boyer had been assured that the Puerto Rican Planning Board would recommend an appropriate solution to inadequate roads to Dorado in the near future. As for promotional aid for the resort, Boyer noted, "Teddy Moscoso has stated that out of the Board of Tourism annual budget of $300,000 the Dorado project would receive equal treatment with all other hotels in San Juan and that we could expect definite help in pre-opening expense." With regard to environmental concerns, Passalacqua had already stationed meteorologists at Dorado Beach to study wind velocity, temperature, and humidity in relation to the built environment of the new resort. As landscape design for the new resort took shape, Boyer also looked to the Puerto Rican government for assistance. He noted that it "could furnish us with plant stock and seeds from Governmental Agricultural Stations with soil data applicable to Dorado." Finally, Boyer was highly concerned about navigating labor issues in a volatile Puerto Rican context. Recent strikes and uncertainty concerning minimum wage requirements led Boyer to believe that the Puerto Rican government might provide the appropriate information regarding labor relations for RockResorts, but he also conjectured regarding "the extent to which we might count on Government intervention on our behalf." Finally, PRIDCO's previous willingness to serve as advocate for Dorado Beach in Puerto Rican bureaucratic circles only heightened Boyer's hopes for further assistance in relation to labor issues. "In fact, Teddy might be willing to undertake a special study or survey regarding labor relations and the Dorado project," Boyer observed. "This may be one of the most troublesome problems we will have in operating the project."[37]

Rockefeller's personal records regarding the evolution of the PRIDCO-RockResorts deal do not include the final date and amount of the financing agreement. However, PRIDCO's continued role as advocate for RockResorts in Puerto Rican political and bureaucratic circles ultimately reveals that an initial loan package of approximately $1 million mushroomed in the course of a year into a $1.3 million deal, over twice the initial 1953 offer for financing. As soon as RockResorts became a developmental partner with PRIDCO, in December 1955, new concerns regarding logistics and infrastructure surfaced. In a letter to Passalacqua, Laurance Rockefeller noted, "Since the present road system in the vicinity of Dorado is so unsatisfactory, I think we are all agreed that a new direct approach road from San Juan will contribute greatly to the success of the project." Rockefeller was somewhat surprised at Passalacqua's view that RockResorts "could not expect any commitment from the Government for a new access road." Expressing disbelief, Rockefeller informed Passalacqua that he would "appreciate some reassurance that your organization will do everything possible to help in seeing that a satisfactory access road is provided." As a parting shot, Rockefeller wrote, "I am hopeful, too, that PRIDCO will help us in our negotiations with the utility companies to achieve an equitable division of costs for bringing utilities to the site."[38] Rockefeller's tendency to turn to PRIDCO as his handmaiden in Puerto Rico is understandable, given the business partnership in which both parties were involved. The dynamics of the private-public resort development model, however, well illustrate the ways in which cooperation tends to distribute risk in distinctive ways that neither solely private nor public development might replicate.

Public absorption of a higher degree of risk, as indicated through larger economic commitments to the partnership as the project evolved, manifested itself as RockResorts developed the resort's extensive infrastructure, including water, sewage, electricity, and adequate transportation facilities. While water and electrical connections were achieved with relatively little conflict, road access to the resort from San Juan continued to concern RockResorts. Less than a month after Rockefeller's December letter to Passalacqua requesting PRIDCO assistance in road development, Passalacqua informed Rockefeller that he was doing all in his power to include an access road to Dorado Beach in government construction programs. The sheer volume of worthy projects across the island, however, made the success of PRIDCO's efforts less than certain.[39] By the following year, PRIDCO had succeeded in securing funding for an access road to Dorado Beach. Acknowledging the organization's role as advocate on the island for RockResorts, Rockefeller lauded Passalacqua's efforts, observing, "I am delighted that such excellent progress is being made with the access road and am most appreciative of the work you are doing with the Department of Public Works."[40] Less than three weeks later, Rockefeller reiterated his gratitude to Passalacqua for additional project financing, as PRIDCO had expanded the $1 million loan for resort development to $1.3 million to account for partial development of the access road. With funding secured for the project, Rockefeller continued to encourage Passalacqua to advocate for completion of the project through the Bureau of Public Works.[41] Ultimately, the personal relationship of the main parties—principally Laurance Rockefeller, Carlos Passalacqua, Teodoro Moscoso, and Governor Luís Muñoz Marín—helped retain the concept of a true partnership between the two private and public entities involved. PRIDCO's role as intermediary during both negotiations and development appears to have been the crucial element to success of the initial development process.

*   *   *

On December 2, 1958, Laurance Rockefeller convened a group of friends and dignitaries to inaugurate the Dorado Beach Hotel. He recognized those individuals who had helped RockResorts and PRIDCO create what Puerto Rican tourism consultant Jose J. Villamil later called "organic tourism," a new genre for most of the Caribbean that emphasized building new tourism infrastructure and superstructures within preexisting built and natural environments.[42] Clara Livingston's sensitivity to the preservation of the estate and landscaping dovetailed with Rockefeller's own sense of preserving elements of the original plantation. "That is a source of great satisfaction," Rockefeller mentioned in reference to the existing estate, "and [it] also means a great deal that we have been able to help to try to bring together a beautiful natural setting with people that need to be more aware of being part of nature and who need opportunity to try and live more in harmony with nature." Similarly, Robert Trent Jones Sr., who designed the hotel's golf course, accomplished the feat with attention to preserving the landscape. "The fact that his artistic and wisdom sense of right involved going around the Lake, which was a large mangrove swamp," Rockefeller recalled, "doubled the original estimate just for the fill and the drainage problem and pumps that were involved, but that was only one of the details of our development." He also acknowledged the impact of jet travel, as well as Juan Trippe, founder of Pan American Airways; Eddie Rickenbacker, president of Eastern Airlines; and

Caribbean airline entrepreneur Dionísio Trigo, for "laying the foundation of an air transport system which is really the core of the lifeline of the tourist industry which we are all so anxious to participate in the development of." Nothing could have been truer for an untested tourism pole like the Dorado Beach Hotel. Finally, Rockefeller also made mention throughout his speech of the assistance that Puerto Rico's people and legislators had given toward development of the project. Rockefeller's alternative to mass tourism, the Dorado Beach Hotel, was merely a philosophical reflection of Governor Muñoz Marín's Operation Serenity, which consisted of "project[ing] a better life and new purpose out of the existing prosperity."[43] Ultimately, Rock-Resorts' relationship with PRIDCO during the early negotiation for and development of Dorado Beach demonstrated the limits of private-public development in the international context, as well as the assessorial role that state agencies found necessary to offer international hotel developers if they hoped to attract the developers' services to Caribbean islands. Economically, the Dorado Beach Hotel was a phenomenal success, with positive returns materializing during the first five years of operation and constant expansion plans that more than doubled the number of rooms, from 136 in 1958 to 306 in 1967.

To sum up the first phase of Dorado Beach resorts, the match between PRIDCO and RockResorts featured two entities concerned about the extent of risk each would assume in an innovative resort project. When each side recognized the negotiating limits of the other, the concerns were resolved, and development of the project began by June 1955. RockResorts' choice of a partner for continued development at Dorado Beach in the late 1960s and early 1970s, Eastern Airlines, would demonstrate the limits of tourism development when two partners possessed very different objectives.

5

A Second Marriage

Even as Laurance Rockefeller celebrated the opening of the Dorado Beach Hotel on December 2, 1958, he was already contemplating the expansion of the resort. Rockefeller had acquired the services of architect Bill Reid, who had been working for Nelson Rockefeller's International Basic Economy Corporation (IBEC) housing project in Puerto Rico, and charged him with planning "apartment houses, with another hotel down the Beach, a residential development, [and] another golf course."[1] The initial success of the Dorado Beach Hotel fueled expectations for growth. From 1959 until the middle of 1966, annual occupancy at the Dorado Beach Hotel never dropped below 55.9 percent. By the end of 1965, the Dorado Beach Hotel enjoyed a twelve-month average of just over 80 percent occupancy. This steady growth was even more impressive given the almost constant expansion of the hotel itself. From 1959 until 1962, one hundred more rooms were added to the hotel property. Then, between 1964 and 1966 another seventy-two rooms were added. Net profits and losses followed an almost linear curve from 1959 to 1966. From a net loss of $2.3 million during the first year (1959), profits rose to an all-time high of just over $1.6 million for the six-month period ending on April 30, 1966.[2]

About this time, Laurance Rockefeller, a longtime stockholder in Eastern Airlines, turned to its new president, Floyd Hall, and the two corporations began talks concerning Eastern's development of tourism in the Caribbean and the strategic role of the Dorado Beach Hotel in those plans. Hall's international vision for Eastern Airlines, when he assumed the CEO position in the mid-1960s, involved an ambitious plan to capture routes throughout the Pacific Rim region and in Latin America. Tourism served as a means to providing Eastern with the rationale for developing flight routes to the Far East and throughout the Caribbean basin. For Rockefeller, the proposed sale of 80 percent of the shares of Dorado Beach and a 40 percent stake of Rock-Resorts promised an infusion of capital that would unburden RockResorts of sole financial responsibility for the enterprise and, more important, offer substantial assistance from Eastern to bring his dream of a second hotel, residential developments, and a new golf course to reality. In other words, if RockResorts had felt some degree of leverage in dealing with PRIDCO in 1957, its pairing with Eastern Airlines would relegate it to a less dominant position in completing the development of Dorado Beach.

By 1967, the RockResorts/PRIDCO development of Dorado Beach had elevated the resort and the surrounding community to one of hemispheric importance. As a result, other hotel operators, namely Hilton International, had opened hotels adjacent to the Dorado Beach Resort. By the time Eastern and RockResorts began discussing a possible merger, land values had escalated to an estimated $5,500 per acre for the 503 acres apportioned to the Dorado Beach Hotel. The remaining 1,000 acres were valued at between $2,500 and $22,000 per acre, the latter figure pertaining to oceanfront land designated for new hotel construction adjacent to the Dorado Beach Hotel. In total, Stone and Webster Engineering Corporation appraised the entire resort in 1967 at approximately $29 million, a far cry from the approximately $2 million that RockResorts and PRIDCO invested in the initial hotel.[3] In its own assessment of the appraisal, Eastern Airlines downgraded the value of the project to between $21 million and $26 million, questioning some of the internal cash flow conclusions reached by the appraiser.[4] Nevertheless, on December 1, 1967, Eastern Airlines turned over 171,736 shares of its own stock to Laurance Rockefeller for 80 percent of the shares in the Dorado Beach Hotel Corporation and its subsidiaries, as well as paid $20,000 for a 40 percent share of RockResorts.[5]

The new partnership began with great optimism for the synergies both corporations could realize and the foreseeable evolution of Dorado Beach from a resort to a tourism community. Laurance Rockefeller wired Floyd Hall in Manila on December 1, 1967, advising him: "Hotel transactions just concluded on schedule. . . . Great new era begins officially today."[6]

RockResorts also issued a five-year financial projection for the years 1969 to 1973. With the emergence of the 747 airplane, capable of disgorging close to five hundred passengers almost anywhere in the world, as well as the possibilities of supersonic travel, tourism in the Caribbean looked very promising. With the Concorde, for example, RockResorts projected, "The Caribbean will then penetrate new markets on the west coast and perhaps in Europe, and Hawaii will penetrate new markets on the east coast and perhaps in the Far East." The report also projected a strong economy through 1973, with a rise of 8 percent in discretionary spending among Americans, totaling a projected $680 billion. With an additional prediction that World War III would indeed be avoided, and that Cuba, Haiti, and the Dominican Republic would not offer serious competition for tourism in the rest of the Caribbean, RockResorts began to look specifically at its own plans for Dorado Beach's evolution. Despite predictions of political and economic stability, the report also noted, "[Private] investors have not planned a sufficient number of hotel rooms in Puerto Rico, despite government encouragement, to meet projected demand." As a result, Eastern Airlines and RockResorts would move forward with the development of a resort on Brenas Beach, later named the Cerromar Beach Hotel, a massive modernist structure housing approximately five hundred rooms and designed primarily for business conferences. New residential condominiums would also create revenue streams at the hotel restaurants, bars, and golf club. The success of the Dorado Beach Hotel justified rate hikes throughout the resort over the ensuing five years as well. Like too many business projections, however, the prognosis for the future was based too much on the success of the past and did not take into account the growing pains that the new partners would experience.[7] Perhaps the crowning conceptual development for Dorado Beach involved the creation of a master plan for the entire resort. Designed by Sasaki, Dawson, Demay Associates, the 1969 master plan envisioned the evolution of Dorado Beach from a self-contained resort to a resort community, including high-density housing (745 units), a shopping center, a cultural center, two schools, maintenance and staff housing, single family housing (411 houses), condominiums (962 units), restaurants, a beach club, a horse farm, a church, a second hotel (Cerromar Beach), and three new golf courses (five total).[8] Flush with Eastern's capital and Floyd Hall's interest in developing tourism via jet travel in the Pacific and Caribbean, the two companies also cultivated hotel management opportunities everywhere from Mexico to France.

Ultimately, the Cerromar Beach Hotel would be the central creative product of the Eastern/RockResorts relationship. During July 1969, the accounting firm of Harris, Kerr, Forster and Company conducted a market study of the proposed hotel at Brenas Beach. While the report ultimately recommended construction of the five hundred–room hotel, it also contained enough warnings against building the hotel that should have alerted Eastern/RockResorts executives to the potentially costly risks of building the hotel in a declining Puerto Rican tourism market. Perhaps the biggest potential problem involved oversupply of hotel rooms, particularly in the conference hotel category, around the island. At the time the report was written, forty-two hundred additional hotel rooms were projected for construction by 1971 in San Juan. Additionally, apartment buildings were projected for hotel conversion in that time frame as well. Despite the growth of tourist arrivals during the 1960s, the report nevertheless noted the potential for oversupply of hotel rooms. Harris, Kerr, Forster, and Company contended that if the supply of hotel rooms in San Juan remained the same as in 1968, the market would continue to reach 70 percent occupancy. In 1968, 572,094 hotel registrants had spent a total of 3,171,700 nights in the San Juan area. With the addition of approximately forty-two hundred rooms, 1,920,000 additional guest nights would be needed to reach 80 percent occupancy (the optimal occupancy level for a new hotel like the Cerromar Beach Hotel). Achieving such a feat—or a 60 percent increase over 1968 figures by 1971— would be difficult in Puerto Rico, the accountants observed, "as the growth rate in visitor nights has shown a declining trend since 1964." Consequently, they noted, "it is unlikely that the total demand will reach anything like the number necessary to avoid dilution of overall occupancies in the San Juan Area." As a result of what the accountants termed a "danger of oversupply," it was suggested that "the best located and managed properties will tend to capture the largest part of the market that is available."[9] While RockResorts could classify the Dorado Beach Hotel among the best-managed resorts, the addition of a new convention hotel (at Brenas Beach) similar in scope to other proposed hotels that were located closer to San Juan, placed RockResorts' new property at a disadvantage. One of the biggest problems involved congested Highway 693 between San Juan and Dorado Beach. It often required between one and two hours to traverse the twenty-mile stretch of road, with frequent morning and late-afternoon traffic jams. To add insult to injury, the report predicted, "This difficulty is likely to continue for some years to come."[10]

Furthermore, for many tourists or guests, access to San Juan was a central feature of any trip to the island. One individual surveyed regarding the project noted, "The San Juan market is unique as far as 'remoteness' from downtown. Attendees do not mind being say five miles from downtown where some of the fine hotels are located. But any distance further than five miles would have a cost factor in traveling between the hotel and the shops and the undeveloped areas away from downtown are eyesores to the attendee. They prefer to be where the action is."[11] At the same time, Harris, Kerr, Forster and Company noted that a two thousand–room convention hotel was under development in Boca de Cangrejos, near the Isla Verde sector of San Juan, as well as four additional hotels projected with over one thousand rooms each.[12] Finally, the report cited a study of tourism development in Puerto Rico commissioned by the Economic Development Administration of Puerto Rico in its assessment of Puerto Rican hotel development. Projecting the island's hotel needs through the year 1980, the report suggested that Dorado could sustain one thousand additional hotel rooms apart from the Dorado Hilton and the Dorado Beach Hotel. This figure assumed that the number of tourists visiting Puerto Rico would increase from 731,700 (the 1967 figure) to 2.4 million tourists by 1980, yet it failed to account for the declining number of nights that tourists were spending on the island. Ultimately, comparing present needs versus future projections would justify construction of the Cerromar Beach Hotel, yet Harris, Kerr, Forster and Company contended that by 1980, the thirty-two thousand hotel rooms in the San Juan area, including fifteen hundred in Dorado, would only reach 41 percent occupancy—a disastrous figure in the hotel industry.[13]

While the report concluded that a market would exist for the Cerromar Beach Hotel, it was laced with caveats that later often materialized. In its analysis of demand for a decentralized convention hotel, the report offered a multitude of attractive advantages for such a project, including indirect government assistance for business trips through tax write-offs, the need for many businessmen and women to combine business trips and vacations due to lack of free time, "atmosphere" for serious discussions, greater space than most city hotels, and opportunities to golf.[14] The only foreseeable impediment to the success of such a resort would be a recession or new tax law.

In reality, the economic woes of the early 1970s severely challenged Puerto Rican tourism and were particularly difficult for the airline industry, with the rising costs of energy. At the time the market study was performed, Harris, Kerr, Forster and Company also asserted that tourist and air travel predictions suggested that only two thousand new hotel rooms would be needed by 1971, as opposed to the forty-two hundred that were currently in development. The accounting firm believed that the contracting economy would probably doom some of the projected hotels to failure, but nonetheless observed, "it is entirely possible that some over-building will occur." In their specific analysis of the Cerromar Beach Hotel, the accountants noted that its competition for conventions and tourists would not only come from San Juan but also from "mainland resort hotels such as Boca Raton, the Broadmoor, Greenbrier, the Homestead, and many others that are aggressively soliciting conference business."[15]

With a master plan and economic study completed, Eastern Airlines and

RockResorts moved forward with plans to build the Cerromar Beach Hotel. The hotel project was unveiled at the board meeting of the Dorado Beach Hotel Corporation on September 18, 1969. The original plan called for a hotel with 517 rooms "in single corridor layout, all having a view of the sea and some overlooking the golf course as well." The hotel would feature convention facilities and a ballroom capable of seating nearly twelve hundred participants for meetings. Various dining rooms and upscale shops would cater to conventioneers and tourists. In addition, a third Robert Trent Jones Sr. golf course would be built adjacent to the hotel, along with six tennis courts and a swimming pool. Puerto Rican architects Toro and Ferrer were charged with designing the modernist building, while IBEC-Bland completed construction of the structure.[16]

Optimism ran high regarding the economic synergies the two hotels might generate. Financial projections estimated a return after taxes for both the Dorado Beach and Cerromar Beach hotels of 16.9 percent on monies invested, a higher rate of return than if only one hotel were in operation.[17] With such optimism, few expenses were spared. For example, RockResorts executives "discussed the possibility of securing operators, such as Neiman Marcus, Saks, or Bergdorf Goodman, to operate the shops in the hotel."[18] Ultimately, however, cost overruns tested Eastern's patience to continue funding the completion of the hotel project.[19] A lavish grand opening ceremony January 6–9, 1972—including transporting hundreds of guests, members of the media, and executives from RockResorts and Eastern Airlines to Dorado Beach—matched the splendor of Conrad Hilton's hotel openings in places like San Juan and Havana, but also ignored the financial realities of a hotel project that had been hemorrhaging losses from its inception.[20]

Changes in global tourism, rather than the local forces anticipated by Harris, Kerr, Forster and Company, dealt a serious blow to the projected success of the Cerromar Beach Hotel project. As early as the summer of 1969, the Dorado Beach Hotel began to feel the effects of a decline in tourism in Puerto Rico. At a RockResorts board of directors meeting on May 12, 1969, Richard Holtzman predicted as high as a 22 percent downturn in occupancy at the Dorado Beach Hotel during the summer of 1969. In explaining the reasons for such a development, Holtzman noted, "Puerto Rico was falling into disfavor with continental Americans as a vacation destination because of deteriorating service and poor employee attitude; Dorado Beach was less unique than it once was and, as a result, is facing greater competition; and, the former Administration's urging against foreign travel last summer created a latent demand now manifesting itself for European travel among potential Dorado Beach vacationers." It was also noted in the meeting that Caribbean travel was down 25 percent, while European air travel was up 23 percent.[21] At a RockResorts marketing meeting the following October, Holtzman reiterated his conviction that price wars on transatlantic routes significantly contributed to growth in the European tourism market and to declines in the Caribbean and Hawaii markets. Local conditions also adversely affected Puerto Rican tourism, as an emphasis on mass tourism in San Juan negatively affected the island's image.[22] The following year, the downward trend for summer travel continued. Holtzman informed the board of directors that "Caribbean tourism during the summer months was expected to fall 30% to 35% below the poor summer of 1969."[23]

In the final analysis, the decision to build the Cerromar Beach Hotel dealt both Eastern Airlines and RockResorts significant setbacks in developing tourism in Puerto Rico. However, the downward spiral began well before construction of the mammoth hotel was complete. While RockResorts executives chafed at Eastern's inability to market RockResorts destinations through its superior marketing channels, Eastern executives were highly sensitive to the need for almost immediate profit streams. As early as August 1970, Eastern executive G. A. Coleman informed Eastern's president for financial operations, W. R. Howard, that structural changes in the economy did not bode well for profitability at Dorado Beach. "All analyses generally indicate a dramatic deterioration [of profits], attributable principally to the softening of the economy, increased operating expenses and higher interest expense (Dorado)," Coleman grimly predicted. "Furthermore, there does not appear to be any readily apparent extrinsic factor which will result in a rapid turn-around situation."[24] Subsequently, Howard wrote to Floyd Hall concerning the lower than expected occupancy rates at the Dorado Beach Hotel, whose profits Eastern had hoped to invest in the $34 million Cerromar Beach Hotel. Eastern's finance department subsequently projected that "the decline in cash flow below projection will result in additional cash requirements, over the $34.5 million committed to general financing, of $8,300,000, instead of RockResorts' original estimate of $700,000." To add insult to injury, Howard observed that financing for the hotel, which would be underwritten by Connecticut-General Insurance Corporation, would probably be subject to higher interest rates, a condition, Howard noted, that "caused me to have some very real doubts about the viability of the Cerromar Hotel." Howard presented two ultimatums: first, both RockResorts and Richard Holtzman should begin managing the hotels on a profitable basis. Or, Howard boldly asserted, "a second possibility would be to use these figures, and refinements thereof, as the basis for deciding whether Eastern wants to reverse the entire LSR-EAL [Laurance S. Rockefeller–Eastern Airlines] hotel transaction, returning both the hotels to LSR in exchange for the preferred stock and some cash and securities."[25]

At the same time that the Cerromar Beach Hotel was under construction and in its early operations, RockResorts and Eastern Airlines went forward with plans to develop 123 condominiums, collectively denominated Villa Dorado, for residential tourists, primarily from the United States. Sale of the approximately thirty home lots at Dorado Beach had gone slowly, but the lots were eventually sold during the early stages of the Eastern/RockResorts partnership. The first condominium units would be built adjacent to one of the Dorado golf courses, "with spectacular views of the ocean framed by giant palms." Costing between $80,000 and $100,000 each, the Villa Dorado condominiums would be priced in the top tier of luxury condominiums on the island, a housing type that had not found great acceptance in Puerto Rico. Much as Hilton International and Intercontinental Hotels had used their hotel properties to launch larger undertakings in Europe and Asia, Richard Holtzman observed, "If results of our survey indicate a demand, we may develop resort condominiums near our other resorts, located on Virgin Gorda, British Virgin Islands, Mauna Kea Beach in Hawaii, Woodstock, Vermont, and the Grand Tetons in Wyoming."[26]

RockResorts conducted a survey among past customers regarding the desirability and marketability of such units. While the results of the questionnaire certainly favored construction of condominiums at Dorado Beach (345 respondents out of 536 questionnaires), most of those surveyed preferred a beachfront condominium to a golf course condominium (313 to 162 respondents). Given RockResorts' environmentally conscious clientele, it is not surprising that only 52 respondents desired "a unit in a high rise resort hotel," and 38 preferred a unit next to a hotel. In terms of cost, only 60 of the more than 500 respondents expressed a preference for a condominium costing more than $80,000, with the mean response falling in the $50,000 to $60,000 category (155 respondents). The vast majority of those filling out questionnaires were interested in purchasing a condominium between $30,000 and $60,000. Ironically, the marketing survey does not appear to have taken into account the residential preferences of the host market, Puerto Rico.[27]

Two years later, as Eastern was trying to dispose of excess land in the Dorado Beach master plan, executive Lew Hucks produced a report on real estate development around Puerto Rico that illuminated consumer preferences on the island. Dorado Beach executives learned of the paucity of luxury condominiums ($75,000 and above) throughout the island (three thousand in total). Puerto Ricans may have stayed away from the RockResorts condominiums due to the preference among Puerto Rican women "living in upper price range houses . . . to [want to] live close together for family and social reasons." Furthermore, Hucks's evaluation of the master plan pointed out that upper-class families also preferred to "be near the private schools to minimize the children's transportation problem." Proximity to a husband's place of employment would also be significant, as upper-class Puerto Rican women "[sought] to have their husbands home for lunch whenever this is possible." Extensive marketing research also revealed what RockResorts might have learned much earlier about the Puerto Rican housing market: "Without knowing the existing Puerto Rican mores and customs of higher income people, it would be very easy for anyone familiar with the 'Scarsdales' and the Westchester Country Club type situations in the U.S. [a possible reference to RockResorts executives] to conclude that it should be readily possible to do a 'Scarsdale' at Dorado."[28] Huck's thorough research also cast doubt on the preference of Puerto Ricans for "garden-style" condominiums, should they prefer a second home in a resort setting. In contrast, most Puerto Ricans interested in condominiums, as evidenced by the profile of the San Juan skyline, preferred "high rise living, which might exist among the present approximately five hundred Puerto Rican luxury, high-rise, first-home condominium owners."[29] In the immediate vicinity of the Dorado Beach Hotel and the Cerromar Beach Hotel, for example, at least two large-scale condominium projects were under way by 1972. E. H. Gutiérrez Enterprises was also in the process of developing three hundred moderately priced units west of the Cerromar Beach Hotel. When Hilton International pulled out of Dorado, developer Rabino Ladd began developing a condominium-based resort community, with the Dorado Hilton being transformed into condominiums.[30]

In 1970, Dorado Beach Estates issued its prospectus for the initial group of thirty-three condominiums. The condominiums, as noted above, were located adjacent to the Dorado Beach Hotel golf courses, "about one-half mile from the beach on a gentle ridge having an elevation varying from three to 20 meters." Landscaping, including palm, laurel, and flamboyant trees, surrounded the condominium site, and, as the prospectus promised, "the landscaping [provided] for numerous open spaces and vistas while maintaining and supplementing much of the more desirable natural vegetation." The proposed condominiums were offered in seven floor plans, ranging from studios to four-bedroom units. Much like the Dorado Beach Hotel and the Cerromar Beach Hotel, the architectural style of the condominiums, constructed by IBEC's Puerto Rican subsidiary, IBEC Construction, would be modernist in design and modular in structure. A pool, two tennis courts, and a main office housing lockers would provide entertainment and privacy for prospective owners. A rental pool also allowed condominium owners to earn money on their investments while at their primary residence or traveling. Ultimately, the condominiums offered potential buyers a permanent version of the RockResorts appeal to the outdoors. Such an interface between humanity, nature, and the built environment exemplified the design philosophy of RockResorts, which stated that "successful resorts could be built in underdeveloped areas, even with the high standards of construction, conservation, and development that we consider essential."[31]

Despite its ambitious plans to build more than one hundred condominiums, RockResorts only sold and constructed thirty-four of the condominiums by March 1972.[32] From the perspective of Eastern Airlines' financial executives, a multitude of problems, including an apparent lack of marketing research prior to execution of the prospectus and condominiums themselves, plagued the project from the beginning. Eastern's C. J. Simons presented a searing report to Floyd Hall in November 1971, shortly before the termination of the sales program for the condominiums. In the broadest financial context, Simons could not believe the extent of the losses on both the Cerromar Beach Hotel and the Villa Dorado condominiums, as Rock-Resorts had promised substantial returns on a "minimal equity contribution from the principles of $.7 million." According to RockResorts, cost overruns and losses associated with the two projects reached $9.9 million by 1973. Eastern tabulated losses on the projects as high as $11.5 million. In reference to the condominium project, Simons chided Richard Holtzman of RockResorts for turning over almost every phase of the project, including architecture, interior design, marketing, sales, legal counsel, and construction, to outside groups. Simons argued that once Eastern Airlines assigned Lew Hucks to oversee the project, he uncovered a multitude of problems. First, design changes were made following the issuance of the prospectus and in the wake of establishing a sales and marketing team. As a result, the sales team had to try and sell condominiums for which final prices had not been established. Simons also argued that RockResorts' inability to provide a firm number of condominiums needed for the project to break even further complicated the financial analysis of the project. The discovery of problems with the Sasaki master plan caused additional cost overruns in the neighborhood of $500,000. In a meeting with Simons in October 1971, Holtzman upped the number of condominiums necessary to break even from thirty-three to fifty, and admitted that Sasaki had been a poor choice as architect for the condominiums and site plan. Simons proposed that the condominium project be discontinued after completion of approximately thirty units.[33]

Eastern Airlines considered the first—and final—stage of the condominiums to have been a success, as it was able to lower the losses to $32,000 through considerable accounting acrobatics. The tension between RockResorts and Eastern remained palpable, however, as such loss reductions were accomplished "in spite of numerous obstacles including the accounting inaccuracies at the Dorado properties."[34]

Only six months after the lavish opening of the Cerromar Beach Hotel, Simons presented Hall with a laundry list of additional failures in the Dorado Beach experiment with RockResorts. Simons cited lack of responsible management by RockResorts as the chief cause for the failure. "[The] profit and loss projections for both of the Puerto Rico Hotels and the related projects [in reference to the condominium debacle] have deteriorated to such an extent," he fumed, "that Eastern is presently facing the prospect of substantial losses from these properties over the next few years which were never anticipated and quite the reverse of the glowing picture painted by RockResorts for the Dorado properties." In documenting the downward spiral, Simons cited heightened loss projections for 1972 ($1 million higher than originally expected), lower than expected occupancy rates at the Cerromar Beach Hotel, higher than expected capitalization requests from RockResorts, and the bombing of the Cerromar Beach Hotel during the Miss USA Pageant in 1972 as reasons for the losses. Simons was even more perturbed to find out that on the Monday following the bombing incident, RockResorts executives were nowhere to be found. "Dick Holtzman was in Hawaii," he observed, "Bill Faber was on his way to Chicago and Digby Brown, after a short visit to Cerromar, was leaving for Hawaii." "In my opinion," he continued, "the limited or complete unavailability of the key RockResorts personnel at such a time of crisis indicated an attitude of less than appropriate concern for the owner's interest."[35] The following year, Simons joined Howard in his call for a reevaluation of the Eastern/RockResorts partnership. In a confidential memorandum to Hall, Simons pointed out that Eastern had invested $34,385,798 in stocks and cash in the Dorado properties while losing over $2 million during the same period on the investment. At the same time, Eastern had doled out more than $4 million in dividends to Laurance Rockefeller. Based on Howard's most recent estimates, the hotels would lose $14 million over a five-year period and suffer a negative $7 million cash flow. Citing the dismal earnings from the hotels, projected losses, labor problems, low appraisal of the properties, and expected lack of profitability from remaining lands, Simons enjoined Hall either to sell the hotels or radically improve hotel management (including a proposal that Eastern replace RockResorts with its own management team).[36] Two months later, Simons revisited the topic in light of a new RockResorts profit plan for 1974. He complimented RockResorts for providing more realistic projections of expected losses; however, with Holtzman, he also broached the subject of "closing one or both hotels for the summer, major service revisions for the summer season, [or] headcount efficiencies."[37]

One of the most negative aspects of the relationship that recurred throughout the rocky eight-year partnership involved the joint marketing of the two brands. Eastern Airlines was known as a high-volume air carrier, and RockResorts was considered to be an upper-echelon resort company. In a March 16, 1973, letter to Charles W. Cramer Jr., RockResorts' John B. Squire voiced his concerns concerning the impact that Eastern's image exercised on RockResorts properties:

> There is some history here, and maybe it is now played out. As you may not know, when EAL acquired an 80% ownership position in the Dorado Beach property, the adverse agent reaction was immediate and violent. Hence, we backed off on the EAL/RockResorts connection. Like all situations of its kind, that one solved itself, and I began plugging for more and more EAL involvement in marketing. . . . I have been trying to get EAL behind the promotion of these properties to the point where I became a pest. In fact, [an Eastern Airlines executive] has put it in his inimitable way: "We hired a dog (RockResorts—no criticism intended) and now we are being asked to bark." That must be an old English saying. . . . Anyway, the fact is there: RockResorts, and the properties, on their own, do not (and did not) have the clout to get big Cerromar off the ground.

As a result, marketing efforts to promote Cerromar Beach largely centered on associating the property with other RockResorts properties, instead of with Eastern Airlines. "I think, frankly it has worked," Squire noted. "I don't think we would have had some of the groups we had in the house in the first year if clients had not felt that such a quality operation was behind it, if they had felt that they were going to walk into a first year schlocky operation. They found a good operation and we had many repeats coming out of that year's operation, and many, many plaudits on service and handling."[38]

Despite new marketing approaches calculated to boost occupancy rates, particularly at the Cerromar Beach Hotel, persistent challenges doomed the property to lower than expected performances in 1974 and 1975. RockResorts began a two-pronged marketing approach attempting to increase Puerto Rican tourism at the hotel and budget-minded tourism from the United States. During June and July 1974, for example, Puerto Rican registrants at Cerromar Beach accounted for about one-third of the guest days at the hotel.[39] By the spring of 1975, Eastern and RockResorts marketing experts had created a budget-minded "all-inclusive" package for Cerromar that would be available from April 1 to December 20. The package included unlimited greens and tennis court privileges at the Golf and Tennis Club for an extra $20. According to company documents, "This one package, with its all inclusiveness and low rate, will be the thrust of virtually all of Cerromar's non-group advertising budget this year." At the same time, the two groups continued to focus on the Puerto Rican market, investing $100,000 in a Spanish-language advertising campaign for newspapers, magazines, and local radio stations. In addition, another marketing specialist had been added to the staff, "to concentrate on Caribbean and other Latin American markets."[40]

Continued blows to Puerto Rico's tourism image, however, still plagued the success of Cerromar Beach, despite the shift to mass tourism in 1974 and 1975. Cancellations of conferences emerged as a significant problem for the Cerromar Beach Hotel in the early 1970s. The summer of 1974 was no exception. The hotel lost two clients during that time, which contributed to a loss of over twenty thousand room nights between June and November 1974. The overall impact on cash flow and profits was significant, as the two clients accounted for more than 11 percent of the annual planned revenue, or $933,000.[41] Eastern executives went as far as to prepare for the possibility of closing both hotels, as long as the casino licenses would not be affected. Additionally, Eastern's Lew Hucks had discussed "possible [Puerto Rican] government guarantees to obtain low cost Arab money to refinance the mortgage."[42] The hotels remained open, yet tourism in Puerto Rico declined 17 percent over the previous year for the six months ending June 1975. In October, Hall vowed to meet with the Puerto Rican governor to impress upon him the importance of the tourism sector on the island.[43] By that time, however, it appeared too late for a turnaround. Significant damage to the image of Puerto Rico as a tourist destination affected the entire sector, not just the Dorado Beach Resort properties. Eastern Airlines learned that 75 percent of five hundred travel agents polled in the New York City area "were not selling Puerto Rico." In assessing why travel agents chose to exclude Puerto Rico, Eastern learned that "[almost] without exception, the replies received stated that . . . Dorado and Cerromar were being hurt by the reputation of many of the San Juan area hotels [specializing in mass tourism] and by the negative publicity of the New York bombings."[44] Bombings in Puerto Rico on January 1, 1975, coordinated with Nelson Rockefeller's visit to the island, also undermined the image of stability on the island. Four bombs exploded, including two at San Juan branches of Chase Manhattan Bank. At the time,

"Rockefeller, [Secretary of State Henry] Kissinger, their wives and the Rock-efellers' two sons [were] staying at Dorado Beach Hotel."[45]

By the end of 1975, the enigmatic Floyd Hall, who left very little personal evidence concerning the relationship between Eastern Airlines and Rock-Resorts, recommended that Dorado Beach Hotel Corporation negotiate the sale of its Puerto Rican hotel properties, as well as all additional real estate and residences adjacent to the properties.[46] In the era of his successor, Frank Borman, Eastern moved to sell off its hotel interests. Of the hotel operations, Borman observed: "They're gone in my mind. . . . We're no longer going to be in any kind of business but running an airline. We failed in the business of operating hotels. Now that's behind us. We'll either sell or dispose of them in some way."[47] Borman's thoughts reflected a growing trend throughout the airline industry to dispose of interests not directly associated with airline management. TWA would eventually sell off Hilton International during the 1970s as well. By the early 1990s, Pan American Airlines would be forced to part ways with Intercontinental Hotels. In both cases, Hilton International and Intercontinental Hotels, two of the American pioneers of luxury hotels that began operations in the Caribbean and Latin America, ended up in British hands. RockResorts quickly followed Eastern Airlines in departing from Dorado Beach. Laurance Rockefeller had created a new paradigm for resort development in Dorado Beach, but found that vision undermined in the union of RockResorts and Eastern Airlines. In 1977, Rockefeller turned management control of the Dorado Beach Hotel and the Cerromar Beach Hotel to Regent International Hotels.[48]

The Real Cost of a Wedding in Paradise

In January 1975, Charles A. Bell, executive vice president for the Western Hemisphere and Corporate Technical Services of Hilton International, observed, "From a hotelman's point of view, making a reasonable profit on a resort hotel in the Caribbean is a much more difficult problem than doing the same in other types of hotels in other parts of the Western Hemisphere." Bell argued that the process of tourism development was more costly in the Caribbean than elsewhere in the Americas. "The resort hotel," he noted, "is much more expensive to build with beach development, tennis courts, swimming pools, and extensive grounds and recreational facilities, and in many cases expensive infrastructure installations such as sewage treatment plants and partial power generation. Lower labor costs do not offset the fact that a large percentage of building materials and furnishing must be imported as well as skilled supervisory labor."[49] In terms of programming costs, decentralized resort hotels often incurred higher entertainment costs than a business hotel, given their isolation from urban entertainment areas or city centers. Furthermore, government involvement with the development process could also impact profitability, as some Caribbean governments failed to limit the number of hotel rooms built in a single region or failed to provide commensurate advertising and promotion for the properties already at the location in question. The quality of local products and agriculture, at times not up to the global standards demanded by tourists and the international hotels, often required importation of goods with heavy tariffs. Moreover, the lack of appropriate hotel training schools created additional training costs for the resorts.[50]

Bell assessed the special requirements of Hilton's seven Caribbean resort hotels in comparison to its three Canadian and three Latin American city (Sao Paulo, Caracas, and Bogotá) hotels. Occupancy at the Hilton Caribbean properties was only 68.5 percent in 1973 compared to 81.8 percent at Latin American hotels and 80.9 percent at Canadian hotels. As with the Dorado Beach properties, the seasonality of Hilton's Caribbean properties made it "hard to move people to the Caribbean in the spring and fall, and there is no fill in market except for group travel or meeting business, often at giveaway prices."[51] Furthermore, Bell noted the instability of Caribbean locations in relation to social, economic, and political conditions. "These vacation travel oriented hotels are highly sensitive to the slightest hint of a recession," he commented, "and the slightest sign of a negative attitude on the part of the local population, or political instability in the country." To further complicate the financial difficulties of Caribbean resorts, Bell observed that even though rooms were more expensive in the Caribbean, guests spent less money in the hotels during their visits than at the Canadian and Latin American city hotels. He contended that the need for more labor in operating a resort than a city hotel, including "gardeners, beach attendants, social staffers," also hurt profit levels. In addition, the cost of imported food and beverages increased during periods when transportation costs escalated.[52]

These factors help explain, at least in part, some of the challenges that Eastern and RockResorts faced during their collaborative activities at Dorado Beach in the late 1960s and early 1970s. RockResorts needed added capital to build the Cerromar Beach Hotel, an additional golf course, and a small number of condominiums. While RockResorts benefited from the added capital available for development from Eastern, the airline's insistence on a quick profit from the joint investment probably contributed to the decision to build a five hundred–room convention hotel, the Cerromar Beach Hotel, in an already saturated hotel market. The Dorado Beach Hotel's isolation from San Juan had initially been an asset in attracting tourists to the out-of-the-way resort, yet the distance of the Cerromar Beach Hotel from San Juan in a more aggressive conference hotel market ultimately served as a liability once additional hotels had been built in San Juan. In the final analysis, Dorado Beach and its two hotels remained a relatively low-density project, but served as a magnet for higher-density hotels in the Dorado area in later years. The short-term relationship between RockResorts and Eastern Airlines, from 1967 to 1976, also illustrated the Puerto Rican government's tolerance for business alliances in shaping domestic tourism. Finally, Eastern's short-term commitment to tourism development in Puerto Rico, as well as its lack of knowledge in the sector, revealed why alliances between American air carriers and hoteliers generally did not produce mutually beneficial tourism development relationships.

6

Destination Cuba!

For all of its propaganda, Mikhail Kalatovoz's film *I Am Cuba* (1964) teaches profound lessons about Cuban national identity during the Fulgencio Batista dictatorship and in the immediate aftermath of Castro's coup. Perhaps it is no surprise, given the ubiquity of casinos, nightclubs, and private beaches in Batista's Cuba, that Kalatovoz and the film's writers, Russian Yevgeney Yevtushenko and Cuban Enrique Pineda Barnet, chose travel and tourism as the initial point of departure for this moving cinematographic discussion of Cuban identity.

The film begins with twisting aerial shots above the Cuban coast; white foam surf laps gently at the coastline, its bays, and its lagoons. The moving camera pans forests of thick palm fronds, while the somber voices of a chorus collide like waves with the crashing sounds of the surf. The camera stops at the base of some palms trees near the coastline, suspended against the blue sky. Shortly thereafter, the scenery shifts from the idyllic coast to a platform high above the Capri Hotel in Vedado, modern Havana. Floor shots angle upward to a young guitar player and two musicians wearing dunce caps, capturing the frenetic pace of this tourist wonderland. High above the swimming pool, on an elevated platform, bathing beauties wearing high heels and floppy straw hats effortlessly twirl on a makeshift catwalk, as a sunglass-masked disc jockey urges the crowd on the pool platform below to applaud and support their favorite contestant. The menagerie of people in suits, dresses, and flowered shirts below clap frantically, as waiters armed with martinis try to dodge lawn furniture. All the while, less-engaged tourists watch the Malecón below from glass enclosures suspended at the edge of the pool's platform. *I Am Cuba's* opening scene, one of several vignettes in the film, offers a significant critique of Cuban tourism during the Batista years. In perhaps the film's most lauded cinematographic sequence, tourists at the Capri Hotel go about their activities suspended above the Cuban landscape. All of these activities, which became associated with Cuban tourism, were in fact, in this stunning metaphor, not a part of Cuba at all. In effect, the director and writers of *I Am Cuba* use the opening frames of the film to separate Cuba from the activities that had come to define Cuba in the capitalist world.[1]

I Am Cuba may be the most dramatic contemporary critique of Cuban national identity through the lens of tourism that has been produced. Nevertheless, since the 1920s Cuban statesmen and businessmen, developmental agencies, and international corporations set forth competing visions of Cuban identity through the myriad tourism programs they suggested for the country. The purpose of this chapter, set against the backdrop of a long national history of tourism development, is to understand that during the 1950s, Batista's Godfatheresque tourism regime was not the only alternative for national tourism development—though it was the most prevalent. Foremost among the tourism reformers, Armando Maribona, the artist, journalist, and longtime promoter of Cuban tourism, proposed significant reforms that would have turned the focal point of Cuban tourism from casinos and private beaches to Cuban heritage and the island's stunning landscapes, flora, and fauna. The second part of this chapter suggests a similarity between Maribona's ideas and the revolutionary tourism program espoused by the new Castro regime and its national institute of tourism, the Instituto Nacional de la Indústria Turística (INIT). In addition to drawing similarities between Maribona's ideas and the revolutionary regime's nationalist tourist program, this chapter suggests that a packaged model for national tourism that truly reflected Cuban cultural, environmental, and social realities could only be created once the island's relationship with the United States had been severed. In many ways, then, *I Am Cuba* served not only as a means of exposing the lack of Cuban nationality and values in the tourism of the Batista era but, more important, also as an entrée for Cuba's revolutionary tourism—a development model that drew on existing ideas from Cuban tourism reformers.

For the years 1898 to 1960, Latin American scholars have provided a fairly well defined picture of the succession of developmental models for Cuban tourism. In *On Becoming Cuban: Identity, Nationality, and Culture*, for example, Louis Pérez Jr. illustrates how American hoteliers and service providers quickly filled the needs of American tourists and soon-to-be Cuban residents in the aftermath of the Spanish-American War. Additionally, Rosalie Schwartz's *Pleasure Island: Tourism and Temptation in Cuba* illustrates how local Cuban businessmen and politicians during the Machado regime tied their dreams for economic development to American hotel and real estate developers, such as John M. Bowman (Biltmore Hotels), in an effort to remake World War I and Prohibition Havana into a Caribbean Paris. For the 1950s, Pérez and Schwartz both explore the consequences of mass tourism (and its impact on conceptions of Cuban nationalism) developed by Batista and the American mob. Cuban authors have also supplemented our understanding of Batista's corrupt tourism program. For example, Enrique Cirules's *The Empire of Havana* dwells on Batista's willing dependence on the American mob, the U.S. government, and financial interests in the United States during his regime. Cirules highlights not only Batista's indiscretions but also the excesses of Meyer Lansky, the ringleader of this empire in Havana. In contrast, Evaristo Villalba Garrido's *Cuba y el turismo* offers a broader scholarly assessment of Cuban tourism from the years after the Spanish-American War through the early 1990s. Villalba Garrido's careful study includes a seemingly endless catalog of legislative and legal measures that supported tourism during the 1950s, as well as a more measured, but nonetheless scathing, critique of the excesses of Cuban tourism during the Batista period. His study differs from Cirules's and Schwartz's in that he includes a fairly exhaustive section regarding Cuban tourism following 1959. For Villalba Garrido, the lack of any alternatives to Batista's plan gives Castro's tourism measures a revolutionary veneer. This chapter challenges all of these studies by suggesting that there were nationalist alternatives to Batista's tourism program, and those alternatives may well have influenced Castro's tourism plans in the immediate aftermath of his triumph in 1959.[2]

*   *   *

By the 1950s, Cuban tourism faced serious questions regarding its long-term viability. First and foremost, the legitimacy of the Batista regime and its tolerance of a tourism program allied with organized crime raised significant concerns. Second, a lack of public and private support for tourism since the repeal of Prohibition placed Cuba's initial role as a tourism leader in the Caribbean in question. The apparent financial success of Batista's plan, however, overshadowed reformist currents within Cuban tourism during the 1950s. These models set forth alternative visions of Cuban tourism development, which also suggested new projections of Cuban identity to visiting tourists. The International Bank for Reconstruction and Development issued the first of these alternative models in 1951. Francis Adams Truslow's seventeen-member committee, in consultation with the Cuban government, published its findings in the *Report on Cuba*. Tourism was not the main concern of the committee's activities. Indeed, the chapter on tourism is stuffed back in the forty-first chapter of its ponderous report. Nevertheless, the members' remarks on the state of tourism in Cuba at the outset of the 1950s, and their prescriptive remedies as to how the Cuban government might best alter its tourism program, are revealing.[3]

The Truslow committee painted a less than flattering image of Cuban tourism at the midpoint of the twentieth century. In essence, Cuban tourism operators had attempted simply to perpetuate the island's reputation as a well-to-do watering hole, which it had developed during Prohibition, and the government and private industry had made few efforts to modernize the infrastructure and tourism program. "By comparison with other countries, such as Mexico," the study noted, "which have done much to stimulate tourism, those in the tourist business feel that [Cuba] has not even begun."[4] The report was also quick to subtly prescribe the audience toward which Cuba's tourist programming should be directed, if the government were to maximize its economic opportunities through tourism development. "It is necessary to consider what Cuba is doing to meet increasing competition [from other Caribbean basin countries]," the report observed, "and to exploit to the full her advantages of climate and proximity to the United States."[5] This statement reflects upon the nature of reforms embodied in the Truslow report. As emissaries of a developmental agency based in the United States, the committee preferred programs that guaranteed continued links with the U.S. economy. This preference for strong U.S.-Cuban economic relations precluded a reformist overhaul of Cuban tourism that better matched Cuban identity, rather than one that simply catered to the preexisting perceptions of the tourists coming to Cuba.

In their assessment of Cuban tourism, the members of the committee commented on the island's basic attractions from the perspective of the American tourist. "From the American tourist's point of view," the report noted, "Cuba offers a 'foreign atmosphere,' Cuban music and a freedom from certain restrictions—[including gambling]—which exist in certain parts of the United States." Other key aspects of why Cuban tourism was attractive to American tourists had little to do with programming content, but instead with the island's proximity to the United States and the lack of "currency problems or troublesome formalities."[6]

The committee found Cuba's hotel infrastructure and offerings to be below the expectations of American tourists: "A high proportion of the rooms listed are not the kind likely to attract the average tourist." "In a great many cases," the report continued, "sanitary arrangements, cleanliness and food would not be acceptable in a sub-standard American hotel." Not only might a tourist have to share a bathroom with another guest, as might be common in Europe or in the rest of Latin America, but the water was only potable in a few locations. In the report's final assessment, not more than two thousand of the more than six thousand hotel rooms on the islands were "of acceptable tourists standards."[7] In sum, the idea of asking tourists to adapt to local conditions stood squarely in the way of Cuba boosting its foreign exchange.[8]

The committee also sharply critiqued the lack of available attractions and the perceived low level of service offered to tourists. Not only were tourists—mainly Americans—suspicious that they had been conned and gouged by hotel, restaurant, and attraction operators, especially in the casinos, but the general level of "service" did not meet their standards. "One American convention of 700, for instance," the report noted, "which had been booked to stay for only three days was so dissatisfied with prices and conditions that many members returned home even before the end of that period." As a result, few Americans stayed very long in Cuba or bothered to return.[9] Lack of appropriate amusements also hurt the island's competitive chances for American tourists:

> In the whole of Cuba there is no public golf course and the only tennis courts available to the average tourist are those which some hotels provide. Public beaches are few and disappointing by comparisons with those in nearby Florida. An exception is Varadero Beach which is quite outstanding, but the accommodation is relatively limited. The best beaches and golf courses are those of private clubs to which the average visitor does not have the privilege of admission.[10]

These comments, couched within the context of developmental tourism aimed at strengthening ties to the United States, are highly ironic, given the fact that revolutionary tourism, in the immediate aftermath of the Revolution, would be responsible for opening up the beaches and many of the elitist activities to greater "public access." The report also went on to recommend improved accessibility throughout Cuba by building additional roads, which would facilitate automobile tourism throughout the island. The only truly unique Cuban aspect the committee recommended was the transformation of mineral springs, most notably at San Diego de los Baños, into healing baths.[11]

To be fair, the Truslow report needs to be understood within its Cuban and organizational prerogatives. First, the report qualifies as a reformist model of Cuban tourism in that it did not overtly promote and condone the Prohibitionist-era legacy of tourism culture that had been popularized in Cuba. In fact, the committee cast a suspicious eye on pension fund raiding schemes that the Batista government would take advantage of to build large hotels in late 1950s Havana, including the Habana Hilton. The report noted that the Sugar Workers' Retirement Fund invested $725,000 in a luxury hotel in Varadero, Cuba (probably the Hotel Internacional). In response, the report noted, "the Mission believes that it is highly doubtful whether such as investment is a proper one for a workers'. retirement fund because of the risks inherent in the operation of a hotel."[12] Despite these wise prescriptions, the *Report on Cuba* imagined a new identity for Cuba through a reformed tourism policy, but did so within the context of Cuba's continued dependence on U.S. tourism and private investment from the exterior. The catalog of official recommendations illustrates the dependent relationship between the two nations, as if it were a sine qua non for national considerations of tourism policy. Those recommendations included an increase in the number of "English-speaking Tourist Police," government encouragement for an auto ferry between Miami and Havana, and strict intolerance on the part of the Cuban government for any organized labor demands that "are detrimental to the development of the tourist industry."[13] Ironically, it would be the absence of American tourists and a lack of American investment that would bring about a definitive transformation in Cuban tourism.

The Truslow report had a significant impact on contemporary and historical debates about the nature of Cuban tourism in the 1950s. From the orthodox revolutionary historical tradition, Enrique Cirules views the Truslow report as a document that offered Cuba a blueprint for mixed agricultural and industrial development at a time when the United States dominated Cuban sugar production. Nevertheless, Cirules argues that the collaboration of the Cuban government with the Mafia, American financial institutions, and the U.S. government during the Batista regime doomed the island to continued dependence on sugar production and service industries (including tourism). He cites President Harry Truman's desire to visit Cuba as proof of this hegemonic effort to keep Cuba dependent on U.S. interests.[14] In Cirules's mind, Batista's ascendancy to power in 1952, followed by his subsequent subordination to American political, economic, and criminal elements, is proof that the Truslow report was never intended to be implemented—except in the case of tourism. Soon after Batista's coup, Cirules notes, "the regime began remodeling for a dazzling Havana to provide the infrastructure for the most important business affairs of the Mafia families. This plan included roads connecting important tourist regions, grand avenues, the construction of tunnels and highways, as well as a group of buildings for housing the administrative apparatus of a modern state."[15]

From the same revolutionary perspective, Evaristo Villalba Garrido critiqued the Truslow report as a justification for shaping Cuban tourism according to the desires of American tourists and investors. To this point, Villalba Garrido argues that most of Cuba's administrations since the formation of the republic had "served as careful custodians . . . of the interests of American capital." Furthermore, the report's critique of inadequate hotel accommodations and its identification of Cuba's lack of restrictions on tourists served to "deface and demerit the [hotel] worker and present him/her as an imposed obstacle to the 'just' access of the [North American] investor to the profits."[16]

On the other hand, at the time the report was offered, one Cuban journalist, Armando Maribona, agreed with the essential critiques of Cuban tourism offered by the Truslow committee. Like the committee members, Maribona believed that Cuban tourism needed to promote decentralized tourism outside of Havana, promote more modern hotel facilities throughout the island, and offer tourists a fair product for the price demanded. Maribona's assent to the conclusions of the Truslow report would not be unusual had he not been an individual of such unusual talent. Maribona's position as a correspondent for the *Diario de la Marina*, Cuba's oldest and one of its most conservative newspapers, was only one of the many hats that this Cuban Renaissance man wore. To understand his background and myriad talents is also to understand how his lifelong assessment and critiques of Cuban tourism offered a substantially different model of tourism to that proposed by the Truslow report. Although they agreed essentially on some of the deficiencies of infrastructure and the capitalist context of tourism promotion and production, Maribona's deep love of Cuba led him to advocate a tourism program that better matched the ideas of Cuban nationalism, particularly in terms of cultural and natural tourism.

Born in Havana on June 23, 1894, Maribona showed early promise as an artist, studying in Havana, New York, and Paris, where he would also have exhibitions. Maribona's talents in the plastic arts were complemented by a passion for writing. He served as a correspondent for Cuban and Latin American newspapers throughout Europe, eventually finding a home at the *Diario de la Marina*, where he was a correspondent from 1930 to 1959. The author of numerous books—including books on Cuban tourism and art as well as original novels—Maribona became a fixture in Cuban art schools until retiring at the end of the 1950s. In addition to his artistic, literary, and academic activities, Maribona traveled widely, enjoyed urban planning, and participated in the formulation of Cuban tourism policy throughout the majority of his adult life.

Since his early days as a correspondent at *Diario de la Marina*, Maribona advocated reforms in Cuban tourism that centered on nationalist themes. He published two substantial books on the development of Cuban tourism: *Turismo y ciudadania* (1943) and *Turismo en Cuba* (1959).[17] Maribona did not delineate a codified tourism policy for Cuba; however, his justifications for tourism centered on the rights of citizens to be able to travel and to be able to see and learn about the world. Maribona's second book on tourism, *Turismo en Cuba*, is the most intriguing, given the context of its publication. The text was ready for publication in December 1958, but this was postponed, in all likelihood, by the events surrounding Batista's flight from power and Castro's triumphant entry into Havana. It would not be published until October 1959.

Maribona served as vice president of the Instituto del Turismo Cubano (ITC) from 1952, when the Batista government created it, until 1959. While Batista conducted most of his tourism development activities through unofficial channels and with mob bosses, the ITC served as an "official" agency geared toward tourism promotion and development. Villalba Garrido, for example, lambasted the ITC for doing little to improve the Cuban content of tourism during its tenure. He charged that the ITC "demonstrated to the visitor the negative aspects of a society dominated by corruption and the zeal for profits."[18] Instead of promoting Cuban culture, folklore, and architecture, Villalba Garrido observed, "gambling and the wide market for [prostitutes] were the central attractions of the sightseeing packages in planned trips from New York, Miami, Chicago, and other North American cities."[19] Villalba Garrido does not stop short of laying the blame for the warped Cuban perspective presented to tourists at the feet of the ITC. He charges: "Thus it was that the roulette table and the dice reached the height of the tourist attractions and especially for the tours organized from the United States, whose objective was the casino."[20] It appears, however, from Maribona's writings—both in the 1940s and 1950s—that Villalba Garrido imputed the ills created through Batista's channels for doing tourism business to a largely powerless ITC. Maribona outlines the extensive ways in which the government either did not act on ITC's recommendations or manipulated the organization's finances. Furthermore, the reputation of Maribona and the ITC could easily be called into question if Maribona had only written his second book in 1959 as a way to defend himself against the new regime. The nationalist ideas that he promotes for tourism in the late 1950s are simply reiterations of the same ideas—including showcasing Cuban landscapes, dancing, folklore, and architecture—he outlines in his 1943 study, *Turismo y ciudadania*. In fact, many of his ideas in the 1943 study go back to the early 1930s, when he began his career as a correspondent for the *Diario de la Marina*.

For three decades, Maribona dedicated his tourism development efforts to cultured activities (in large measure a reflection his own avocational interests) that could be tailored to the middle classes. While Cuban governments and entrepreneurs had spent a great deal of money, particularly during Prohibition, to attract wealthy tourists to exotic attractions like casinos, nightclubs, and race tracks, Maribona argued that the most effective way to build Cuban tourism at midcentury would be to present Cuban attractions that would accent local culture and build a strong customer base for return visitors. "The error consists," Maribona noted, "in imagining that by simply putting on an expensive tie we are then elegant and that with [brief] festivals, isolated details and attractions like the Marianao Beach, the Hippodrome, the Casino, and the Opera season, in an unorganized and unprepared city for tourism that it can develop itself and constitute a stable industry."[21]

Despite his zeal for nationalist content in the tourism program, Maribona was well aware of the cultural and economic context within which Cuba would launch its activities aimed at tourists. With Cuban tourism on the decline between 1932 and 1954, Maribona watched as nearby Caribbean islands, including Bermuda and Jamaica, quickly rose to the fore as tourist destinations. Lacking the casinos, racetracks, and other "spirited" infrastructure that had given Cuba so much business, yet detracted from its reputation, these neighboring islands emphasized their natural landscapes, beaches, and environment to attract tourists for long stays—much like the spas of Europe or the northeastern United States. Maribona noted, at length:

> Without casinos, without a race track, without jai-alai, without automobile racetracks, without "winter festivals," Bermuda, Nassau, Jamaica and other islands receive vacationers, men, women, and children, who find trees and flowers, palm trees and pines, beaches, hotels of many categories, at prices in keeping with their luxury, but all very clean and attended by very friendly (*amabilísimo*) personnel. They go to enjoy the relaxation, to swim, to tan in the sun, to play golf, to fish . . . to be treated with exquisitely respectful courtesy, and no one molests them nor charges them abusive prices.[22]

In terms of his own island, Maribona was fascinated by the advantages that Cuba's landscapes, beaches, weather, and environment offered for augmenting tourism.

Maribona believed Cuba, blessed with hundreds of miles of beaches and mineral springs, could attract a sizable middle-class tourism base to the island. He observed, "When international [tourists] know that in Cuba there are beaches and mountains of exceptional beauty and extraordinary natural attractions, where the [tourist] is able to practice his favorite sport, live comfortably, tan oneself all year long with our sun, whose rays and atmospheric conditions have excellent healing virtues, he/she will prefer to spend his/her summer or winter period of vacations in our country."[23] While Maribona clearly hoped to match the same types of activities offered to international tourists in Bermuda or Jamaica, he also sought to open the island—outside of Havana and Varadero—to international tourists. In that context, Cuba's flora and fauna would become an integral part of the "packaged vacation."

To that end, Maribona believed that Cuba should modernize its beach tourism offerings, yet he also recognized the importance of Cuba's cultural and historical heritage. This stemmed not only from his love of Cuba but also from his desire to protect Cuba's heritage from the ravages of modernization. Maribona cited movies as one of the standardizing factors that accounted for the gradual homogenization of global culture. As a result, he lamented, "everything becomes monotonous, vulgar. Samurais wear tuxedos, motorboats are substituted for gondolas . . . and automobiles . . . are substituted for camels in the sandy deserts."[24] Modernization also impacted tourism. "First class hotels are the same all over the world," he commented. And how did globalization affect Cuban culture? "The 'daiquiri,'" he observed, "and other cocktails of Bacardi rum are [now] drunk universally."[25] Maribona's theory for limiting the impact of globalization on tourism was based upon the idea that tourists search for "*exoticismo.*"

As a result, Maribona suggested that the Cuban government and private groups give more attention to the value of historical structures, including homes, governmental buildings, and religious buildings. He lightly chastised Rotary and Lions clubs in Trinidad for not recognizing the colonial splendor of their city's architecture. After making mention of European heritage sites, he argued, "The nations that promote tourism, looking for prestige, conserve and promote attractions that, even when they are only of interest to refined and cultured visitors, allow them to worthily 'sell hospitality.'" Maribona then turned to the Cuban reality in the 1940s to emphasize the importance of heritage tourism: "On the other hand, the cabarets, the hotels, the theatres of variety, the horse tracks, the roulette table, etc., are not sufficient in the list of attractions of a city or country that respects itself and pretends to conserve an honorable place in the concert of civilized nations."[26] Much of Maribona's zeal for developing heritage tourism derived from feelings of guilt that arose while listening to the U.S. secretary of state, Cordell Hull, lecture neighboring states on the value of historical preservation in the late 1930s. Maribona subsequently observed, "We take a quick look at how much we have destroyed [architecturally] for business sake, for stupid idleness . . . for utilitarianism, for indifference towards the past; for lack of artistic concepts."[27]

Toward the end of the Batista era, Maribona codified a list of attractions that the ITC should develop in order to amplify the island's offerings for tourists. Among these, Maribona not only listed museums, conferences, and opera but also historical and archaeological sites. "While it is true that Spanish colonization did not leave [Cuba] palaces and temples of the magnificence of Mexico and Peru, neither fortresses as great as that of Cartagena (Colombia), it did leave us interesting examples that, linked to their respective histories and legends, are tourist attractions."[28] Despite this tremendous legacy, Maribona warned, looters and lack of care had intervened to desecrate these sites. Modernization and the transformation of Cuba during the twentieth century had further hampered preservation. Havana's fortresses remained intact, but had not been properly cared for, with hundreds of cannons being sold to Americans as scrap metal. Historical houses had also been destroyed. "Each demolition is justified with the . . . phrase, 'under the banner of progress,' as if our territorial extension was so lacking that progress could not flourish parallel with conservation of that which we inherited from Spain."[29] Citing Trinidad, still unrenovated in 1958, as a nearly complete example of colonial architecture and design, Maribona argued for greater attention to the "national patrimony." Finally, Maribona also cited the preservation of religious sites from the colonial period as an important element of national heritage, as well as a possible draw for religious festivals.[30]

Armando Maribona retired from the *Diario de la Marina* in 1960 and died four years later. There is no record of his interaction with the Castro regime in the wake of the Revolution's triumph. Nevertheless, the nature of Castro's tourism policies—and much of the Cuban Revolution itself—leads one to believe that his policies were gathered from existing material and fashioned to fit the needs and aims of the Revolution. In fact, Castro's tourism program depended less on revolutionary new ideas and programs and more on the ability to reorder the island and its possibilities in the image of a socialist state able to stand up to the United States. As far as his tourism program was concerned, there were three necessary elements: nationalistic tourism ideas, a tourism infrastructure, and a clean break from the United States—as an investor on the island and as a source of tourists.

Looking back, the break with the United States seems to have been the most critical element in constructing national tourism. As Louis Pérez Jr. has illustrated throughout *On Becoming Cuba*, from 1898 until 1959 American films, commercials, products, and styles largely influenced Cuban identity. Hence, the relationship surely would have had a significant impact on Cuban identity as reflected through its tourism program. "In growing numbers Cubans were arriving at the realization," Pérez has written, "that emulation could not produce authenticity, that North Americans could not deal with them on any terms other than instrumental ones . . . and that [the] meaning of 'Cuban' had come to imply submission and subservience. They were learning that 'Cuban' was defined simply as North Americans' exotic and tropical Other."[31] This was especially true in regards to tourism. While in consumer culture Cubans had mimicked U.S. styles and fashions, in tourism Cuba had projected to American tourists what they expected and desired to see as "Cuban." As long as Cuban tourism was dependent on American tourists and responsive to the concept of Cuba as a place of "freedom" and lack of responsibility, there would be very little chance that an emphasis on Cuba's beautiful landscapes, history, and culture would command the attention of package tour operators and tourists. Maribona's ideas represented one strain of tourism reform that best reflected Cuban nationalism. Unless a reorientation of the economy, culture, and politics away from the United States could be effected, however, those ideas would have little currency. As a result, President Eisenhower's ban on trade with Cuba and the subsequent U.S. Treasury Department restrictions on spending money in Cuba brought the number of American tourists traveling to Cuba to a trickle.

With the break from the United States, Castro could then speed ahead with his plans to transform Cuban tourism into a sector reflective of Cuban identity. In reference to Cuban consumer culture, Pérez has noted that in the wake of the Revolution, "the proposition of *Cuban* resonated across the island. Once more consumption became a way to affirm nationality, but now the products were Cuban made. Advertisers stressed the virtues of locally produced merchandise."[32] Cuban tourism followed suit. There are two stages of tourism during the Castro regime. The first, lasting from 1959 until approximately 1981, can be designated as "revolutionary tourism." Reflecting Castro's synthetic thought process, "revolutionary tourism" comprised a limited international aspect, which catered to the small number of international visitors still visiting the island, and a larger domestic tourism project. On both accounts, Castro's program was meant to showcase the achievements and talents of the Revolution, and the beauty and hospitality of Cuba, and to retain valuable foreign exchange on the island.

By 1961, the new Cuban government had nationalized foreign-owned property in the tourist sector. However, Castro began laying out his new vision of Cuban tourism less than forty days after entering Havana. His program combined an effort to retain foreign exchange, either from tourists visiting Cuba or Cubans leaving the country, with an effort to showcase the Cuban environment through a massive domestic tourism program. On February 19, 1959, Castro discussed the topic of tourism within the context of the Revolution. During a four-hour television appearance, he stressed the importance of tourism to the national economy. He also emphasized that the nature of tourism, which had been dominated by gambling and catering to the elite, would have to be changed in order to stress the nation's natural beauty. Always the pragmatist, Castro noted that the gaming tables in the large hotels would remain open in order to keep full employment.[33] In June 1959, the revolutionary government approved the creation of the Junta de Fomento Turístico, with Fidel Castro as its leader.

The Junta de Fomento Turístico initially worked through channels already established to plan and develop tourism: namely, the ITC, for which Armando Maribona had served as vice president since 1952. While there are no documents to corroborate the transfer of Maribona's plans for tourism development throughout Cuba, his ideas seem to pervade much of the new regime's tourism strategies. In September 1959, the new Cuban government began to promote its plan for tourism development, an ambitious program that would take three to four years to complete and would involve tourism infrastructure development throughout the island. Fifty million dollars was set aside for the first year of development, during which funds would be used to build roads to improve access throughout the island and to construct hotels in remote locations. While a new air-conditioned airport would be completed in Havana, most of the money would be used to "show the tourists that there is much more to see in Cuba than the capital." The new director of the Cuban Institute of Tourism, Carlos F. Almoina, also announced the construction of a hotel near Viñales in rural Pinar del Río; reconstruction of a pool for the thermal waters at San Diego (noted by both the Truslow report and Armando Maribona); 150 beach cabanas at the beaches of El Megano, El Salado, and Arroyo; a dock for boats at Puerto Esperanza; motels at Jibacoa and La Rotilla; completion of the Hotel Jagua in Cienfuegos; and a motel in Trinidad. In the eastern part of the country, which the director characterized as "the future of Cuba," the government would build a hotel of 150 rooms at Santiago de Cuba; motels at the beaches of Siboney, Guarda la Barca, and Castillo Español; and a motel at Manzanillo. Almoina's remarks, carried in the *New York Times* and then reprinted in the *Diario de la Marina* (Maribona's newspaper), had a hint of Maribona's influence. Almoina noted that the institute's "new" plan was to "present a wide and novel portrait of Cuba as a tourist attraction. The campaign of the Institute proposes that the tourist not only go to Habana, but also to the interior of the island, underscoring the historical interest of places like Trinidad."[34] Two weeks later, on September 23, 1959, the revolutionary government announced the dispersion of more funds for eastern Cuba, dedicated primarily to the construction of more public beaches and roads from the Sierra Maestra to eastern beaches.[35]

The following spring, Castro emphasized the national component of Cuba's new tourism program. "Cubans used to go to Paris, or Florida, and so on and spend huge sums abroad," he noted. "The revolution is promoting a tourist trade here at home." Castro outlined that workers would have paid vacations, but would enjoy them somewhere in Cuba. Envisioning the leisure empowerment of the working class, Castro mused, "The tourist trade will boom. Today the people who never before were able to travel are taking trips and seeing the marvels of our country." The Revolution not only changed the geographical focus away from international travel but also highlighted its new activities. As a result, Castro declared, "almost all the tourists go to see the towns we are building, the new schools, the cooperatives. So there will be more and more things to see in Cuba." Castro also hit on one of the new activities of tourism that would dovetail with the Revolution: a nascent form of ecotourism. Visiting the countryside or the beach offered an opportunity to contemplate the beauty of Cuba and to remember the struggles of the revolutionary forces against Batista. "When July 26 comes," he stated, "we will organize tours to the Sierra Maestra region."[36]

To this point, Castro's tourism program and its emphasis on opening up the private beaches for Cuban use have been explained from a class-based perspective. According to that analytical approach, the main reason for opening the beaches was to illustrate to the masses the democratizing effects of the Revolution. While that perspective is certainly valid, it overshadows Castro's own love affair with Cuban landscapes, whether on the beaches or in the mountains. Castro's own experience growing up goes a long way to explain the nationalist emphasis on the environment and outdoor activities in the new regime's tourism program.[37]

*   *   *

By the beginning of the 1970s, as international tourists were beginning to trickle back into Cuba, INIT had integrated revolutionary tourism into its offerings for foreign travelers. The INIT publication *El sol de Cuba: Panorama turístico* offers a glance at the ways in which revolutionary nationalism was packaged into suggested island attractions.[38] The few advertisements throughout the booklet feature those attractions that had made Cuba famous over time, including the Tropicana ("a paradise under the stars"); the old Du Pont mansion in Varadero, Restaurante Las Américas (with the provocative invitation: "The Dupont [sic] family was accustomed to passing the summer here in this very luxurious mansion of Varadero. How would you like to eat here now?"); Havana Club (rum); and La Cueva del Pirata, a nightclub in Varadero ("Take drink with Morgan and Drake"). An ad for Cubana Airlines—with service to Havana from Barbados, Trinidad, Guyana, Mexico, Lima, Madrid, Berlin—promoted Cuba's 137 beaches.

These advertisements, geared toward international tourists—as much to convince them of Cuban sophistication as to invite them to its most popular attractions—provides a framework for discussing Cuba's tourism panorama. Overall, the Cuban tourism offering favored Cuba's history and natural setting. Sections on Cuba's flora, fauna, geography, museums, and folklore accompanied sections on tobacco, rum, and nightlife. The Revolution played a mediating role between pre-Castro activities (nightlife) and revolutionary tourism. While disavowing revolutionary achievements and activities as tourist attractions, the guide boasted that "a large number of visitors are highly interested in our social, cultural, and economic advances and are anxious to learn about them." Visits to the Revolutionary Plaza served as a highlight for some tourists, as did visits to farms and recently constructed dams for others. "It is frequent to see many [visitors] ask for a . . . hat, some gloves, and [a blade] to also cut sugar cane," the guide continued, "and treasure the memory of having given a symbolic hand to our first industry."[39] Interspersed throughout the rest of the thin guide are similar sections that serve to link Cuba's traditional tourist activities and more nationalist endeavors with the meaning of the Revolution. "Revolución y logros" (Revolution and accomplishments), for example, highlights the lack of illiteracy on the island. Cuba's lack of unemployment, high levels of hygienic cleanliness, and advanced medical practices are also underscored. This paradise in the Caribbean, the booklet further boasts, refuses to pay athletes for their efforts, nor does it charge admission to cultural events. Furthermore, "thanks to the growing economic development and without necessity of means of control, panhandling disappeared in Cuba, as well as prostitution, the use of drugs, criminal classes and other blemishes."[40]

In 1973, the Cuban tourism organization, INIT, began a shift toward enticing international tourists to return to Cuba. This slow change also signaled a shift from "revolutionary tourism" to "postrevolutionary" tourism. Under the former, the nationalist content and socialist character of Cuban tourism reinforced the validity of the revolutionary movement. However, as tourism increasingly became the economic engine of the state, both the nationalist content and revolutionary content of Cuban tourism were muted. Beginning in 1973, and culminating on May 16, 1981, the social ethic of Cuban tourism—and not necessarily the nationalist content of tourism—profoundly changed. On that day, Castro announced that Cuban citizens would enjoy their vacations at camping sites around the country. While this indeed reflected nationalistic values for domestic tourists, it also undermined the social concept of equality embodied in Article 42 of the 1976 constitution, which declares: "The state consecrates the right won by the Revolution of that its citizens, without distinction of race, color or national origin: . . . May live in whatever sector, zone or neighborhood of the cities and stay in any hotel; be waited on in all restaurants and other establishments of public service . . . enjoy the same swimming pools, beaches, parks, social circles and other centers of culture, sports, recreation, and rest."[41]

Without enforcement of constitutional access by the general public to tourism facilities, the nationalist content of Cuban tourism was, in a sense, diluted to match the preferences of the global tourist. Today, small shrines to the Revolution in opulent international hotels—which everyone passes and few take too seriously—reflect the attenuation of revolutionary Cuban nationalism as a tourist offering.

Despite the decay of revolutionary tourism after 1981, Armando Maribona, were he alive today, would probably identify the bulk of his ideas as the centerpiece of postrevolutionary Cuban tourism. Beach tourism, ecotourism, and cultural heritage tourism remain the predominant offerings for international tourists in Cuba. Nevertheless, the economic imperatives of tourism, particularly in the wake of the fall of the Soviet Union, were accompanied by greater toleration of exclusive restaurant and hotel properties for international tourists, as well as a decline in beach tourism opportunities for Cubans. Perhaps no one better expressed the demise of revolutionary ethos of Cuban tourism better than musician Carlos Varela in his song, "Tropicollage," which lambastes tourists who come to Cuba yet see very little of the country during their time holed up in tourist enclaves.[42]

Ironically, Cuban tourism has come full circle, with artists like Varela suggesting the need for reforms in what tourists should do and see in Cuba. Despite ideological and practical incongruities between revolutionary and postrevolutionary tourism, reformist (or nationalist) impulses continue to play a significant role in Cuba's tourism program. Beach tourism, of course, has been dominant, albeit in a less than open setting. Increased revenue streams from tourism, moreover, have allowed Cuba to undertake an ambitious effort to restore its architectural heritage, particularly in Old Havana. The irony here rests on the fact that preservation of Cuba's architectural heritage has really only been possible within the context of global capitalism. Through the 1980s and into the 1990s, Cuba turned outward for help in renovating and refurbishing hotels and decaying colonial-era buildings.[43]

*   *   *

In my own research, I have also made a mistake that the directors and writers of *I Am Cuba* exposed forty years earlier with their provocative film: I conflated global tourism in Cuba with Cuban tourism. The response to my faux pas reinforces the contemporary relevance of coming to terms with the emergence of nationalist tourism during the 1950s and 1960s. To a certain degree, this is a distinction—global tourism in Cuba versus Cuban tourism—that Cubans are quickest to catch, and in some small way they owe a debt to individuals like Armando Maribona.

In February 2004, I found myself in Havana attending a conference on higher education sponsored by the United Nations Educational, Scientific, and Cultural Organization (UNESCO). Included in this global conference was a segment devoted entirely to tourism and higher education. Between the sessions, I struck up a lively conversation with various Cubans, including one who headed a tourism studies program at a Cuban university. I told him that I was going to study "postrevolutionary" Cuban tourism in Varadero following the conference, with a focus on the hotel infrastructure. He shook his head and insisted that tourism at Varadero—now a thriving bastion for European and Asian (and some American) tourists—was *not* Cuban tourism. With other sessions upon us, he insisted he would tell me later what he meant. In a later communication he wrote:

> In reference to Varadero, I wanted to effectively say that it is a very international [tourist pole], that was inherited, in terms of its conformity as a tourist destination, at a stage of development where the criteria of design, construction, and other [criteria] were very different. In Cuba there are other destinations with different characteristics, in which the community is better integrated [to the tourist pole], where the occupancy rates are lower, and which you should get to know. In my personal valuation, I like Varadero a lot; it is beautiful, but I prefer more natural and less built-up places.[44]

My friend's construction of Cuban tourism had as little to do with ideology as it did with the beauty of Cuban landscapes and the rural pace of life in central Cuba. Similarly, in coming to terms with the development of a nationalist Cuban tourism program in the 1950s and 1960s, both reformist and revolutionary ideas served to shape the nationalist content of revolutionary and postrevolutionary Cuban tourism. Armando Maribona, for the extent of his writings and the breadth of his interests, stands as the figure of greatest interest in this complex process of unraveling the sources of influence for these programs. We still do not exactly know the extent of his influence on the ITC, INIT, or Castro himself, but his introduction to *Turismo en Cuba* may offer insight. After copiously listing his credentials and disavowing any political affiliations, he closed his introductory comments by noting: "The *arrivistes* abound. I have read articles and listened to talks in which almost to the letter concepts and comments previously spoken by me were repeated. And as a fact that among Cubans intellectual property does not exist, here my friends, 'Fatten yourself from someone else's [work].' And [this book] will demonstrate one more time that journalists, with a few exceptions, far from being 'opportunists,' . . . [have been] robbed of that which pertains to us: our ideas. It does not matter; my only purpose is that this book is useful to my country, to its administrators, and to my compatriots."[45] Despite these mysteries, suffice it to say that concepts of nationalist tourism in Cuba owe a great deal to creative, prerevolutionary tourism planners like Maribona.

7

Visions of Cancún

As Mexico turned its focus for tourism development to Cancún Island in the late 1960s, planners within the Banco de México began designing a new genre of cities, the tourist city. The Banco de México outlined its objectives for the infrastructure and superstructure of the tourist city with great optimism. As time went on, however, the packaging of the Cancún resort experience underwent a series of rapid transformations that simultaneously validated the initial plan for mass tourism development and presented new challenges that would reshape the resort destination. What Mexican hotel management pioneer Rodolfo Casparius once succinctly noted in relation to hotels remains true for large-scale tourist cities as well: "[they] are not dead, they are alive." Changes in the global economy and adverse weather conditions, as well as deliberate design changes to a resort city, could transform its image on a regular basis. Using planning documents and diagnostic reports, this chapter explores the initial packaging and subsequent repackaging of Cancún between 1971 and 2006.

Cancún Island probably did not look much different to António Enriquez Savignac of the Banco de México when he visited the island in the mid-1960s as it did to adventurer Thomas Gann in the 1920s. "Cancuen [sic] is long, narrow, and flat, nearly ten kilometres in length by less than one kilometre broad in places. Its eastern part is merely a sandbank," Gann observed, "while the western and central portions are covered with scrub and high forest growth interspersed with patches of swamp." Gann noted that the island was home to a coconut plantation tended to by a man from Mérida.

Sailing south for approximately five miles, Gann and company encountered Indian mounds and ruins along the west coast of the island. The only semi-permanent structures on the island, apart from the ruins, appeared to be the makeshift huts used by the coconut workers as homes. Disembarking, Gann examined the various ruins and artifacts that had fallen into disrepair due to vandalism by local workers. Gann's vision of Cancún, which would prevail until development began in the 1970s, emphasized the tropical landscape, a surprising diversity of ruins and artifacts related to Mayans from as far as away as Tulum, and the rustic character of the island's coconut plantation and its workers.[1]

In spite of Gann's adventures, Cancún and Quintana Roo languished as a tourism destination until the 1960s and 1970s. Prior to that time, the colonial capital of the peninsula, Mérida, served as the international gateway to the region. To a large degree, the development of tourism on the Yucatan Peninsula was largely the work of the Barbachano Peón family. In 1921, Fernando Barbachano Peón called for the development of tourism infrastructure on the peninsula, including roads, which would allow tourists to visit Chichén-Itzá, Uxmal, and other Mayan heritage sites from Mérida. Barbachano Peón also built hotels at both Chichén-Itzá and Uxmal. His son, Fernando Barbachano Gómez Rul, extended the family's tourism empire into Quintana Roo, where he pioneered hotels and port development initiatives in Cozumel. Prior to the 1960s, however, the focus of tourism on the Yucatan Peninsula was dominated by visits to Mayan ruins and glimpses into the lives of the contemporary Maya. Chichén-Itzá represented the eastern limit of tourist attractions on the peninsula. As Lawrence Martin and Sylvia Martin's *Standard Guide to Mexico and the Caribbean* stated in its 1958–1959 edition: "The Chichen Itza [*sic*] road goes on beyond the ruins to Valladolid and is being extended to the east coast, where it is hoped that soon a Havana ferry service will connect Yucatan with the Havana-Miami tourist circuit and make it easy for vacationists to bring their cars." The combination of new tourists and automobile access to the east of Chichén-Itzá would "open up interesting new country in the almost unknown state of Quintana Roo, and make accessible the island of Cozumel, said to be well provided with tropical beaches."[2]

Indeed, had tourism experts in Mexico been queried in the late 1950s and early 1960s as to where a beach resort infrastructure and hotel super-structure should be built in Quintana Roo—the idea of what Cancún would become—they probably would have selected Cozumel for at least two reasons. First and foremost, coral reefs protected turquoise waters and marine life of unparalleled beauty, whose renown grew with visits from individuals such as Jacques Cousteau in the early 1960s. Second, the trail of Barbachano family investments, centered in Mérida, Chichén-Itzá, and Uxmal, eventually shifted eastward to Quintana Roo in the mid-1950s and 1960s. During the 1950s, Fernando Barbachano Gómez Rul carried the family's hotel and tourism empire into Quintana Roo. Trained at Harvard University, with a bachelor's degree in anthropology and Mayan archaeology, Barbachano Gómez Rul modernized the hotel industry in Cozumel by opening a hotel school there in 1954 and operating the Hotel Playa. Had Barbachano Gómez Rul simply opened a string of modern hotels in Cozumel, he would not be remembered as one of the great innovators of Mexican tourism. Frustrated by the lack of air service from the United States and central Mexico, however, Barbachano Gómez Rul also attempted to start his own airline, Aerolinea Aeromaya, to improve transportation between Mexican cities and Quintana Roo. Stymied by the protectionist policies of government-owned airlines, Barbachano Gómez Rul turned to cruise-ship tourism as Cozumel's avenue to economic development. As his successes multiplied in Cozumel, Barbachano Gómez Rul next looked to the islands north of Cozumel, including Cancún and Isla Mujeres, to expand his tourism empire at the outset of the 1960s. In 1962, he "acquired [an] important extension of the beaches of Cancún and a small lot of two hectares with beaches on Isla Mujeres." His acquiescence to the Banco de México team desirous to create the "idea of Cancún" on Cancún Island was essential to its success. Antonio Savignac visited Barbachano Gómez Rul at his home in Mérida, explained the new project to him, and asked if Barbachano Gómez Rul would sell his land there. In exchange for his willingness to sell his lands on Cancún Island and Isla Mujeres, the Banco de México awarded Barbachano Gomez Rul's personal bank, Banco de Yucatan, the first banking location in Cancún; the Banco de México provided important loans for the expansion of his Hotel Cozumel Caribé in Cozumel; and he received an invitation to participate in the creation of one of Cancún's first hotel projects, the Hotel Cancún Caribé.[3]

The same year that Barbachano Gómez Rul purchased his prime property on Cancún Island and Isla Mujeres, 1962, officials at the Consejo Nacional de Turismo (CNT) began to discuss plans for development of tourism infrastructure on the "Mexican Caribbean" in the northern Yucatan Peninsula. As a result, the idea that would become Cancún began as something very different under the direction of Miguel Alemán Valdés, former president of Mexico, head of the CNT, and father of Acapulco's tourism infrastructure. By 1965, the CNT had met on at least two occasions to formally discuss tourism development in the Mexican Caribbean. At that point, it was time for

Figure 3. Packaged vacation, Puerto Maya, Cozumel, Mexico. Puerto Maya welcomes hundreds of cruise ships and thousands of foreign tourists each year. Mexican history, architecture, and identity are part of the tourism product. (Author's photo)

the CNT to carry out statistical and in-field studies in relation to Caribbean tourism. This would involve research trips to Miami, the Bahamas, Jamaica, Barbados, Curaçao, and Puerto Rico. The research was carried out with an emphasis on finding successful practices from the surrounding Caribbean islands and tourist poles and then adapting them to unique elements of Mexican culture that would accent tourism development in the Mexican Caribbean. In a more practical vein, the report compiled by the CNT researchers as a result of their visits throughout the Caribbean emphasized the logistical challenges of bringing more tourists to the largely isolated Yucatan Peninsula. The pre-Cancún (1968) literature related to the development of a major tourism pole in the Mexican Caribbean is suffused with tones of respect for those nations that had already initiated mass tourism developments in the Caribbean. The search for innovative and successful practices throughout the region provides the first images of what could make a Mexican tourist pole in the region unique.

For example, CNT researchers traveled to Miami to better understand how the metropolitan area had acquired its image as a tourist paradise in the United States. "In its totality," the study noted, "Florida exercises a particular fascination over the North American tourist, a reason for which year after year it is visited by thirteen million people." For the low price of sixteen cents a tourist, the local tourism board publicized the region around the country. Five million tourists a year, in turn, spent an average of $210 each during their trips to the Miami metropolitan area. Observing tourism in Miami was important for Mexican officials not only because of its massive scale and profitability but also because Mexican authorities had clearly targeted American tourists as the primary clients for whatever tourism pole was created in the Mexican Caribbean. Understanding the emotional reasons that attracted so many Americans to Miami was as important as understanding how much money they spent there.[4]

If Miami reinforced the importance of creating an image that would perpetually attract tourists to the sandy beaches of Quintana Roo, the CNT's other in-field visits emphasized the changing nature of global tourism in the 1960s. In the Bahamas, for example, Mexican officials learned about the growing decentralization of tourism away from a single urban pole. By 1965, the preference of tourists to visit Bahaman islands other than Nassau had grown by 38.5 percent. The need for added amenities at these peripheral sites also became apparent. "They are creating new tourism centers [in the Bahamas]," the report stated, "and they are working to give them as many facilities and attractions as Nassau could bring together in a given moment; all of this . . . conforms to new and intelligent methods of planning and touristic integration."[5] To the astonishment of the Mexican officials, these hotels combined all of the services, including restaurants and nightclubs, on the hotel grounds. "These establishments, which are of the highest category, have in the majority of cases beaches as well as private swimming pools," the report noted, "to the which should be added the fact that the local tourism authorities have worried, from time to time, about the function of the public beaches with first class services. Their beauty and natural landscapes are extraordinary."[6] On a more practical note, the Bahamas held an important place in understanding the tendencies of American tourists, as 80 percent of its tourists hailed from the United States, and the majority of these tourists came from the states of Florida, New York, Illinois, Pennsylvania, California, and Ohio.[7]

If the CNT had been pressed to name Mexico's greatest future competitor in the Caribbean in 1965, it probably would have named Jamaica. Like the Bahamas, the exponential growth of tourism there in the 1950s and 1960s had been staggering. Special airfares from the United States served as the most important factor for attracting tourists from a logistical standpoint. But the beauty of Jamaican tourism in 1965 grew out of Jamaican authorities' understanding of the need for a barrage of activities to keep tourists focused on leisure in decentralized tourist poles: "Jamaica presents, without a doubt, an endless number of attractions for the visitor, among which we can cite: nine excellent golf courses of the highest quality, two polo fields, a racetrack, four yacht clubs, varied and abundant fishing, . . . excursions and happy night life, full of color, that develops in localized and equipped centers, being in the most part integrated to the stupendous hotels that are complemented by well planned beaches."[8] Added to this, the successful exploitation of duty-free shopping, an activity mentioned for most of the locations visited in the Caribbean, rounded out the never-ending parade of attractions in Jamaica. Ultimately, Mexican officials cited the Jamaican government's indefatigable support of tourism, low airfares, and the availability of a seemingly endless number of activities for visiting tourists as lessons to integrate into the development of tourism in the Mexican Caribbean.[9]

CNT officials also lavished praise on other Caribbean islands, including Puerto Rico, Curaçao, and Barbados, for their ability, despite small populations, to provide strong government support for tourism and excellent air and sea transportation options for potential tourists. In terms of tourism programming, the study dwelled at length on the success of casinos in Puerto Rico (Lázaro Cárdenas had banned casinos in 1935 over concerns that Mexico's identity was being tarnished) as well as the island's associated relationship—largely through transportation logistics—with the Virgin Islands. In Barbados, CNT officials were most impressed by the prevalence of decentralized tourism centers, complete with restaurants and nightclubs.[10] Despite the country's relatively small size, the collective will of Barbadians to support tourism generated high revenues from duty-free shopping. Given the growing national importance of establishing decentralized beach tourism in the Yucatan Peninsula in the 1960s, it is difficult to judge which of these observations played a direct role in the creation of Cancún. Nevertheless, this early report brings together many elements from around the Caribbean that would eventually be integrated into the Banco de México's vision of Cancún.

In addition to its field surveys, the CNT also laid out its vision of a tourism pole in the Mexican Caribbean. It emphasized the depressed economic condition of the region, particularly in the territory of Quintana Roo. Henequen cultivation, fishing, subsistence farming, and logging occupied the time of an isolated population. Despite these discouraging realities, the establishment of tourism in Mérida, Cozumel, and the surrounding archaeological sites offered the distinct possibility that tourism could be established in the Mexican Caribbean. The CNT's vision included the development of a resort city at Playa del Carmen, an hour south of Cancún, as the center for Mexico's Caribbean resort development. With the addition of an airport, a port, and 1,540 hotel rooms, Playa del Carmen could serve as a land-based center for an expansive tourism corridor. According to the CNT, Playa del Carmen would "come to represent, without a doubt, the backbone of the development and not merely a complementary economic activity."[11] CNT planners promoted Playa del Carmen's proximity to American cities, focusing particularly on the proximate distance between New York City and Playa del Carmen versus the distance between New York City and San Juan or Kingston. The CNT predicted that with competitive airfares, 120,000 international tourists would book airplane tickets for Playa del Carmen to enjoy its beaches and the surrounding attractions.[12] In addition, thousands of Mexican tourists who would normally travel abroad could now keep their money in Mexico by vacationing in the Mexican Caribbean.

As the CNT planners learned during their excursion to Miami, a well-built hotel infrastructure could be found nearly anywhere in the Caribbean, but the unique image of the location was of equal importance. Yachting, first-class hotels, and a cruise-ship port with commensurate duty-free shopping opportunities would provide the infrastructure and tourism superstructure necessary for an enjoyable vacation. Additional strategic elements would make the Mexican Caribbean unique. First, the number of attractions should be overwhelming. The CNT argued that ten nightclubs would be necessary in Playa del Carmen, with three of them integrated into hotels. In addition to nightclubs, "a bullfighting arena, a shopping center principally destined for the exhibition and sale of handmade products, a museum, convention center, theater, marina, golf club, restoration and conditioning of archeological monuments and other small investments" would be needed.[13] The *Mexicanización* of cultural activities would bear a strong resemblance to efforts taken on the northern border through the Programa Nacional Fronterizo (PRONAF) (National Border Program).[14] Indeed, the Museo de la Ciudad Juarez, constructed by PRONAF in the early 1960s to teach tourists about Mexican history and culture, served as a prototype for a similar archaeological museum projected for Playa del Carmen. Publicity campaigns for the city would emphasize themes, including "[Mexico's] traditions and legends, its music and folklore, as well as its rich regional cuisine."[15] Finally, the report emphasized the need to encourage visitors to purchase as many Mexican handicrafts as possible, if even to the exclusion of foreign goods sold duty free. "It is believed to be preferable to induce the tourist to acquire goods from among the many varied products made in Mexico," the CNT report observed, "more than anything in the branches of jewelry, silver, and we repeat, the extraordinary handiwork products." In contrast, local selling of duty-free items could simply make Playa del Carmen more dependent on foreign manufacturers.[16]

By 1968, Banco de México researchers had identified Cancún Island as their choice for developing a major beach tourism installation. Nevertheless, alternative plans for beach resort development in Quintana Roo continued to emerge, this time from the results of a private report on tourism development in Mexico. At that time, the consultancy of Booz, Allen y Hamilton de México, S.A. de C.V. undertook a major survey of Mexican tourism in an effort to increase North American participation at key tourism centers around the country. Impulsora de Empresas Turísticas, S.A. de C.V. funded the study, with the full cooperation of the Mexican Department of Tourism and its director, Agustín Salvat. The study identified eight regions most likely to attract American and Canadian tourists in Mexico and then devised strategies, mainly in the fields of transportation, hotels, and cultural attractions, to effectively increase North American tourism.[17]

The study pinpointed the corridor from Mérida to Cozumel as one of the areas most susceptible to growth from North American markets. Until Cancún was created in the mid-1970s, Mérida reigned as the capital of Yucatan Peninsula tourism for most of the twentieth century. The one-time colonial center of the peninsula had become increasingly dependent on tourism as the twentieth century went on. It was the main aerial link to the outside world as well as the only starting point from which to visit Uxmal and Chichén-Itzá in the Yucatan's interior. Booz, Allen, y Thompson sensed a shift in the preferences of tourists in the late twentieth century to beach tourism, and relegated Mérida to a complementary role in the emergence of the "new" Yucatan that Mexico would offer to American and Canadian tourists.

In contrast, the report christened Cozumel as the future center of tourism on or near the peninsula, and in Quintana Roo specifically. Ironically, Cozumel's lack of development and Mérida's decadence made Cozumel more attractive to the analysts as a potential site for the installation of luxury hotels. Despite significant challenges related to the supply of water to the island, which relied almost exclusively on the exploitation of underground sinkholes for fresh water, and shortages of construction materials and workers, Booz, Allen, y Thompson believed that the possibilities for developing beach and cruise-ship tourism could best be served by Cozumel Island. In order to carry out such a plan, they asserted that substantial planning and urban design would be necessary. "An urban development company with experience could be in charge of the construction in order that these developments contribute to the creation of an environment of luxury," the report noted.[18] Golf courses and two hundred new first-class hotel rooms would be helpful, but one thousand hotel rooms would ultimately need to be completed by 1973 to meet the needs of the projected 77,900 expected tourists during the first year. Nightclubs and fishing boats would diversify tourist activities, while new roads would decentralize tourism to other beaches on the island. Cozumel held a double attraction in its ability to attract cruise ships, should the appropriate ports be built for European and American vessels. Sensitive to the power of imagery and experience, the authors equated cruise-ship stops as advertisements for future business in Cozumel and the Yucatan Peninsula. "If the passengers take away a good impression of the island," they noted, "it is possible that many of them [will] return to enjoy a longer period of vacations there."[19]

While Mérida had once been the central focus of Yucatan tourism, the "White City," as it had been named, would eventually become a gateway for Cozumel, given its more advanced infrastructure, including warehouses and airline connections. Nevertheless, Mérida would continue to cater to tourists interested in either the region's colonial heritage or archaeological sites, such as Chichén-Itzá. In order to bring the surrounding features up to the levels expected by international tourists, the report insisted, one hundred new hotel rooms should be built near Chichén-Itzá. Additional suggestions for the Mayan city included "a library which brings together all the knowledge that is available about the Mayan culture." And, perhaps aware of North Americans' preference for the "technologic sublime," the report also urged inclusion of a "light and sound" show there. Finally, the addition of bilingual plaques at major points in Chichén-Itzá and Uxmal was believed to be necessary to improve tourist receptivity to those sites.[20]

The Impulsora de Empresas Turísticas plan also suggested a subordinate role for Playa del Carmen in its designation of Cozumel as the luxury resort center of the Mexican Caribbean. Instead of serving as the main resort town in the region, as suggested by the earlier CNT report, this private plan designated Playa del Carmen as a major agricultural center to supply food to Cozumel. With the addition of adequate irrigation systems and an appropriate port, Playa del Carmen could provide vegetables for the tourist market in Cozumel throughout the year.[21] These ideas, however, emerged too late to have any significant impact on plans within the Banco de México for tourism development in the Mexican Caribbean.

By the late 1960s, and in the aftermath of surveying the Mexican Caribbean for the ideal location for tourism development, the Banco de México, under the close guidance of Secretary of Finance Antonio Ortiz Mena, imposed a new vision of Caribbean tourism development upon the landscapes of Quintana Roo. While much credit has been showered on the Banco de México for its role in the development of Cancún, too little has been attributed to Ortiz Mena, who served as the constant political figure in the transformation of Mexican tourism during the 1960s and early 1970s. In addition to championing PRONAF, Ortiz Mena promoted the creation of the Museo Nacional de Antropologia y Historia in the early 1960s. It is with some sense of poetic justice then, that Ortiz Mena not only initiated conversations regarding a loan for building tourism infrastructure with the Inter-American Development Bank (IADB) in 1968 but also served as the IADB's president in the mid-1970s as Cancún blossomed on the low-land, limestone landscapes of Quintana Roo.[22]

Under Ortiz Mena's direction, the Banco de México created the Fondo de Promoción de Infraestructura Turística (INFRATUR) in 1968 to proceed with plans to develop beach tourism on the Caribbean and Pacific coasts of Mexico. By 1971, INFRATUR set forth a polished version of its vision for Cancún. In its vision of Cancún, INFRATUR emphasized the economic benefits to Mexico of such a project, particularly in the realm of additional employment for the economically depressed peninsula, almost as much as it talked about the process of creating a tourism paradise. The prospect of building a tourist city in Quintana Roo, it believed, would integrate skills already possessed by many of the region's residents into the new project. Agriculture and handicraft production, in addition to hotel employment, would directly contribute to the success of the new tourist city. From 1960 to 1970, the employment structure of Quintana Roo had remained largely static, with over 50 percent of local residents working in agriculture, followed by service sectors. Ultimately, INFRATUR hoped that tourism would become one of the important sectors of employment in the territory, yet not the only viable sector.[23]

A sense of cautious optimism accompanied the selection of Cancún as a location for creating a tourist city. While this type of integrally planned city would be unique in the annals of Mexican tourism, INFRATUR also erred on the side of caution, selecting an area whose "natural resources, beach, sea, and climate are similar and at times superior to the other places of the Caribbean." The primacy of geographic centrality gave INFRATUR planners hope that Cancún would be successful, given its relative proximity (by air) to major cities in the United States and Canada. Its warm and relatively dry climate (by Caribbean standards), averaging 82 degrees Fahrenheit throughout the year and one hundred days per year of appreciable precipitation, endowed the island with arguably one of the most attractive climates in the region. Finally, the first Mexican visions of Cancún were inseparable from the area's wealth of archaeological ruins, which ran the gamut from Chichén-Itzá to Tulum. These seemingly timeless cultural attractions figured into the geographic advantages of the location for Cancún and into the business strategy. "The ruins of Tulum and [Chichén-Itzá] and the abundance of existing vestiges from the Mayan civilization in the region," the INFRATUR report hypothesized, "without being sufficient by themselves to attract a massive volume of tourists, constitute an element that [together] with the other attractions, could help lengthen the average length of [tourists' visits]."[24]

INFRATUR also foresaw a slight shift in tourism on the Yucatan Peninsula as a result of Cancún's construction, but not a drastic transformation, as has been the case. Planners recognized that Mérida was the "actual center of attraction and distribution of the peninsula's tourism streams." In addition, Mérida was the transportation gateway for foreign tourists. By 1970, Mérida boasted fifty thousand foreign tourists each year. To the southeast, Cozumel attracted thirty-five thousand foreign tourists each year, and Isla Mujeres hosted six thousand foreign tourists annually. The peninsula was attractive, then, not only because of Cancún Island's numerous natural benefits but also due to the exponential growth of tourism on the peninsula that preceded its creation. In 1960, only thirteen thousand foreign tourists had visited the peninsula. By 1970, that number rose to around fifty thousand foreign tourists a year. These statistics corroborate that the quick growth of Cancún as a pole for foreign tourists was not a deviation from recent trends in Yucatan tourism. Instead, it was an intensification of growing tourist interest in the post–World War II era.

When one thinks of Cancún today, the physical profile of the island comes to mind. Its built environment distinguishes it from other tourist destinations. Although the INFRATUR plan did not include zoning specifications, the high number of rooms that Cancún's hotels would feature portended a dramatic shift from the size and density of Mexican hotels at the time. According to the INFRATUR report, Cancún would begin operations with 1,000 first-class rooms. In contrast, the Yucatan Peninsula only featured a total of 184 first-class rooms in 1960. The total number of first-class rooms on the peninsula jumped to 431 by 1965 and to 1,085 by 1970. INFRATUR believed that direct flights from major U.S. and Canadian markets would make Cancún a viable tourist center on the Yucatan Peninsula. A clear emphasis on North American tourists would also influence commercial developments on the island.[25]

Finally, the superstructure of Cancún Island—including hotels, airport, golf course, and shopping facilities—also provided insight into the image and vision that INFRATUR wanted to project for Cancún. INFRATUR planners cautiously hoped that Cancún would become integrated as one of several tourist options in the Yucatan Peninsula. As a result, a modest international airport was built, with the capacity to handle DC-9s and 727s. However, INFRATUR left sufficient room to expand the runway into one that could handle "an efficient operation of jumbo jets and similar long-distance [planes]."[26] Hotel plans for the resort town also targeted moderate annual growth. During the first year of operations, 1,000 rooms would be available, with 250 to 500 rooms being added each year. By the tenth year, 4,750 rooms would be operating, and by the twentieth year, 10,000.

If the Banco de México had learned by 1970 that American tourists preferred to fly, rather than drive, to a resort location, they also knew that most North American tourists demanded amenities and attractions—not just sun and sand—on vacation. As a result, the original plan for Cancún included a Robert Trent Jones Sr. eighteen-hole golf course. Perhaps even more important than his ability to design high-quality golf courses was the reputation he had earned. It is not coincidental that Jones is listed in the report as a "designer of international fame whose name is widely known among the aficionados of this sport [who] find special satisfaction playing on golf courses designed by him."[27] Finally, INFRATUR approached its task of capturing tourist dollars with some sophistication. It believed that the most important private investment in the tourist zone would be a shopping center designed specifically for tourists. In this project, one sees the first elements of "destination themeing" in Cancún. As the 1971 report noted: "It is projected to build this commercial section giving some of the more relevant characteristics of Mayan architecture to the [stores]. The architectural motives of this civilization are abundant and it is possible to adapt them to such a degree that they mesh with the practical design of a modern shopping center, converting it into a singular, attractive site that fills its function within a framework that harmonizes with the cultural inheritance [of the Maya]."[28] Needless to say, shopping has become one of the vacation attractions par excellence in Cancún, with many Mexico City residents flying to the peninsula to shop at stores not available in the Mexican capital.

As the IADB moved to the final stages of preparing Mexico's substantial loan for infrastructure development in and around Cancún Island, its planners projected distinctive elements of their visions for Cancún. The IADB also miscalculated the exponential rate of Cancún's future growth. In its projections, the IADB predicted that Cancún could capture, by 1980, between 8 and 15 percent of the annual growth of tourists from the United States who visited the Caribbean; attract between 1 and 2 percent of the total flow of tourists from the United States who visited the Caribbean; receive 50 percent of the annual increase of U.S. tourists to the Yucatan Peninsula; attract 15 percent of the total number of American tourists visiting the Yucatan Peninsula; attract 30 percent of the foreign tourists who would visit the peninsula from countries other than the United States; and attract thousands of Mexicans to the new pole.[29]

The IADB report also addressed the issue of INFRATUR's authority within the bounds of Cancún Island and Cancún City. As part of the integrated city, INFRATUR planned for either the Mexican government or private organizations to build 670 houses for hotel executives and hotel workers on Cancún Island. This permanent presence, as well as the thousands of tourists, would require constant services, maintenance, and support. As a result, INFRATUR would not only develop the city, but it would also maintain it, including maintenance of roads, oversight of the golf course and convention center, operation of electricity and water services and fire stations, insect abatement, garbage collection, and street cleaning.[30] Concern for maintenance of the infrastructure went beyond protecting the investment that Mexico and the IADB had made through their loan. It opened a larger concern of the IADB, namely, the viability of the ecosystem in the face of mass tourism. "The development of touristic centers in Mexico and other parts of the world has meant, in the majority of cases, certain ecological deterioration of the respective zone, because they generally do not take the appropriate measures with enough anticipation to prevent said deterioration," the report noted. As a result, the IADB required INFRATUR to undertake a study of the region in question and formulate recommendations to protect the area's flora and fauna.[31]

Ultimately, the IADB report on Cancún stressed the permanence of this new tourist city. In language that goes beyond concern for return on the initial investment, the IADB dwelled at great length on Cancún's role as both a tourist city and a residential city whose quality of life would be measured not only by the swells of the ocean or the cleanliness of the beach but also by the efficacy of public services offered to those who chose to live there. The IADB report also projected an idealized vision of Cancún as a model for other tourist resorts to follow. As Acapulco declined in beauty and cleanliness during the early 1970s, and as other poorly planned tourist cities in Mexico dealt with transportation and infrastructure problems, the IADB held Cancún up as a potential alternative to traditional beach tourism.

In 1979, five years after Cancún had functioned as a tourist city, the Mexican secretary of housing undertook a comprehensive spatial analysis of Cancún, focusing on the needs of local residents in relationship to the development of tourism. The secretary operated under the assumption that recent tourist developments in Mexico, including Cancún, Ixtapa, and Puerto Vallarta, ran the risk of "an anarchic and unarticulated expansion of urban growth . . . implying high economic and social costs." In effect, this diagnostic assessment of FONATUR's principal tourist centers (Ixtapa and Cancún) hoped to assure that these new towns were developed in the integral fashion originally intended by their creators. While the secretary of housing wanted to provide a diagnostic snapshot of housing, public services, public schools, and commerce in the Cancún area, the report also offered a vision of what Cancún might become by the year 2000. In hindsight, however, the greatest insight from the study involved its identification of Cancún's transformation from a decentralized tourist city to the metropolitan center of an emerging tourism corridor between Cancún and Tulum.

Researchers traveled to Cancún sometime prior to May 1979 to assess conditions for community building in the adjoining areas. One of the most persistent features of the diagnostic study involved the exponential population growth, from 117 individuals in 1970 to 15,000 in 1974, and finally 40,000 in 1979. Cancún, situated in the municipality of Benito Juarez (organized in November 1975), and the surrounding areas drew their population largely from the Yucatan Peninsula (74 percent), Mexico City, Veracruz, and Tabasco. Furthermore, the population of the Cancún area was very young, with 49 percent of the inhabitants between the ages of fourteen and forty, and another 40 percent younger than fourteen years old. Cancún's 1979 population was 57 percent male and 43 percent female. In terms of occupations, 2,357 individuals worked directly in the hotel industry, with 20 percent holding administrative posts and 40 percent working in restaurants and bars, 24 percent in cleaning, and 16 percent in the entertainment sector. In the overall economy, approximately 20 percent worked in the hotel sector, 30 percent in construction, 9 percent in commerce, and 8 percent in public services. Analysis of available housing in the area identified 7,206 homes distributed between Cancún City and the surrounding *colonia*, with an average occupancy rate of 5.6 persons per permanent dwelling. Urban sprawl, the result of continual exponential growth in such a short period of time, had also become a feature of the region. Beyond the *colonia*, there were 1,205 additional living structures in the *ejidos* (Alfredo V. Bonfil, Morelos, Vallarta, Leona Vicario, and Puerto Juarez). According to the researchers, "the conditions of all of these homes are deplorable, with all the deficiencies . . . characteristic of peasant housing, that is to say, regional building materials, dirt floors, walls of mud . . . , except in the case of those located in the Ejido Alfredo V. Bonfil, whose walls are [made of] cement block." Based on 1979 numbers, the report predicted that population growth due to immigration would continue at an accelerated pace until 1982 (at a rate of 16 percent annually), but then slow to a more "rational and stable" rate thereafter. In fact, the report predicted that population growth by natural childbirth in the region would surpass population growth from immigration after 1979. According to this model, Cancún would become a metropolitan area by 2000, with 150,000 inhabitants. The disparity between this number and the actual metropolitan population in excess of 600,000 people in 2007 assumed that the pace of tourism growth in the region, as well as in the surrounding communities, would also slow.

The recommendations made by the secretary of housing were based on very different motivations for regional development from those of FONA-TUR, whose task was to promote tourism on Cancún Island and provide all of the requisite services needed for such development to function. The tremendous growth of the tourist center, however, began to manifest its impact well away from the center. In terms of future tourism development, the secretary's report recommended that tourism be developed where the concentration of new inhabitants chose to live. The report theorized: "The establishment of tourist corridors and circuits in those regions of the country that permit them, provide[s] a more rational use of resources, more than anything, if they promote the establishment of such activities in the areas with high growth or demographic concentrations, now that these represent a great potential for touristic services." While this would take place—to a certain degree—with the decentralization of new resorts to the south of Cancún, the analysis missed the very point as to why people came to Cancún: to stay at a hotel on the island and take in the cerulean views against a growing urban backdrop of large hotels and associated attractions.

In an effort to alleviate potential growth problems in Cancún and the surrounding area, the secretary also called for the decentralization of community services away from Cancún. Playa del Carmen should become the new industrial center of the Cancún-Tulum corridor, with the creation of a regional wholesale warehouse, a large-scale meatpacking facility, and other industrial functions, such as fish and fruit dehydration centers there. Between Playa del Carmen and Cancún, the secretary's study recommended that "Puerto Morelos be destined to fulfill the intellectual and cultural functions [of the region], as well as hygienic and therapeutic functions by way of the establishment of junior high and high schools . . . libraries, movie houses, theaters, and a social center; as well as through the establishment of a specialty hospital." Farther south, Xel-ha would become the national park of choice for ecotourism, with land and sea excursions facilitated by walkways throughout the park. A botanical garden, a zoo, and an aquarium featuring "the different existing species of the region that apart from serving as recreation, function as regenerative elements of the local flora and fauna" would highlight the facility. Furthermore, a prohibition on intrusive buildings and campsites would also enhance the attractiveness of the national park.

Finally, the report took the creators of Cancún to task for not providing enough attractions and low-cost tourism alternatives for Mexican citizens who either lived in the area or desired to visit Cancún. "A preferential focus to satisfy visitors with a high income level, largely concentrated in international tourism, [and] neglecting national tourists that do not have the same economic resources," the report observed, "offers an interesting perspective as much in the magnitude of population that [nationals] represent as for the minimal investment in infrastructure and services that would be required to satisfy the elemental conditions of comfort [for them]." In its concluding recommendations, the report suggested that someone build budget-minded hotels and campgrounds. In addition, the report recommended that FONATUR limit the construction of luxury hotels, examine how credits for hotel construction had been used, and review hotel construction within the context of Article 27 of the Mexican constitution, which prohibited foreign ownership of land within about thirty miles of Mexican beaches.

The secretary's recommendations ultimately revealed the challenges of multiple government agencies working together in the administration of a tourist city. While many of the recommendations in relation to school construction, housing for workers, and infrastructure needs followed a largely technical analysis, the attacks on FONATUR's development of tourism at Cancún presented a new vision of Cancún that departed from its original purpose as a center for attracting international tourists to spend lots of money for the benefit of Mexico's balance of payments. In contrast, the report viewed Cancún as a national good that Mexicans of any income level (at least those living in the region), as well as wealthy foreigners, would enjoy. FONATUR did develop campsites and at least one resort for Mexican youth. Ultimately, the report is valuable in that it pinpointed the transformation of Cancún from a decentralized tourist city into the center of a regional economy that would be serviced to an extent no one had imagined by the surrounding hinterlands.[32]

In 1982, FONATUR issued its own retrospective on Cancún's first seven years of operation, examining the original justifications for the project from meteorological, economic, and developmental perspectives. One unique element of the meteorological justification that did not accompany the IADB report or the INFRATUR report (1971) involved the incidence of hurricanes on Cancún Island. After six years in operation, the island had avoided several cyclonic patterns, including Caroline (1975), Eloise (1975), Frida (1977), Greta (1978), Henri (1979), and Allen (1979). Against the broader backdrop of meteorological history, nearly two hundred tropical storms and hurricanes had passed within proximity of Cancún Island, with only two of these posing any danger to Cancún. While the law of averages suggested that Cancún would be susceptible to three or four tropical storms on an annual basis, planners hoped that trends since September 1961 would continue. Since that time, the book noted, "a storm susceptible of damaging Cancún" had not materialized.[33]

It is fitting, in hindsight, that FONATUR issued a published account of Cancún's creation and early development. In 1982, Mexico had reached a crossroads. Spiraling interest rates and falling demand for oil doomed Mexico to devaluations and economic tourniquets for most of the decade. In contrast, Cancún was just beginning to consolidate its place as one of the premiere tourist destinations in the Caribbean. Ironically, after Cancún had been operating for only six years, FONATUR chose to compare Cancún's statistical base to the tourism statistics of other countries, and not individual tourist poles, in charting past and future growth. The 32 percent growth rate, for example, "permitted Cancún to place itself in 1981, in third place among principal destinations in the Caribbean," the report noted, "only below Puerto Rico and the Virgin Islands."[34] This success and momentum provided the impetus for new visions of growth in Cancún.

It is taken for granted today that the United States has disproportionately influenced Cancún. Until 1983, however, Mexicans regularly visited Cancún in larger numbers than North Americans. Most of these Mexican tourists traveled to Quintana Roo by airplane, as did their foreign counterparts. In Cancún's opening year (1975), for example, 72,200 Mexicans visited Cancún as compared to 27,300 foreigners. By the end of 1981, the two tourist streams were practically even, with 264,000 Mexicans and 276,700 foreigners vacationing in Cancún. In terms of places of residence, early Cancún attracted Mexicans from Mexico City (45 percent), Nuevo Leon (14 percent), Oaxaca, Veracruz, and Tamaulipas (each with 5 percent). The preponderance of North Americans came from the states of Texas (17 percent), Pennsylvania (7 percent), New York (7 percent), Florida (6 percent), and California (6 percent). FONATUR surveys also found that a higher percentage of Mexicans with professional and postgraduate education (26 percent) visited Cancún than did their foreign counterparts (14 percent). In contrast, a higher number of foreign business executives (28 percent) visited Cancún than did their Mexican counterparts (13 percent), while a higher number of Mexican business owners (31 percent) visited the island than did foreign business owners (16 percent). However, relative buying power manifested itself in the dramatically low levels of Mexican tourists who chose to stay in Cancún hotels for more than six days (none). In contrast, 19 percent of foreign visitors choose to stay from seven to twelve days in the region.[35]

By the early 1980s, Cancún's hotel superstructure began to fill the dramatic, multistory profile one associates with the tourism capital of the Mexican Caribbean. Cancún provided its more than half a million visitors in 1981 with 5,225 hotel rooms, up from 1,322 in 1975, its first year in operation.[36] With the vast majority of these rooms associated with first- and second-class hotels, Cancún entered a critical period, as the national economy began to rely more heavily on tourism for aggregate growth. With stated goals of protecting the environment, wisely using natural resources, and highlighting "design of tourist spaces that combines beauty, and functionality," FONATUR looked toward Cancún's future growth.[37] The next fifteen years would see an explosion in hotel construction, with contractors working almost nonstop to keep up with the needs for growth and economic development. As a result, the physiognomy of Cancún adjusted to the ever-pressing needs of development. Zoning laws also reflected the needs of development and maximization of revenue per acre. Lots in the hotel zone on the island ranged between approximately ten thousand square yards in size to twenty thousand square yards. Low-density hotels could only rise 45 feet or three floors. Medium-density hotels varied from five to seven stories, with a maximum height of 90 feet. Medium high-density hotels could be as tall as fifteen floors or 165 feet. Finally, anticipating construction of hotels like the Riu Cancún, high-density hotels could rise as high as 210 feet or twenty floors. In contrast, the maximum height for condominiums in the residential zone was limited to five floors or 54 feet.[38] The preference for scale also played a significant role in the density of construction on Punta Cancún, the physical focal point of the island, and the two arms of the island heading south to Punta Nizuc and east to Cancún City. Punta Cancún housed the preponderance of early luxury hotels built on the island, as well as shopping centers and a convention center, in order to create, "from the point of view of the urban image, a great landmark of identification and urban orientation."[39] These zoning ordinances, creative visions, and growing pressures for large-scale hotel development in the face of falling peso values helped to lay the foundation for Cancún's aesthetic template during the next fifteen years.

Despite the ensuing economic calamities, FONATUR could say by 1982 that its first stage of Cancún Island development had been a tremendous

economic success. From the tip of Laguna de Bojórquez north to Punta Cancún, and then east along Kulkulkan Boulevard to Cancún City, FONATUR
had created an imaginative tourism infrastructure and superstructure. In addition to expansive hotels, including Ricardo Legoretta's signature Cancún
hotel, El Camino Real, perched on the tip of Punta Cancún; a Robert Trent
Jones Sr. golf course; multiple shopping areas; and marine transportation
systems, FONATUR pushed the second stage of development forward in the
early 1980s. The second stage would begin below the Laguna de Bojórquez
and extend south to Punta Nizuc. Planners envisioned over fifteen thousand
hotel rooms on this thin ribbon of sand and coral, as well as spaces for recreation, archaeological preservation, and another shopping center. With the
completion of the second stage, Cancún Island would house approximately
twenty-two thousand hotel rooms. Hotels nearest to Punta Cancún would
have the highest density, while those closest to Punta Nizuc would dimin-
ish in room density to match the narrowing of the peninsula at that point.
If completed according to schedule, FONATUR calculated that the more
than twenty-one thousand hotel rooms would accommodate the 2.2 million
tourists who were projected to visit the island in 2000. The transformation
of Nichupté Laguna would also offer greater recreational opportunities for
tourists and additional sites for hotel construction. Finally, a bold new shopping and cultural center, Centro Comercial El Rey, underscored the creative
optimism of FONATUR's second stage of development in Cancún. Designed
around the El Rey archaeological site, the shopping center would combine
theaters, restaurants, a cycling path, a handicraft bazaar, an archaeological
museum, a children's play area, a supermarket, dressing rooms, and easy
beach access along the Caribbean side of the complex. Nevertheless, the
shopping center was never built, nor was a proposed hotel that would have
been "the best hotel in Latin America." Finally, the continued dream of integrating a marina and cruise-ship port topped FONATUR's list of priorities.
Similarly, although FONATUR wanted to compete with San Juan and Miami
for yachting tourists, lack of capital left Puerto Cancún to languish on planners' boards until the late twentieth century.[40]

The most pivotal year in relation to the potential alteration of Cancún's
image by FONATUR planners may have been 1986. At that point, several
significant developments came together, consolidating Cancún as one of
the most important mass tourism poles in the Caribbean, but also raising
questions about its future. To a large degree, Cancún's future appeared to
be inextricably tied to the devaluations of the 1980s that forced hoteliers
to compensate for the decline in room rates by offering tourists even more
rooms, effectively driving down the economic profile of the average Cancún

tourist. A second, less adverse effect of the devaluations involved the efforts by the Mexican government to court American and European (particularly Spanish) hoteliers to build hotels in the region through the availability of loans and incentives. This set into motion the productive diversification of Cancún's hotel superstructure, which by the early twenty-first century boasted as many European-operated hotels as North American– or Mexican-operated hotels. The question lingered at the outset of 1987, however, whether Cancún would continue to bank on mass tourism or diversify its offerings to attract wealthier tourists.

A 1987 FONATUR study of Cancún provided an excellent picture of Cancún's tourism population to that point. By the early 1980s, the number of international visitors finally outstripped national visitors. For example, 307,400 Mexicans visited Cancún in 1982, while 336,400 international tourists enjoyed vacations there. The following year the number of nationals visiting Cancún dropped to 244,500, and the number of foreigners visiting skyrocketed to 510,200. With all expenses considered, the inflexibility of airline rates in Mexico, in the wake of Mexico's currency devaluations, limited the number of Mexicans willing to fly on their vacations, most opting instead for vacations to auto-accessible Acapulco or Puerto Vallarta. By 1986, 641,900 foreign tourists flocked to Cancún while the number of national tourists languished at 227,400 visitors. Of the foreign visitors, more than 80 percent in 1986 hailed from the United States, with Houston, San Antonio, Los Angeles, and Chicago providing the most receptive markets for travel to the Mexican Caribbean. The declining cost of tour packages also made Toronto a receptive market to trips to Cancún and Ixtapa in contrast to the cost of similar packages in other parts of the Caribbean. To complement the rise in international tourists, Cancún's hotel plant contained 6,775 hotel rooms by early 1987, mostly in the first phase of the project along Playa de Mujeres to Punta Cancún. Just over 5,000 more rooms were on the drawing board, and land had been sold for almost 9,000 more hotel rooms. In addition, 7,096 hotel rooms were under construction. As the report bluntly noted, "The evolution of room prices per night in luxury hotels in Mexico has been held back during the past three years, having favored the foreign guest [through] the constant devaluation of the peso and the consequent strengthening of the purchasing power of the dollar." As a result, FONATUR statistics illustrated that a night in Cancún hotels was "20 to 50% more economic than [prevailing rates] in Europe, the United States, or the Caribbean." The question remained as to whether that was the direction Cancún should continue to pursue.[41]

FONATUR decision makers looked to southern Florida as a reference point for what Cancún could become if it chose to chart a future away from mass tourism. For the future of the Mexican Caribbean, Miami represented "a Caribbean center in clear maturity," and a comparison would be undertaken "with the purpose of identifying those deficient areas that will permit Cancún to maintain the historical levels of growth and diversify its segments of receptive [international] tourism."[42] The FONATUR study determined that spatially, Cancún had an approximately 280-acre deficit of tourist attractions (when compared to Miami), a number that would grow to approximately 1,100 acres if no additional tourist attractions were created in and around the Cancún area. FONATUR focused on several categories that correlated with the new direction in which it hoped to steer Cancún's future. First, it noted that occupancy in Miami's fifty-eight thousand hotel rooms hovered around 67 percent. Nevertheless, of that total number of hotel rooms—almost ten times the number of hotel rooms in Cancún—only 11 percent were in "Grand Luxury" hotels, or hotels with more than five hundred rooms charging rates of over $400 a night per room and offering guests access to golf courses. Through the alchemy of statistics, FONATUR determined that Cancún's biggest attraction deficits, based on a spatial analysis, included golf courses, theaters, bowling alleys, convention centers, a zoo, a horse-racing track, an aquarium, and a recreational center.[43]

The 1987 FONATUR study appears to have exercised a significant amount of influence on subsequent decisions made concerning the third stage of Cancún's development. As noted earlier, the first and second stages corresponded primarily to the massive construction of Cancún's hotel skyline along Bahia de Mujeres and sloping down toward Punta Nizuc (where Club Med had been located and operated by FONATUR as a franchise since the mid-1970s). The third stage involved development of hotels south of Punta Nizuc and attractions around the Laguna Nichupé, and the creation of a marina and port for Cancún north of the urban area on the road to Mérida. In terms of developing the remaining space, FONATUR had a limited number of options to pursue. First, the agency could choose to save the area for future development; second, it could dedicate the land to "the touristic segment of Grand Luxury," which had not been developed with great efficacy to that point in Cancún; third, it could develop the third segment according to the most needed attractions (including golf); or fourth, FONATUR could combine "Grand Luxury" hotels with attractions that were lacking.[44]

Any decision to develop the precious remaining acres of land required the ability to build tourism infrastructure and superstructure as well as a clear goal for tourism programming that Cancún would pursue well into the twenty-first century. One of the least imaginative, but perhaps most lucrative, approaches involved convention tourism. FONATUR planners salivated over the nine hundred thousand conventions held annually by organizations in the United States, with sixty million delegates attending. From the Mexican perspective, convention tourism was well suited to Cancún for at least six reasons: the number of Americans who attended conferences outside of their country was five times greater than the same group of Mexicans; each convention delegate to conferences larger than one thousand delegates spent, on average, $660; Cancún already had adequate airport facilities for large conferences; the existing conference facilities in Cancún were underutilized; the cost of convention services would be lower in Cancún than in other Caribbean conference destinations; and sections of the third stage of Cancún's development could be used to create better convention facilities.[45] While convention tourism has been successful in Cancún, it did relatively little to alter the paradigm of Cancún as a mass tourism pole.

In contrast, FONATUR's evaluation of a second alternative has exercised a tremendous impact not only on Cancún's development but also along the entire Riviera Maya, which in many ways is an outgrowth of a new approach to luxury tourism in Quintana Roo. Planners focused on the "elite or super-luxurious" segment of tourists as a potential market. Such tourists, the report observed, looked for "exclusive sites with significantly higher average [hotel] tariffs as well as [hotels offering] nautical facilities, as well as golf, tennis, health centers, etc." Such an approach would tap into a neglected market, particularly in the United States, where 44 percent of the population earned more than $40,000 in 1986. The fact that ten of the major American resorts catering to such tourists in the United States averaged 75 percent occupancy rates also boded well for a similar approach in Quintana Roo. Finally, FONATUR reported that 1.9 million families in the United States corresponded to this elite segment of international tourists.[46]

With this goal in mind, planners proceeded with development plans for super luxury hotels south of Punta Nizuc and the development of a marina, as long as the new developments did not "propitiate the development of more of the same" (a clear reference to the mass tourism models of Cancún's first and second stages). Even in development section 3A, south of Punta Nizuc, the report noted, "[the area] can orient itself towards new tourist attractions or a touristic offer of super luxury, without competing with what already exists, when the second stage of development has been effectively built."[47] As a result, space would be utilized for attractions catering to the elite tourist, while plans for a horse-racing track, zoo, recreational fields, and botanical garden would be tabled.

The most creative of FONATUR's new visions for Cancún involved efforts to construct a marina, which had been an integral element of the master plan since 1971. Based on a French model, Puerto Cancún would ideally attract cruise ships, as well as yachts from around the Caribbean. Under the 1987 plans, Puerto Cancún would occupy approximately six hundred acres, with 14,500 hotel rooms. But Puerto Cancún would be much more than hotels and yacht slips. In an effort to capture a larger percentage of the Caribbean's super elite tourist market, the project would integrate twenty-seven acres for hotels, seventy-nine acres for condominiums, thirty-five acres for villas, and twenty acres for mixed commercial uses. The move toward a residential tourist component in the tourist zone, outside of the residential zone of Cancún City, as well as the focus on yacht tourism, laid the foundation for Cancún's diversification during the twenty-first century. Optimistically, FO-NATUR planned for the construction of Puerto Cancún to begin in 1988 and be completed in three years, with condominiums and hotels operational by 1995. The project would languish on the drawing board until the late 1990s, when American investor Michael Kelly invested several billion dollars in the project.

The move toward a decentralized, upscale orientation for the third stage of Cancún's development was already beginning to take root in the late 1980s south of Cancún, between Puerto Morelos and Tulum. The Riviera Maya catered largely to condominium and villa buyers, as well as to smaller, more intimate hotels. These hotels presented something of an anti-Cancún ap-pearance, focusing on a horizontal rather than vertical orientation. Size also differed, with the typical Riviera Maya hotel between twenty-five to seventy-four acres in size, with much lower price tags ($20 to $70 per square yard) than in Cancún ($120 per square yard).[48] According to FONATUR, hotel chains, including Sheraton and Princess, had announced their intention to build "super-luxurious hotels" in the region, integrating golf courses and ex-clusive real estate, in the form of villas and condominiums, into their resorts. Spanish hoteliers in particular would invest in this region in the 1990s and after the turn of the century, consolidating the region as one with even more hotel rooms than Cancún by 2005 and presenting the state of Quintana Roo, the Mexican government, and FONATUR with new planning challenges. In the 1980s, however, the spillover effect of tourism from Cancún toward Chetumal represented the benefits of tourism development in the region. As the FONATUR report mentioned: "This situation has been well received by the state authorities, because of the positive effect in [distributing money throughout the region], and definitely fits in the schemes of priorities of regional touristic development toward other different zones from Cancún, because it is considered that this does not require great impulses or in the last case its flow continues in the hands of FONATUR with success guaranteed."[49]

While resort growth pushed Cancún out, it also began to demonstrate the urban challenges of growth in Cancún City. It is fitting, perhaps, that life in Cancún City was often understood through the lens of tourism. FONATUR used two streams of data to arrive at Cancún City's future population projections: one involved basing population growth on "the accumulated offering of tourist hotel rooms," and the other on natural birth rates. Based on past and present population growth, FONATUR projected that Cancún's population would grow to nearly three hundred thousand inhabitants by 1994. With such high levels of growth, new wells would need to be drilled in order to maintain the region's water supply. Intense energy demand had not taxed the city's electrical supply, but hotel construction in the second stage, south of Punta Cancún, raised the need for new energy generators that could accommodate construction of approximately five thousand more hotel rooms by 1989.[50] The utility most taxed by continued, exponential urban and touristic growth in Cancún was telephone service, with as many as nine thousand lines lacking service at the end of 1986. Simultaneous urban and touristic building often induced such a crunch. As one diagnostic report noted, "Towards the future it is believed that there will be an increment in the demand because of the construction of new hotel rooms, as well as additional houses [in the urban area], because of which the foreseen expansion for the current year (3,400 lines) does not solve the problem, requiring, therefore, a significant enlargement of 10,000 lines in the short term and another 5000 towards 1995."[51] Finally, Cancún City lacked the necessary recreation space for its inhabitants. Future growth, however, presented even more daunting challenges, with 927 acres needed to meet the recreational needs of the city's growing population by 2000.

In August 1997, FONATUR's Dirección Adjunta de Desarrollo convened to update Cancún's master plan. At that point, Cancún had been a magnet for more than two decades as a premiere "sun and sand" destination in the Caribbean. Nevertheless, national currency devaluations in the 1980s and 1990s made Cancún dependent on the volume of growth in hotel rooms per year. As a result, Cancún hotels targeted, for the most part, budget-minded vacationers from the United States and Canada. The 1997 adjustments to the master plan attempted to enhance the image of Cancún, as well as its attractions and offerings, with an emphasis on catering to upscale tourists.[52] Hearkening back to issues discussed in the 1987 report on Cancún, FONATUR planners observed that if Cancún was to successfully cater to elite travelers, current aspects of Cancún's appearance and capacities would have to be altered. The airport needed to be enlarged, and the areas around the airport deserved better care as they provided "the first impression for visitors." Though largely undeveloped areas, "they lack[ed] the adequate treatment in their areas of contact with the touristic and urban zone, which affects the general image of the development." The study also stressed that while Cancún Island and Cancún City were interdependent economically, their development was "badly balanced and unequal." For example, Cancún City would need to take on the appearance of a city that called itself the "Port of the Caribbean." Unregulated construction and development lacking the appropriate infrastructure and services reinforced this division in the image of Cancún's two halves. Fast levels of growth, sustained over the lifetime of the development, encouraged urban sprawl, leaving the city without a true urban center. Congestion in the city's transportation infrastructure and reliance on one main thoroughfare in the tourist zone (Kulkulkan Boulevard) demanded attention. Additionally, the high concentration of attractions at Punta Cancún, which had been designed, ironically, to attract attention, was ultimately contributing to the tourist zone's congestion and declining image.[53]

In order for Cancún to tap into more exclusive tourist markets, as well as maintain a position of leadership in the Caribbean, FONATUR planners reiterated that Cancún would have to reposition itself and remedy the deficiencies brought on by focusing on mass tourism. "The Cancún of the future," the study noted, "conceptualizes itself as a touristic destination of high quality, positioned and consolidated in the Caribbean market occupying the top position among its touristic destinations and one of the most important on the world level." To achieve and maintain this lofty goal, FONATUR proposed expanding the airport to include a second runway. In addition, golf and yachting enthusiasts would be the target of Puerto Cancún, which would link golfing, yachting, luxury hotels, and shopping on the Bahia de Mujeres. Punta Cancún would also receive a makeover in order to decongest the island's center of attention. Construction of a zoo, a botanical garden, and a theme park, "Mundo Maya," might reinforce the natural attractions of the region in general and "dignify" Tulum Boulevard between the city and the airport. In keeping with the theme of the Yucatan Peninsula's ancient past, renewed efforts to consolidate attractions around the El Rey archaeological site, an area that languished after Centro Comercial El Rey was not built in the mid-1980s, would complete the second stage of Cancún's development.[54] This rehashing of goals set in the late 1980s underscored the decline of funding for sophisticated projects in Cancún in the late 1990s, but also reiterated the vision of a "New Cancún" for the twenty-first century.

Figure 4. Hurricane damage, Puerto Maya, Cozumel, Mexico. Nature as well as human forces shapes the evolution of tourist poles throughout the Caribbean. Hurricane Wilma destroyed much of Cozumel's tourism infrastructure. (Author's photo)

Nature, as well as human ingenuity, played a significant role in shaping visions of Cancún. Cancún Island suffered its first direct hit from a hurricane with the arrival of Gilbert in 1988. Nearly a decade later, in 2005, Hurricane Emily buffeted the Mexican Caribbean from July 16 until the early morning hours of July 18, when it arrived in Cancún. Not twelve hours after Emily left the peninsula, President Vicente Fox met with municipal, state, and federal officials to assess the damage from the storm and make plans for recovery and reconstruction. Fox's experience with previous natural disasters during his presidency helped craft a unique philosophy for dealing with these unfortunate events. In the course of his remarks to those attending the meeting in Cancún in the wake of Hurricane Emily, Fox enunciated this philosophy, which would become contagious in Cancún after the even greater devastation Hurricane Wilma wrought in October 2005. Reflecting on previous experience with hurricanes in Cancún, Fox observed:

> At the same time that all of us together have learned that . . . the people
> have the right to demand that we attend to them with quickness; we
> have also learned that if we [integrate] reconstruction to resolve the

immediate problem, as a reconstruction based on the medium and long term, when we attend to other needs of development, it is very beneficial for us. The economy of the Yucatan [during a previous hurricane] not only addressed the problems of emergency, but also with the injection of resources that were made available it was surprising how that economy recuperated its strength in a short period of time and surpassed the [current] levels of Gross Internal Production, of employment, and of economic growth that they had before the passing of a previous hurricane, and therefore, I would ask the federal agencies that we [view this situation] a little more with this vision, not only to mend, but also to see if we can go deeper to activate the economy and resolve the problems with greater depth.[55]

If Cancún escaped Hurricane Emily with minimal damage, Fox's vision for disaster recovery planted the seeds for a much more daunting task with the arrival of Hurricane Wilma.

After Cancún took a direct hit from Hurricane Wilma on October 22 and 23, 2005, Vicente Fox returned to Cancún on October 27 and 28 to tour the affected areas and coordinate recovery efforts with municipal, state, federal, and private interests. Damage estimates on Cancún Island alone reached $1.5 billion. Approximately 22,750 homes were reported damaged throughout Quintana Roo. With residents and tourists evacuated in an orderly fashion to safe shelters away from the island, Wilma heaved the Caribbean Sea onto the bottom floors of Cancún Island's sturdy hotels. Deadly winds yanked palm trees out of the ground and laid them low across roads. Couches, brushed by sand and palm fronds, lay inverted in the road, hundreds of feet from their original location. Decaying commercial buildings suffered involuntary condemnation as Wilma raged against stucco exteriors and smashed glass against the walls. Electrical lines dangled from the inside of damaged buildings like mangled pendulums whistling in the storm's fury. Punta Cancún suffered extensive flooding and wind damage. Not only were schools closed in Cancún City, but also the exotically painted school bus in front of Coco Bongo was surrounded by rubble, impeding entrance to the nightclub. Most important, Cancún's beach had dissolved like fine crystal sugar into the Caribbean.[56]

President Fox held two meetings at the Hotel Le Meridien in order to receive reports from government entities and petitions from labor groups and hotel owners. Before the initial meeting with hotel owners, Fox reiterated his vision of reconstruction. First, he urged hotels to maintain their normal workforce in order to avert massive unemployment due to the destruction of the beaches and hotels. The sooner the city was functional, the sooner it could continue to generate revenue for local, state, and national development. With that in mind, he set the date of December 15, 2005, for the "relaunching" of Cancún as a tourist destination. To make this feasible, it would not only be necessary to restore Cancún to its previous self but also to improve upon it. Fox noted, in words similar to those embodied in his recovery philosophy enunciated during Emily: "The idea is to protect not only the short term and immediate earnings, but also the idea of protecting the long term, to assure ourselves, to return to offer the product of better quality and higher excellence on a global scale in the field of tourism, to all the clients that you already have, to all the clients and visitors that are already in the [Riviera Maya]."[57]

Fox then listened to the petitions of hotel owners and tour operators in the Riviera Maya and Cancún region. Many were as concerned about the reconstruction of Cancún's image as about its physical recovery. Pablo Azcárraga, vice president of the Mexican hotel group Posadas de México, expressed his concern for the restoration of the beach, but then proceeded to emphasize the almost equally pressing issue of rehabilitating Cancún in the minds of tourists. He requested that Fox serve as the face of Cancún, much as Rudy Giuliani did for New York City in the wake of the attacks on the World Trade Center. While money for physical structures was important, funds for public relations were of equal importance for Azcárraga. Such efforts could contribute to an improved product. "We have very clear cases of other destinations, we can think of Jamaica, that recently had a very strong hurricane problem, that not only pulled itself up from its problem, but truly improved its business," Azcárraga noted. In dramatic fashion, he concluded his remarks by proclaiming: "We hotel owners are convinced that inside of the bad of the hurricane there are also great opportunities. It is a great opportunity to launch anew the Mexican Caribbean as an important global destination. I am convinced that there have been bad practices in the past, that this opportunity presents us, in truly launching the destination again and looking, not only for the quantity of business, but the quality of business."

After Azcárraga's petition, Francisco Ortiz, representative for the Consejo de Promoción Turística, elaborated on his organization's activities to coordinate the new and improved image for Cancún in the wake of the storm. Ironically, with all the discussion regarding the improvement of Cancún's product, Ortiz's plan appeared to launch Cancún as a mass tourism destination. Comparing Cancún to a shopping center or retail establishment, Ortiz announced the "Coming Soon: Cancún" ad campaign. The Consejo would also try and contract MTV to come to Cancún during the week of December 15, 2005, instead of during the first three months of 2006. A boxing match might also take the place of a golf tournament that would have to be canceled because of a hurricane. Finally, a large parade, ending in Cancún's main plaza, would highlight the event. Ironically, these plans seemed to reinforce the image of Cancún that so many hoteliers, FONATUR planners, and marketing experts were trying to erase.[58]

In the wake of Hurricane Wilma, other professionals set forth their visions for Cancún. Marketing specialist David Cobar, for example, made the most dramatic contribution to new visions of Cancún. In the aftermath of Wilma, Cobar commissioned Michael Maurus to provide photographs of the storm's fury, and Pepita Ramos to accompany those images with a story of Cancún's evolution. Cobar, Maurus, and Ramos viewed the storm as a stage in Cancún's evolution as a city and metropolitan area, marked most notably by the cooperation between tourists and locals during the fury of the storm and the dedication of its citizens and workers in cleaning up the city afterward. The collective images of spiderweb-like electrical lines, extensive flooding, defaced buildings, and long lines for food and water could not stop this transformation. As a result, cooperation prevailed, and high regard for public officials, the military, and police forces won out over cynicism.

The second half of Cobar's book deals with the cleaning and reconstruction of Cancún, emphasizing the efforts of the working class in pitching in to do whatever type of work was needed (while still in the employment of hotels and other private sectors). Restored electricity, new streetlights, and improved traffic lights all set the tone for an improved city, according to Cobar. Cobar's vision ends with futuristic images of Puerto Cancún's marina and vertical skyline. He also links the restoration of Cancún's beaches and lagoons to the improvement of Punta Cancún. "Punta Cancún is a meticulous work that will allow extending roads, pedestrian areas, terraces, and parking facilities," he noted. "The restoration of the lagoon will permit the creation of a levee that will surround a turquoise-blue lagoon." The upscale orientation of Punta Cancún—with added walkways, retail offerings, and entertainment choices projected by Cobar—matched FONATUR's push for upscale tourism in its 1997 master plan changes. Similarly, a Formula One racecourse would further diversify Cancún's offerings and target new tourist groups. Finally, an enlarged airport would "turn Cancún into an electronic node of integration to the world-wide network for the Caribbean, [Central] and South America."[59]

In Cobar's estimation, Cancún has moved beyond simply being a city, and has "incorporated a large regional basin, connected with America, Europe and possibly Asia, [which will] grow until becoming one of the most powerful regions of the world, touristically speaking." In line with FONATUR's vision for the region, Cobar also sees the Mexican Caribbean expanding south toward Chetumal and five Central American nations. In terms of marketability, Cobar asserts: "I believe that the success of any brand depends heavily on the consistency of its activity over a long period of time. Cancún was born as a tourism success that today is one of the most globally recognizable brands. Thus it should continue, growing and enriching itself to maintain its attractiveness."[60]

Cancún, like any hotel or resort, according to Mexican hotel doyen Rodolfo Casparius, is a living entity. Even its selection as Mexico's choice for state-developed beach tourism was never a foregone certainty. During the 1960s, competing state tourism agencies and private interests vied to locate new tourism infrastructure in cities along the Riviera Maya, including Playa del Carmen, Cozumel, and eventually Cancún. State and international interests, in the form of the IADB, attempted to regulate the growth and development of the city in a sustainable fashion, taking into account the needs of residents as well as tourists. Internal FONATUR studies addressed the conundrum of developmental success in a shifting global market comprised of international tourists with increasingly sophisticated needs and desires. Finally, the torments of nature offered opportunities to reconfigure the vision of Cancún for another period of time. In early July 2006, Mexico City's *El Universal* newspaper provided a glimpse into some of the possibilities for that future. In the wake of beach restoration and hotel reconstruction, the newspaper detected "a change in the profile of [Cancún's] tourist." "First of all," the article observed, "the Mexican tourist begins to be more numerous. Second, there are segments of the international market that now have greater affluence on these beaches, whose sand, certainly, will never be the same." While North Americans still predominated in Cancún, "Russian and Japanese tourism is more present, and the Chinese, from Hong Kong, begin to be more notable." As a result, hotels such as Fiesta Americana Coral Beach hired two specialists in Japanese tourism, as well as a culinary consultant. Everything was adapted to Japanese tourists, including foods imported from Japan.[61] Ultimately, the constant stream of Mexican employees searching for El Dorado in Cancún, a growing number of Mexican tourists, and the increasingly varied stream of international tourists have come together to create Mexico's first tourism megalopolis, stretching from Cancún to Tulum, initiated specifically for the purpose of tourism. Whatever its challenges and advantages, its dynamic evolution will continue to inspire a myriad of visions concerning its future.

PART 3

The Global Caribbean

8

A Means of Last Resort

In the spring of 1898, as Spanish hopes for retaining Cuba, its final Latin American colony, dimmed with the entry of the United States into the Spanish-Cuban conflict, Ramon Blanco, the leading Spanish authority on the island, desperately appealed to his Cuban adversary, Máximo Gomez. He declared: "We Spaniards and Cubans now find ourselves face to face with a stranger of a distinctive race and of an acquisitive nature, whose intentions are not only to keep Spain from raising its flag on Cuban soil, but also to exterminate the Cuban people, because of its Spanish blood. . . . Therefore, the supreme moment has arrived in that we forget our past differences and that united, Cubans and Spaniards, we reject the invader for our own defense."[1] If Blanco's desperate appeal to the Cuban independence movement appeared absurd at the time, and even less relevant during the following years as American hotels and retail establishments poured onto the island, the economic difficulties of socialist Cuba in the late 1980s and 1990s made such a union a patent reality. Despite the fact that American consumer culture dominated Cuba during the first sixty years of the twentieth century, the United States' subsequent embargo of trade with the island, coupled with Europe's willingness—and Spain's in particular—to capitalize on the American absence in a new global era, clearly tilted the Cuban hotel industry in the direction of Europe, returning the island's elite, in a sense, to the cultural milieu that had prevailed there during the Spanish colonial period. At the same time, Fidel Castro's enthusiasm for European excellence in hotel management illustrates his willingness to reconcile capitalist tactics for the sake of a socialist revolution: in theory, both required discipline and an accountability that were just as much at home in a free market economy as in a command economy.

The European Reconquest

By the mid-1980s, Fidel Castro began looking for new forms of exchangeable currency to supplement the sagging Soviet-subsidized economy. More important, Castro recognized the folly of trying to manage hotels and retail establishments without the proper expertise to be competitive in the global marketplace. Castro touted tourism as the economic future of Cuba, investing in the airport and road infrastructure that would be necessary to make Varadero Beach a world-class destination again. "You have a great resource in this province," he told a local crowd, "and that is the Varadero Peninsula. That peninsula has great unexploited possibilities."[2] Castro predicted that during the next three years, five thousand rooms would be added to the two thousand rooms that existed there in 1988.

The one thing that Castro knew he lacked was the expertise necessary to operate a world-class tourist destination. "The better the service and the more quality rooms," he asserted, "the more we will earn." Castro then proceeded to explain to the audience in Matanzas province the way in which such expertise would be acquired: "Some hotels . . . will be jointly owned with [European] firms with a lot of experience in tourism, which is what we need: experience in tourism. How to run a hotel, how to treat a tourist. If there ever was anything like that here, there is none of it today." Running a hotel also demanded a capable workforce. "You have to train for this," Castro noted, ". . . discipline must be rigorous. Without discipline, there's no [chance] to develop those natural resources. Dealing with foreigners requires good qualifications and training."[3]

Contrary to conventional wisdom, Castro began the turn toward Western Europe and its management-rich corporations prior to the Soviet pullout. This would not have been possible without a reciprocated interest by the European Union (EU). At a time when the United States was turning back the clock on U.S.-Cuban relations (President Carter had started the process of normalizing the relations, only to have those advances reversed by President Reagan), the EU seized on the opportunity to invest in the Cuban economy. Spain positioned itself at the vanguard of this economic revolution. Its shared history and cultural heritage with the island made Spain the natural leader in the Europeanization of the Cuban economy. The fact that the Socialist Party ruled Spain at the time provided ideological connections that further fused the interests of the two countries.

No company better represented the European conquest of Cuba than Sol Meliá, the international hotel empire of Gabriel Escarrer Julia. In 1956, at the age of twenty-one, the ambitious Escarrer began managing hotels in the Balearic Islands, a string of islands in the Mediterranean Sea off the southern coast of Spain, where an increasing number of Northern Europeans, particularly Britons and Scandinavians, elected to pass their vacations. He later turned to the acquisition and management of hotels on the Balearic Islands, the Canary Islands, and the Spanish peninsula. Much like the Spaniards had carved an empire out of existing empires in the fifteenth and sixteenth centuries, Escarrer bought up competing hotel chains and integrated them into his emerging Sol Meliá chain. One of the first major acquisitions involved the purchase of the HOTASA chain, which provided Escarrer with a major network of hotels throughout the Spanish peninsula. In 1987, when he outbid the likes of Hilton for the Meliá chain, he fortified his commitment to the creation of an international chain of hotels. In spite of this multitude of acquisitions, the strength of the Sol Meliá portfolio remained its ability to manage world-class facilities, as well as provide the attendant services for hotel architecture, supply, and marketing.[4]

The true beginning of international expansion for Sol Meliá began in 1985. After locating his first resort in Bali that year, Escarrer focused his attention on the market segment he knew best, vacation resorts, and the two regions best known as European playgrounds for sun and sand: the Caribbean and the Mediterranean. Escarrer's decision to expand in the Mediterranean basin was a natural fit, given the proximity of existing hotel properties. The move into the Americas was more risky, but followed historical precedents going back to the fifteenth century, when Spanish landowners used the Canary Islands as a springboard to the conquest of the Americas. The opening to establish a foothold in the Caribbean basin emerged in the form of Mexico's currency crisis in the 1980s. At that time, the Mexican government appealed to various Spanish and American hoteliers to come to its planned resort communities, particularly Cancún, which had only been in commercial existence for eleven years, and take advantage of the opportunities for investing in a new market.[5]

The Spaniards lay claim to the title of the "kings of Caribbean tourism" as a result of their bold entrance into the market in the mid-1980s. Sol Meliá did not enter the Caribbean alone but went abroad with other Spanish hoteliers, including Barceló (the dominant hotelier in the Dominican Republic) and Oasis (a competitor in Cuba as well as in Mexico). Later, the Iberostar, Riu, Hotetur, Occidental, Tryp, Guitart, and Fiesta chains would join this Spanish conquest. Sol Meliá initially planted four flags in Mexico, opening the Meliá Cancún, a hotel inspired by the pyramids of ancient America; the Meliá Turquesa (also in Cancún); the Meliá los Cabos; and the Meliá Puerta Vallarta. These four hotels gave Sol Meliá a foothold in the major FONA-TUR-planned tourist communities and set the stage for further expansion into Mexico in succeeding decades. The foray into Mexico was followed by an invitation to build a resort community, the Meliá Bávaro, at Punta Cana in the Dominican Republic.

As Sol Meliá laid the foundation for an American empire in Mexico and the Dominican Republic, even greater opportunities presented themselves in Cuba. In the mid-1980s, the Cuban government sent representatives to Spain to promote the island as a tourist destination. Curious, Escarrer saw the potential of Cuba as a tourist destination for Canadians, Latin Americans, and Europeans, and joined forces with one of Spain's wealthiest businessmen, tobacco grower and hotel builder Enrique Martiñon.

For Martiñon, the venture into Cuba was a risk, but one worth taking since he saw a lot of the same tourist potential in Cuba that he had seen in the Canary Islands, his home base. The union between Martiñon, Sol Meliá, and other Spanish investors was known as the Corporación Interinsular Hispana S.A. (CIHSA). After meeting with Castro and Cuban officials regarding the possibility of entering the Cuban resort industry, CIHSA entered into an agreement with Cubanacán, the Cuban agency charged with developing tourism, in 1987. The union between CIHSA and Cubanacán produced Cubacan, a mixed enterprise in which Cubanacán would own 51 percent of any hotel built by the joint group, and CIHSA would own 49 percent. In 1987, this historic consortium agreed to set its sights on building three world-class hotels at Varadero Beach, the old home of Irénée Du Pont's vacation home, Xanadu.[6]

While there were scores of European hotel companies that entered or desired to enter the Cuban market, several factors explain why Sol Meliá was able to shape the Cuban tourist sector in its own image. Escarrer's personality and nonpolitical approach to Cuban tourism placed his group in a position of strength with the Cuban government. Most important, however, was the management approach that Sol Meliá offered the Cuban government and the application of its global model to a particular locality. Perhaps the biggest challenge for a hotel company in entering a market like Cuba involved personnel. Because of the management vacuum created by the Cuban Revolution, it was very difficult to begin from the ground up and create

Figure 5. Varadero, Cuba. In the 1920s, Irénée Du Pont, heir to the Du Pont family fortune, built a vacation home (center) on Varadero peninsula in Cuba. His development of the peninsula's infrastructure made mass tourism there today possible. On the right is the Sol Meliá Las Americas. (Author's photo)

a competent hotel staff that could cater to discriminating customers. Sol Meliá adapted to Cuba by making its human resources vice president, Gabriel Cánaves, head of Sol Meliá's Cuban division. Working together with the Cuban government, Sol Meliá not only trained Cuban professionals for the tourist sector but also worked to transfer knowledge and training to Cuba through interactive teaching programs originating in the Balearic Islands. This commitment to help the Cuban tourist industry grow placed Sol Meliá in a position to become the dominant leader in the Cuban hotel industry and a cornerstone of Cuban tourism since the late 1980s.

Another advantage that helped Sol Meliá dominate the Cuban hotel industry related to cultural integration into the community. After directing the construction of numerous hotels in Cuba and the Caribbean, Enrique Martiñon cast down his roots in Cuba, electing to make Havana his official residence. Furthermore, Martiñon planned for his wedding to a Cuban bride to coincide with the opening of the Meliá Habana hotel in 1998. Around October 1, 1998, Escarrer, Ian Delaney (Canadian partner in several of the CIHSA hotels and president of the Sherritt International), and Fidel Castro looked on as Martiñon married Janet Martínez Morán. Martiñon's wedding was significant not only because it coincided with the opening of CIHSA's fourth hotel on the island but also because it followed a long-standing European pattern of social integration into the foreign society in which one chose to do business. At the end of the wedding, Castro proclaimed, "Meliá, Sherritt, and socialism! . . . a symbol . . . of this era."[7]

CIHSA's pioneering work in Cuba also helped forge political and cultural ties between the Cuban government and the provincial governments in the Balearic Islands and the Canary Islands. These connections further reinforced the position of Sol Meliá and Martiñon in the Cuban tourism market. This was evident in the winter and spring of 2000, when the presidents of the governments of the Canary Islands and the Balearic Islands made official visits to Cuba, including personal visits with Castro and cabinet officials. An overriding theme in the meetings between Francesc Antich Oliver, president of the Balearic Islands, and Carlos Lage, the Cuban vice president, was the link created by tourism between the two regions, which Oliver also stressed in his six-hour meeting with Castro. Antich Oliver also visited the resort of Varadero, site of the highest concentration of Sol Meliá's beach resorts. Vice President Lage further emphasized this connection: "Baleares is a region of Spain with a great deal of tourist development. Wherefore, for a country like ours where tourism is the most important activity . . . the possibility of exchanging experiences, establishing relationships, is really very significant."[8] Sol Meliá's position as the key link in the Balearic-Cuban relationship was evident at the state dinner held in honor of Antich Oliver's visit. Gabriel Cánaves, director of Sol Meliá in Cuba, was one of the guests of state. Later that year, the president of the Canary Islands made a similar state visit to Cuba, meeting with Castro for five hours, and reminding those present at the dinner of lobster, lamb, and wine that Enrique Martiñon was the pioneer who established the first tourist relations between the Spanish islands and Cuba.[9]

With these advantages, CIHSA and Sol Meliá pursued their development of Varadero Beach. The master plan called for construction of three hotels that would appeal to different tourist segments. Designed to reflect the architectural style of Sol Meliá hotels in the Canary Islands, the horizontal orientation of these properties blended into the beach landscape. With over six hundred rooms and villas, the structure of the Sol Palmeras faced onto the beach. It was inaugurated on May 10, 1990. The second hotel, the Meliá Varadero, a four-and-a-half-star property, lay cloaked in the flora of the island's tropical brush. It opened in December 1991. Finally, the Meliá las Américas, a five-star property, sat next to Du Pont's former Xanadu mansion and was later complemented by the refurbished and expanded golf course, which was christened the Varadero Golf Club. The Meliá las Américas opened for service in July 1994. A convention center and a shopping plaza, Plaza Américas, located between the two properties, connected the Meliá las Varadero and the Meliá Américas.[10]

Castro followed the development of Varadero, as well as the Meliá hotels there, with great interest. On September 27, 1988, he visited the peninsula, mentally mapping out the expected thirty thousand hotel rooms he hoped to build there. Reminiscent of his yearly sugar goals, Castro insisted that Cubans could build five thousand hotel rooms by 1991. He reiterated a point he had made earlier in the year related to hotel management: "We've lost the idea of how to treat a tourist during all those years without them. It is a culture we must acquire."[11]

At the inauguration of the Sol Palmeras hotel, Castro also addressed the important lessons in hotel management that Cubans were learning from their partnership with Sol Meliá. While he stressed the high level of culture and education of Cuban hotel workers, he also bluntly conceded, "I should honestly say that we know nothing about hotel administration. Not even the most efficient of our administrators who might be around here knows a thing." Castro confessed that in the 1970s and 1980s, Cuban hotel operators had learned how to run hotels by the multitude of errors made in tending to guests. "They wanted to serve them but did not know how," he noted. "Someone said once . . . a Cuban is the most hospitable man or person in the world, the most pleasant and thoughtful, but once he puts on a waiter's uniform he is terrible."

At the hotel opening, Castro also outlined broader goals of transferring knowledge to young Cuban professionals in order that state-run ventures would improve. "We are going to acquire an enormous amount of experience on how to manage a hotel," he asserted. "This is not an ideological matter, it is a technical matter, it is a scientific matter. . . . We have told [the Spaniards] to manage the hotel for many years until we have cadres who can do the job the way they do, with the experience they have." Recognizing the competitive struggle that Cuba found itself in with reference to the global tourism game, Castro challenged the workers to achieve the type of efficiency that would allow Cuba to rise from the bottom of Caribbean tourism to loftier heights, all on the shoulders of Sol Meliá's experience.[12]

One year later, at the inauguration of the Meliá Varadero, a short walk up the beach from the Sol Palmeras, Castro reiterated the value of the joint partnership, particularly as it enriched Cuban knowledge of planning, designing, building, and operating world-class hotels. "Our country did not have much experience in hotel management," he stated. "We did not have any experience in the field of tourism. The experience we had was very out-dated and underdeveloped. We really did not have much experience in preparing hotel projects. It was a field that was truly new to us."[13]

Castro's speech revealed how he had thrust himself into the project of creating tourism infrastructure with the same precocious zeal with which he had learned every other facet of running a country. Castro boasted that the efficiency of the Sol Palmeras provided a source from which to improve the wholly Cuban-owned hotels in Varadero. After one year, Castro brimmed, "the number of workers [at the Punta Arenas and Paraiso hotels] has been reduced." The Sol Meliá hotels became the standard, and Cuban hotels would be measured against the performance of the joint-venture hotels. "I believe we would not [have] learned as much without the privilege of gaining knowledge from the international experience, from the experience of being part of this Spanish hotel chain." He further lauded the Spaniards for their ability to plan the cost of hotels on a per-room basis and then acquire the products at a better price than he had been able to. Castro's observations also extended to resort planning. One of Cuba's advantages in the development of resort infrastructure was the ability to learn from what had and had not worked in other locations. It is difficult to separate, in hindsight, however, where Castro's emulation of Sol Meliá and his own original ideas for resort planning part ways. Castro advocated a low-density approach to resort planning in beach sectors, citing poor examples of building large hotels right next to the water in Europe. "We have been thinking a great deal about all this," he observed, "and about truly knowing what vacationers want. For example we have learned that people do not want skyscrapers for hotels, because they became a cage."[14]

Ten years later, at a conference on tourism, technology, and nature, Escarrer elaborated on his own theory of resorts, architecture, and the environment. Following the pioneering work of Sol Meliá's one-time architect and pioneer in the development of ecoresorts, Alvaro Sans, Escarrer asserted, "The vertical shoe boxes have no room in the travel industry today. . . . Hotels have to respect the environment." More than likely this parallel vision of Escarrer and Castro regarding hotel design came from the innovative work of Spanish architects who worked hand in hand with Cuban architects. Some of the earliest hotels built at Varadero during the Revolution looked like high-rise Soviet apartment buildings, which still stick up, out of place, against the Varadero sunset.[15]

Sol Meliá was not the only Spanish chain that revolutionized the Cuban hotel industry in the 1990s. The Guitart Hotel Company, another chain primarily based on the Spanish peninsula, also took advantage of the Cuban government's invitation to transfer know-how to the island. Guitart undertook the management of several beach hotels, as well as the island's premiere business and diplomatic hotel, the Habana Libre. Although the Guitart hotels in Cuba would eventually become part of the Sol Meliá family of hotels, Guitart set the standard against which the Cuban government measured its progress in managing urban hotel properties in the early 1990s.

At the same time that Cuban architects and builders, in conjunction with Spanish experts, were working on the Meliá las Américas, the Habana Libre had been passed to Guitart, and Castro was very intrigued to see what types of management improvements would be made as a result of foreign expertise. A November 17, 1993, meeting of the Cuban Communist Party, attended by Castro, city historian Eusébio Leal, and several other party delegates involved with tourism, revealed the profound impact that the Guitart management team had wrought in the few short months Guitart had been in control of the Habana Libre. The main concern of those attending the meeting was the renewal of tourism to Havana, which had once been the crown jewel of Cuba's tourist offering. Castro applauded the discipline with which the Guitart team had enacted its reforms, noting the benefits of foreign, instead of Cuban, management. "When two Cubans get together," Castro noted hypothetically, "one says: this is my cousin; he has to put up with and tolerate everything I do; he cannot demand anything from me." In contrast, Castro stated, "they listen to everything the Spaniard tells them." "The psychological make-up of the Cuban people is quite a sight," he mused. "They listen to a Spaniard; but when a Cuban speaks, they do not listen."[16]

Party delegates later answered Castro's questions about the Habana Libre. The number of employees at the hotel had dropped from 999 to 577 since June 1. The following dialogue ensued:

CASTRO: Why were there so many workers?
FIRST DELEGATE: Commander, in 1989 there were 1,200 workers.
CASTRO: There were more. There were 1,200. Go ahead. Now you have fewer than half.
FIRST DELEGATE: It was because of their inefficiency.
CASTRO: What were all those people doing there?
FIRST DELEGATE: I guess they wandered around, because today we do the job with 577 and we get the job done right. . . .
CASTRO: How many people who should not have been eating there were eating at the hotel?
FIRST DELEGATE: Seven hundred twenty workers.
CASTRO: How many?

FIRST DELEGATE: Seven hundred twenty.

CASTRO: Who were not workers at the hotel?

FIRST DELEGATE: They were not workers of the hotel.

CASTRO: But they ate at the hotel.

FIRST DELEGATE: Yes, they ate at the hotel.

CASTRO: Do you think a tourism industry can prosper that way? I ask you, comrades, tell me the truth: Do you think a hotel where approximately 700 people with nothing to do with the hotel are eating can be a hotel for tourism? In what country of the world? Until when did that go on?

FIRST DELEGATE: This went on until June.

CASTRO: June, this year?

FIRST DELEGATE: Until 1 June, when the Spaniards took over.[17]

The meeting also brought to light other transformations at the Habana Libre as a result of Spanish management. Under Cuban management, the Habana Libre suffered 10 to 11 percent absenteeism among employees, but the percentage had been cut to 2 percent under Guitart management. Regularization of workers' hours also took place in the wake of the transfer of management. In addition, the workforce became younger, in step with the higher demands placed on tourism workers.

The Cuban experience with Spanish management at the Habana Libre paved the way for more efficient national management of tourist properties and hotels. Even Castro was forced to recognize his indebtedness to the Spaniards:

CASTRO: Was the experience of the Spaniards who joined the hotel not worth anything?

THIRD DELEGATE: We have done this thanks to that, because alone, as a Cuban, I would not have been able to do any of this. This is what makes the difference.

CASTRO: Then we had to import Galicians?

THIRD DELEGATE: Yes, at least initially.

CASTRO: Right, but you think that one day we can do this by ourselves?

THIRD DELEGATE: I am fully convinced of this but I also have to be given the powers that were given to him.[18]

The delegates at the meeting revealed that the joint-venture partners, like Guitart, had achieved higher levels of efficiency and occupancy as a result of their ability to work around, rather than through, the politicized Cuban economic structure. Whereas the Guitart chain had the ability to order food and set its own menu and prices in the hotel, Cuban hotel managers were required to carry certain foods requested and priced by party officials. "My hands were tied," one Cuban hotel official complained. "In his case," referring to the joint-venture partners, "this does not happen. He estimates the cost and he sells at a profit and no one gets in his face or sets fines or takes him to court." A party delegate at the seminal November meeting asserted, "Commander, I also believe that the Habana Libre experience . . . has helped to energize the rest of the hotels." From marketing, to human resources, to client attention, Guitart set the mark for Cuban tourist departments to follow.[19]

The Helms-Burton Act

From the fall of the Berlin Wall in 1989 until completion of Escarrer's and Martiñon's three resorts at Varadero in 1994, the United States had taken several measures to capitalize on the implosion of Soviet support for Cuba and the resultant economic uncertainty on the island. The fall of the Soviet Union sent a rush of optimism through the U.S. State Department. An internal memo dated January 24, 1990, outlined the increasing economic strains that a collapsed Communist bloc in Eastern Europe portended for the Caribbean island. "As a result of lost markets," the memo predicted, "Cuba's balance of trade will further deteriorate, shortages of food and other consumer goods will become more acute, and hard currency reserves will be further depleted." The ousting of Manuel Noriega in Panama provided even more evidence that the end was in sight for Castro's regime. Panama had been the main offshore acquisition point of first-world consumer goods and capital for Cuba during the embargo.[20]

In 1992, Democratic senator Robert Torricelli of New Jersey, in conjunction with the chairman of the Cuban American National Foundation, Jorge Mas Canosa, masterminded a further tightening of the 1961 trade embargo against Cuba. Until 1991, hundreds of subsidiaries of American countries had legally been trading with Cuba. They simply had to ask for permission from the State Department on an annual basis. In the lead-up to the 1992 election in the United States, the Torricelli bill proposed a ban on U.S. subsidiaries trading with Cuba, regardless of where they were based. Mexico, Argentina, and the European Community expressed their opposition to the law. Canada and Britain did heed the legislation once President George H. W. Bush had signed it into law. Many experts claimed that its purpose was simply to help either the Republican or Democratic presidential candidate carry the Cuban-exile-rich state of Florida, with its twenty-five electoral votes. A lawyer representing Cuba in the United States, Michael Krinsky, put it this way: "Those votes in Dade County, Florida, mean more to George Bush right now that the whole of the [European Community] and Canada put together." Jorge Mas Canosa placed the bill's significance within the context of wresting control of Cuban consumer culture from the Europeans at the end of the Castro regime: "[When Castro falls] a market of 11 million consumers will open up overnight; a market that will need everything from toilet paper to the most sophisticated computer. And most of that will come from Florida."[21]

Anti-Castro groups also applied extralegal pressure. Sol Meliá and Guitart hotels, as well as other European-managed hotels, became targets of vigilante terrorism aimed at scaring tourists and companies away from Cuba. According to a Cuban report submitted to the United Nations Security Council, attacks on hotels began almost as soon as Europeans were allowed to operate in Cuba. On October 7, 1992, four Miami-based terrorists launched an armed attack on the Meliá Varadero from a boat off of the peninsula. The following January, the report alleged, the leader of the group Commandos L announced that more hotel attacks were imminent and that "from now on, we are [at] war." Cuban diplomats further charged that in November 1993, a spokesperson for the Miami group Alpha 66 allegedly warned tourists to stay away from Cuba. "Those who stay in Cuban hotels," he allegedly warned, "are considered as enemies." The following March, the Spanish-managed Guitart Cayo Coco Hotel was peppered with gunfire. The same hotel was attacked again on October 6, 1994. Several months later, in May 1995, another terrorist attack targeted the same property. The attacks subsided for about two years, but then gripped Havana and Varadero anew when a string of explosions rocked the Caribbean capital in the spring and summer of 1997. On April 12, 1997, a bomb exploded in the Meliá Cohiba hotel. Later that month, another explosive device was found at the hotel. In July, bombs exploded at the Cuban-run Capri Hotel and the Hotel Nacional in Vedado (Havana). On August 4, 1997, another bomb exploded in the Meliá Cohiba. Finally, a bomb exploded at the first of the three hotels built by CIHSA in Varadero, the Sol Palmeras, in August 1997.[22]

If terrorism and threats to American subsidiaries trading with Cuba were not enough to asphyxiate the Cuban economy, the ascension of Republican Jesse Helms of Virginia to the chairmanship of the U.S. Senate Foreign Relations Committee set the stage for the most daring attempt to thwart the European conquest of the Cuban economy. Several factors contributed to the drafting of the infamous Cuban Liberty and Solidarity Act—or the Helms-

Burton Act (1996). Ironically, for a bill with such far-reaching international implications, its motivations were primarily domestic. Domestically, some considered this a veiled message from Republicans to President Bill Clinton that he needed to get tougher on Cuba. Second, the Helms-Burton bill, approved by a majority Republican House and Senate, reinforced the political importance of Florida in national politics. The Helms-Burton Act would punish the executives of companies that trafficked in alienated property from former owners in Cuba with revocation of their visas (Title IV), as well as open up the possibility of being sued in American courts for using those properties (Title III). As a side effect, the new law would also create uncertainty for Cuba's trade partners, a condition that might ultimately benefit American corporations.[23] The bill did not, however, take into account the overwhelmingly negative international reception to a law that suggested the U.S. Congress could directly punish foreign businesses for activities in a third country. Furthermore, the law would be applied retroactively (for business decisions made in the past) and for the benefit of many who were not American citizens at the time their property was confiscated.[24]

In theory, the Senate committee operated from a secretive, inquisitorial list of names of companies suspected of occupying land or using resources nationalized from American or Cuban American exiles by the Castro regime. The Cuban American National Foundation allegedly drew up the list from the primary investors of each country in Cuba. The Senate Committee on Foreign Relations would then draw up its own list from which investigations would be made. In practice, the companies that were publicly targeted were those that had been identified by Cuban-exile families or their lawyers (many of whom advertised their services specifically for the Helms-Burton Act). Lawyers then pressed the Foreign Relations Committee to act on their behalf.[25]

On May 22, 1996, Madrid's *El País* newspaper reported that Sol Meliá would be included on a list of companies to be investigated for their operations in Cuba. The Sol Meliá case focused on the location of the Meliá las Américas, which was adjacent to the Du Pont mansion. In response, the Du Pont family diplomatically observed that "the global economy is dependent on reliable rules of trade and those rules would be jeopardized by the friction that would result [if the law took effect]."[26] If Sol Meliá were found to be in violation of the law, its executives, including those who worked at subsidiary offices in the United States, would be denied visas for travel to, from, and within the United States. The article also noted, "In diplomatic circles it is believed that Washington is choosing to punish those emblematic businesses from the principal investors in Cuba with the clear purpose of dissuading them from continuing investment there."[27] In response, Sol Meliá announced that it would rather pull out of its two resort hotels in Florida—one a collection of 150 villas in Orlando near Walt Disney World, and the other, a 271-room hotel on Miami Beach—than risk losing its more lucrative business ventures in Cuba. At the same time, Sol Meliá pressed ahead, announcing new investments and operations in Cuba, including a new hotel in Havana (the present-day Meliá Habana); the Sol Club las Sirenas (Varadero); and a cruise ship, the *Meliá Don Juan*, on the southern coast of Cuba.[28] A *Miami Herald* report on October 8, 1996, announced that the U.S. government would not continue to pursue a case against Sol Meliá for the time being.[29]

With strong support from the Spanish government and the EU, Sol Meliá avoided the dreaded "letter" from the State Department apprising it of sanctions under the Helms-Burton Act. In 1997, the Spanish legislature reiterated its disapproval of the Helms-Burton legislation and its support for Spanish businesses in Cuba. Spain's approach to Cuban investment reflected European policies toward Cuba in the 1990s: while European nations disapproved of human rights violations and the undemocratic nature of the Castro regime, they believed that dialogue was more valuable than an embargo. Furthermore, Spain's business presence in Cuba was becoming too formidable to terminate. Having responded to Cuba's calls for help in the late 1980s, Spanish investments in Cuba had reached fifty-four million pesetas in 1996. Ironically, Cuba's inability to pay back debts to lender nations made the presence of their corporations on the island even more vital. However, the Spanish legislature noted in a report, "In general, the investments are bottomed out now that the general climate generated by the said Helms-Burton Law is discouraging Spanish investments as well as investments from other countries." The report concluded by calling for a defense of Spanish interests on the island.[30]

Undeterred, Sol Meliá pressed on in its efforts to become the leader in Cuban tourism. The furor over the Helms-Burton Act seemed to be in abeyance, particularly after U.S. secretary of state Madeline Albright agreed with leaders from the EU on May 18, 1998, to work with the U.S. Congress toward a suspension of Title IV in exchange for a commitment by the EU not to take the matter to the World Trade Organization.[31] The same month, Sol Meliá officially captured the title of leader in Cuban tourism. By that time, it managed eight hotels on the island and committed to build and manage more resorts in connection with the Canadian mining interest Sherritt International. It had also opened the new Meliá Habana in the Miramar district across the street from the new Monte Barreto complex, a business center comparable in function to the World Trade Center. Attended by Castro, the inauguration of the Meliá Habana further cemented the strong relationship between Martiñon, Sol Meliá, and Castro.

In 1999, the Spanish government staged the ultimate protest of the Helms-Burton Act by publicizing President Aznar's stay at the Meliá Habana during the Inter-American Summit. At the summit, Castro singled out Sol Meliá for its importance to the Cuban economy. The pressures of the U.S. Congress amounted to an "assault against the most important foreign company of tourism with which Cuba has relations."[32]

In the wake of this revelry, however, Senator Helms renewed the fight to catch Sol Meliá in violation of the Helms-Burton Act, based on its operation of a new resort in Holguín, Cuba.[33] Sol Meliá was not alone. Given the fact that tourism had passed sugar production in the early 1990s as the chief generator of foreign exchange in Cuba, tourism-related businesses found themselves the targets of investigation. The German hotel company LTU and the French-based Club Med also received letters of inquiry from the State Department related to their operations in Cuba.[34] On July 30, 1999, the State Department served Sol Meliá with a letter of inquiry regarding its operations of the Sol Rio de Oro Hotel on Santa Lucia beach in Holguín province. The hotel sat on land once owned by the Rafael Lucas Sánchez family, where they had operated the Central Santa Lucía sugar plantation.[35] Lawyers for the family leaked rumors to the press later that fall that sanctions would soon be imposed on the hotel chain, although nothing ever came of the matter. In an awkward move, the State Department, which was never as interested as the Foreign Relations Committee and Jesse Helms were in applying the Helms-Burton Act, encouraged the two parties to agree to a settlement. Sol Meliá, citing a ban on such compensation by the EU, rejected the proposal and continued to operate hotels in Cuba. In fact, the turmoil only strengthened Sol Meliá's resolve to expand its operations in Cuba. To add to the irony, Escarrer was invited to the Palace Hotel in New York City to accept the award of Hotel Man of the Year from the International Association of Hotels and Restaurants in November. The subject of praise, he insightfully noted, "The American hotel operators are dying of envy because they cannot enter the Cuban market."[36] In December 1999, Escarrer, undeterred by the Helms-Burton Act, emphasized the next phase of hotel management in Cuba, which included joint-venture projects at Cayo Coco and Cayo Guillermo.[37]

During the 1999 crisis, Sol Meliá received its strongest support from provincial, national, and international bodies (the EU).[38] The most persuasive arguments against the Helms-Burton Act emerged during discussions in the Spanish Congress of Deputies following Sol Meliá's receipt of the State Department letter of inquiry. At a September 29, 1999, meeting, Minister of Foreign Relations Juan Matutes apprised the deputies of the contents of the letter. He assured the delegates that the letter was simply a request for information about the Sol Meliá hotel in Holguín, Cuba. However, Matutes also blasted the letter for its ambiguous implications of possible punishment and condemned the law for its extraterritorial and retroactive nature. He faulted the United States for not living up to the pledge that Albright had given in February 1998 to push Congress to deactivate Articles III and IV of the Helms-Burton Act. Matutes argued that the Spanish government had a responsibility to defend Sol Meliá, given the fact that the fate of other Spanish companies in Cuba hung in the balance with that of Sol Meliá.[39]

The controversial nature of the Helms-Burton Act broke down traditional party divisions in the Spanish legislature. Legislator Rodríguez Sánchez objected to the fact that the letter had been sent directly from the State Department to Sol Meliá and not through corresponding channels of the Spanish government. "It is [arrogant] that a Department of State would direct itself unilaterally to a private business from another country," he noted. "In the field of international relations, I believe that this would be worthy of study. Apart from being a political intimidation, it is a sword of Damocles that is always [hanging] above us." Sánchez also welcomed news that Club Med and LTU had received letters from the State Department. This would only strengthen support from members of the EU against complying with the law. Robles Fraga, from the Grupo Popular, gave the most stinging rebuke. Perhaps recalling the painful experience of Spaniards following the Spanish-American War in 1898, Fraga observed:

> Our businesses in Spain, assuming risks and naturally looking for the logical benefits, find themselves in the necessity of arriving at agreements with a government [the U.S.] that has an important original sin: For one part, that they do not respect nearly any of the international norms of protocol and, for another, that, in its own day, [its citizens] expropriated and confiscated determined properties from thousands of legitimate owners that had worked to acquire them, among whom, certainly, I will remind one more time, were thousands of Spaniards.[40]

Fraga concluded by urging the EU to oppose the extraterritorial practices of the United States. Balletbo I. Puig (Socialist Party) noted that the most damaging effect of the law was its tendency to create a sense of doubt among

European investors. "What is happening," she observed, "in these moments has already had an effect that is creating instability in Spanish and European investors . . . who tend to be very prudent by definition." She also noted that the law discouraged free trade, something the Americans had actively promoted in the late twentieth century. The session ended in unanimity, with the ideas of historical irony and free trade conspiracy fresh in the air.[41]

Meanwhile, on the other side of the Atlantic, the lack of action on the part of the State Department helped explain why the Helms-Burton Act had created smoke and mirrors, but little in the way of actual sanctions. Furious at the State Department's unwillingness to carry out his recommendations, Jesse Helms made a desperate attempt to see sanctions served on Sol Meliá. On November 16, 2000, Helms wrote to Undersecretary of State Thomas Pickering, demanding that his department carry through with recommended actions against the Spanish hotelier. Helms emphasized that he had worked with the Sanchez family for three years in bringing sanctions against Sol Meliá. He accused the State Department of dragging its feet on the mailing of the July 30, 1999, letter and admonished Pickering to carry out the mailing of sanctions to Sol Meliá.[42] This was one of Helms's last-gasp attempts to punish the company. It brought to light the reluctance on the part of the State Department to proceed on the matter, perhaps because of conflicting interests with the European desks of the State Department. The following year, Helms retired from Congress. The Senate Foreign Relations Committee has not assailed Sol Meliá since sending it a letter of inquiry in the summer of 1999.

Europe's success in transforming Cuba's tourist sector into the most productive sector of the Cuban economy did not go unnoticed by American corporations, the American government, or special interest groups, such as the Cuban American community in Miami. If the purpose of the Helms-Burton legislation was to discourage foreign investment in Cuba, it did nothing to close loopholes that permitted American business executives to visit the island and plan their own post-Castro conquests. In 1995, the year prior to passage of the law, approximately thirteen hundred American business executives visited Cuba to make their market assessments, including those from Colgate Palmolive, Proctor and Gamble, General Motors, K-Mart, Gillette, Johnson and Johnson, Sheraton, Radisson, and Royal Caribbean Cruise. Ultimately, these developments, coupled with the tacit approval of business arrangements taking place between American companies and Cuban officials, led some Europeans to believe that the purpose of the Helms-Burton legislation had more to do with punishing the Europeans for getting to the island first, before the embargo was lifted.[43]

Europe and the Cuban Hotel Industry

During the last half of the nineteenth century, Cuba was Spain's most "loyal" colony, and Paris, London, and Madrid largely ruled the cultural preferences of its well-heeled residents. The Spanish-American War in 1898 brought an abrupt transformation not only in the way Cuba was governed but also in the precipitous domination of the consumer arena by American companies and styles. In the 1950s, Batista further encouraged American investment in the retail and hotel sectors, only to be toppled by the improbable success of the Cuban Revolution.

Castro's rise to power was accompanied by the creation of a consumer culture vacuum with the decommercialization of Cuban society and the flight of American investment and capital from the island. Perhaps Castro's greatest error was his belief that Cuba did not need management experts in order for the Revolution to survive. Castro's opening to Western Europe in the 1980s was a tacit admission that the island could not survive without some expertise in the fields of hotel and retail management. The arrival of companies like Sol Meliá returned the pendulum to its original point in the mid-nineteenth century, as Cuba's economy oriented itself toward Europe. Ironically, the American hotel and resort infrastructure that was supposedly erased by the Revolution, as in the cases of Varadero and the former Habana Hilton, provided the groundwork for European success on the island. After that success, the Helms-Burton Act represented an extraterritorial attempt on the part of the United States to thwart European domination on the Cuban island.

9

Punta Cana

To a degree unmatched in the rest of the Spanish-speaking Caribbean, the Dominican Republic packaged its tourism offering in the post–World War II era in a predominately urban setting. To a large extent, the urban orientation of Dominican tourism reflected dictator Rafael Trujillo's desire to showcase Santo Domingo, or his Ciudad Trujillo. Trujillo's efforts to promote tourism consisted mainly of luxury hotel development and hosting international fairs.[1] Such a combination created a strange dichotomy, particularly as decentralized tourism began to emerge around the Caribbean. Hotels such as the Intercontinental Embajador (opened in 1956) created a splash for a couple of years, and then tourism would begin to ebb.[2] Ironically, Santo Domingo boasted some of the Caribbean's finest hotels, but lacked the types of attractions and infrastructure that jet-set tourists were growing accustomed to in the 1950s and 1960s in places like Mexico, Puerto Rico, and Cuba. Tour guides gushed about the "modernity" of Trujillo's city, but found it difficult to provide tourists with other options in the Dominican Republic besides Santo Domingo.[3]

Political instability in the early 1960s further stifled tourism development in the Dominican Republic. Trujillo's heavy-handed dictatorial rule, followed by his assassination in 1963 and the subsequent political instability, practically killed the Dominican Republic's tourist trade in the mid-1960s. As stability returned to the country in the late 1960s, the Joaquín Balaguer administration commissioned a series of assessments of tourism development in the Dominican Republic.[4] In May 1968, the consulting firm of H.

Zinder and Associates, Inc., under contract with the Organization of American States (OAS), prepared a comprehensive assessment of the Dominican tourism industry and offered suggestions for immediate improvement.[5] Later that year, in September 1968, UNESCO published A. Arespacochaga y Felipe's report, *República Dominicana: Desarrollo turístico*. A Spanish tourism consultant of renown, Arespacochaga y Felipe had conducted a survey of tourism in Cartagena, Colombia, during the same year for UNESCO.[6] His report on the Dominican Republic focused on the theoretical plausibility of tourism reversing the Dominican Republic's balance of payments woes.[7] He also identified and prioritized the most important decentralized locations for rapid tourism development in the country.

Given the limited tourism development in the Dominican Republic, Zinder and Associates emphasized the importance of tapping into the significant wave of tourism development on the islands surrounding the Dominican Republic, stressing Puerto Rico in particular. "While little has been going on in the tourism field in the Dominican Republic," the report noted at the outset, "tourism has grown by leaps and bounds in Puerto Rico, in the Virgin Islands, and in Jamaica."[8] In an effort to take advantage of its proximity to millions of tourists, the Dominican Republic would need to promote favorable commercial air routes that would only minimally raise the total cost of a vacation for travelers in the Caribbean. Furthermore, given the economic vitality of Puerto Rico, promotion of the Dominican Republic there could yield additional Latin American tourist streams. Finally, Zinder and Associates recommended that Dominican authorities would also need to promote internal tourism to reduce international tourism by Dominican nationals, and the concomitant flight of currency abroad. "Some 80,000 to 100,000 Dominican citizens travel abroad each year," the report observed, "as contrasted to about 45,000 foreign visitors who visit the Dominican Republic. By contrast, Puerto Rico got about 800,000 tourists."[9]

In addition to stressing the need for a government-directed tourism organization with strong links to the business community, the report also illustrated ways in which Dominican officials and private investors could package tourism in more attractive colors for tourists.[10] In 1968, the report observed, most of the "tourists" to the Dominican Republic were business professionals and Puerto Rican tourists. These visitors generally stayed in the Dominican Republic for less than a week and spent approximately $200 per person during their visits. Spatially, tourists remained concentrated in the capital, as "the great bulk of tourists and visitors do not get out of the Santo Domingo area."[11] Initially, this would work to the benefit of a rapid tourism development program, as transportation bottlenecks and infrastructure limitations elsewhere made the capital city almost a mandatory destination. "For all practical purposes, it's an enforced entry point," Zinder and Associates noted, "and partly because it is the capital of the country, and is really the only place in the country with enough first-class rooms to accommodate more than a handful of tourists. Moreover, Santo Domingo and its environs have utilities already available, so that a substantial expansion of hotel facilities could be carried out more economically than in areas where development would to be started from scratch."[12]

In their formal recommendations for tourism development and its packaging for international tourists, Zinder and Associates proposed that the state-operated group of twelve hotels, División Hotelera, either be privatized or managed by foreign management, given the hotels' inability to generate revenues.[13] The consultants dwelled at length on the declining status of these hotels, noting:

> There is no doubt that in almost all cases, existing hotels need a drastic overhauling; and this is particularly true of properties owned by the División Hotelera. If these smaller properties outside of Santo Domingo are to get any reasonable share of future tourism (including local tourism), maintenance will have to be improved, plumbing overhauled, air conditioning installed or repaired, more adequate electricity outlets located in rooms, better lighting fixtures and facilities, and a thorough-going overhaul and improvement of furniture and furnishing, particularly beds. Painting is generally needed; so are light bulbs; so are hangers in closets; and adequate-size soap bars in the better hotels.[14]

If the Dominican government should ever become involved again with hotel financing and developing, Zinder and Associates further opined, it should "make sure that the hotels are built to the specifications of a responsible [presumably foreign] operator."[15] In order to accommodate the projected swell of tourists from approximately 45,000 in 1968 to a projected 270,000 by 1972, the state's tourism development organization should encourage the construction of twelve hundred to fifteen hundred additional hotel rooms in Santo Domingo and the outlying areas. At the time, the first-class rooms in Santo Domingo at the Jaragua, Hispaniola, and El Embajador hotels could only absorb fifty thousand of those tourists in the course of a year. Furthermore, it was recommended that Dominican authorities open a hotel training school, with assistance from Puerto Rican tourism experts and in conjunction with international training opportunities in places like Spain and Puerto Rico.[16]

The Zinder and Associates recommendations dovetailed with the dire economic necessities of the Dominican state and its underemployed populace. The need for mass tourism would affect how the nation prepared itself to receive tourists. At the airport terminal in Santo Domingo, for example, passenger-processing capacity would have to be reevaluated in light of the emergence of new aviation technologies, namely, the Boeing 747. "It's not yet clear when the Boeing 747 jumbo jet will fly to Santo Domingo," the report noted, "but we feel that sooner or later it will, and when it disgorges its 490 passengers, the adequacy of planned air terminal facilities will become strained indeed." Dominican officials were advised to take these factors into consideration before opening the new international airport.[17] Cruise ships would also be enlisted to bring the crush of mass tourism to Hispaniola. While the Dominican Republic received only a thousand cruise-ship tourists in 1967, its neighbor, Puerto Rico, received over one hundred thousand cruise-ship excursionists. In order to capture cruise-ship routes, the Dominican Republic would have to dredge Santo Domingo's harbor from twenty-six feet to thirty-two feet deep, add tug boats for turning ships around, increase the number of light ships for unloading boats outside of the harbor, clean up the port, and add telephone service at the dock to facilitate communication with ships. Finally, given the lack of internal transportation routes in the country, Zinder and Associates emphasized the internal development of air travel in the immediate future in order to jump start international tourism while additional roads were built.[18]

Zinder and Associates mentioned the importance of heritage tourism, particularly around Santo Domingo, but laid greater importance on the potential for "sun, sand, and water" vacations to lure international tourists. Furthermore, the fashion in which these vacations were prepared and sold to potential tourists was almost as important as the activities that the vacations entailed. In accord with the nation's need to increase revenues and maximize profits, Zinder and Associates stressed the importance of packaged vacations. In conjunction with travel agents in the United States, Dominican officials could promote destinations on the island in package format, thus maximizing the potential exposure and receptiveness to packaged tours.[19] Such trips might include a visit to the beaches in Puerto Plata from Santo Domingo and then a visit to the mountains on the return trip to the Dominican capital. However, lack of adequate infrastructure portended difficulties for such decentralized excursions, as "some sections of the road system will have to be improved to reduce danger and make for more comfortable driving conditions."[20]

Zinder and Associates also advised that Dominican authorities and private businesses would have to transform the way in which tourists were treated once they arrived in the country, while they were there, and at the moment of departure. In addition to the need for quicker processing of passengers at the customs and immigration stations upon arrival, the firm proposed a full makeover for the airport, including multiple posters featuring the Dominican Republic, "liberal use of colorful flags, large travel photographs . . . and comfortable chairs for tourists who have to wait." At the time, according to the consultants, none of these amenities had been incorporated into the airport's appearance. Live Dominican music and free drinks for customers might also ease the stress of international travel and warm tourists to the destination.[21] Having taxi drivers approach the hotel zone by driving down George Washington Boulevard near the sea could also make improvements in tourist perceptions of Santo Domingo. Nevertheless, "at various places along the road into town, screening is needed in the form of trees (to mask unsightly areas), and so is landscaping." According to the consultants, "the point here is that initial impressions gained by a tourist are extremely important in determining length of stay." Finally, flowers could be harvested from the countryside to enliven hotel rooms and public areas.[22] Ultimately, the Zinder and Associates report emphasized the need for an organizational structure in the Dominican government to deal with tourism development and a successful marketing strategy to attract tourists already visiting the Caribbean basin, and it offered specific recommendations on packaging tourism in a way that would be attractive for international tourists.

In contrast to the marketing emphasis of the Zinder and Associates report, Arespacochaga y Felipe's assessment of Dominican tourism looked more closely at the spatial possibilities for international tourism in the Dominican Republic, especially in areas outside of Santo Domingo. Yet like Zinder and Associates, he stressed the alchemic ability of beach tourism to attract international tourists and generate revenue. His report carried an unparalleled passion for tourism and its ability to help developing nations leap from subsistence economies to industrial and even postindustrial economies, much in the same fashion that his native Spain had since the end of World War II. By the late 1960s, Spanish tourism receipts often offset a substantial percentage of its imported products. Whether the same could be reproduced in a country lacking basic infrastructure and having been recently rocked by political turmoil remained to be seen.

Arespacochaga y Felipe proposed a plan that would quickly thrust the Dominican Republic into the international tourism market, despite its virtual absence in the aftermath of Trujillo's assassination. One of the Dominican Republic's obvious advantages included its hundreds of miles of beaches available for tourism development. As a baseline, the Spaniard suggested that the Dominican Republic could feasibly develop 60 miles of first-class beaches, 120 miles of second-class beaches, and 120 miles of slightly elevated coastline without beaches. The large number of protected bays and beaches already available could raise their value for tourism as well as help the "fight against the possible threat of sharks in the same [waters]." Perhaps over-exuberant for the potential of beach tourism and hotel development, the Spaniard projected that 500,000 rooms could be developed on the first-class beaches with a density of 100 rooms per 2.5 acres, with another 210,000 rooms on second- and third-class beaches.[23] These fantastic numbers were probably generated in order to reiterate the almost unlimited theoretical possibilities for tourism development with only sea, sand, and hotels. Arespacochaga y Felipe also elaborated on an eight-year program to increase tourism from around forty-five thousand tourists per year in 1967 to over eight hundred thousand tourists in 1975. The plausibility of such results assumed growth rates of anywhere from 25 to 60 percent more tourists per year than in preceding years. While such levels of growth might be feasible in Mallorca or on the Costa del Sol, the Dominican Republic's economic challenges, lack of infrastructure, and image question with international tourists cast suspicion on the apparently fantastic statistics.

Most important, Arespacochaga y Felipe evaluated the regions of the Dominican Republic most apt for tourism development. Given its relatively well prepared infrastructure for hotel development, he identified the Santo Domingo area as the most important region for immediate tourism growth. With its international airport, Santo Domingo offered access to prime beaches within driving distance of the capital, beginning with Boca Chica. Well publicized by travel guides as the nation's most significant beach community, Boca Chica was a far cry from modern developments in Mexico at Acapulco and in Puerto Rico at Dorado Beach. Arespacochaga y Felipe cited urban planning as one tool that could be used to stop the "deterioration of urbanizing possibilities of this beach." Adjacent islands also provided possibilities for local tourism development. Beyond Boca Chica, San Pedro de Macorís offered the possibility for development of "a nice tourist center with a golf course." In addition to hotels, the region lent itself to residential areas with a marina. Farther away, Catalina Island presented possibilities for development of an ocean-front promenade with artificial beaches.[24]

Arespacochaga y Felipe also identified the Playa Dorada corridor on the island's northern flank as an ideal location for decentralized beach tourism.

The zone he targeted stretched from the Bahia del Luperón to Puerto Plata, with a total of at least forty-two miles of beaches of "perfect sand."[25] To the east of Puerto Plata, additional beaches near Playa Dorada offered developers as many as 370 acres of land for infrastructure and hotel superstructure development. Finally, the beaches of Sosua provided excellent access to the Atlantic Ocean. Arespacochaga y Felipe esteemed the Puerto Plata region, taken as a whole, as valuable as Santo Domingo's Boca Chica region, particularly in light of the fact that Puerto Plata and Santo Domingo shared good communication routes. He foresaw the development of eight thousand hotel rooms in the Playa Dorado region at four tourism poles. In the decentralized Santo Domingo region, he called for construction of six thousand hotel rooms at four poles as well.[26]

In total, Arespacochaga y Felipe outlined five different zones for decentralized tourism development in the Dominican Republic. However, three set themselves apart from the others either for their accessibility to be developed or their unparalleled beauty. The areas around Santo Domingo and Puerto Plata exhibited great beauty, but were also his two top suggestions because of their accessibility. Private as well as public development ensued. Gulf and Western International, the conglomerate with significant sugar holdings in the Dominican Republic, decided to build a resort near its headquarters in La Romana, east of Santo Domingo. With a small jet landing strip and large amounts of money that could not be repatriated to the United States, the company tapped Cuban-born Alvaro Carta to develop the Casa de Campo Resort project, which would grow to include hotels, residences, golf courses, a faux European village, and other cultural venues. Gulf and Western's project began with a small hotel, but the company quickly became an innovative leader in decentralized tourism throughout the Caribbean. As marketing consultant David Pearson, a member of the original development team, has observed, "Not only was it a pacesetter, it was *the* pacesetter because before Casa de Campo the only 'resort' in the whole country was the Hotel Santo Domingo. The hotels in Santo Domingo were business hotels that doubled as resorts because there was no other place to go."[27] The addition of a Pete Dye golf course further consolidated the reputation of Casa de Campo as a complete resort destination.

The emergence of La Romana as a tourist destination would have surprised Arespacochaga y Felipe, who saw little tourism potential in the city, but its proximity to Santo Domingo gave it certain advantages over other, more isolated parts of Hispaniola. He identified one of these highly isolated areas, Macao, as the third priority for tourism development in the Dominican Republic. His extended description of the area, located to the north of La Romana, south of Samaná, and east of Higuey, is significant for what followed there:

> This zone of Macao is truly exceptional and among all the tourist beaches that we know in almost all the world, few offer a cleaner water, a greater fineness of sands and a cleanliness of the same exceptional level that one nearly doubts that they are really beaches made with sand, while in its components exist a great deal of detritus of clean shells and mother of pearl that give it a whiteness and a special quality. It can be affirmed without a doubt that this zone of Macao can include itself among the finest beaches in the world.[28]

Despite such beautiful beaches, Arespacochaga y Felipe lamented the fact that the region's infrastructure was so poor. Even though it surpassed Boca Chica's and Puerto Plata's developmental potential, the government or private investors would have to provide roads, electricity, and water just to begin the process of tourism development. The Spaniard suggested that perhaps private companies could come in and develop the beach with the help of the state. The severity of Macao's isolation and its underdevelopment, however, made tourism there a much more daunting task in the short run. In relation to conditions in Macao, he wrote:

> Near these beaches there are not resort installations or houses because of the great difficulty of access. There are not roads of some importance, to arrive at the beaches directly [from the rest of the country]. Nevertheless, the roads that link each of these towns among themselves (Sabana de la Mar, Miches, La Romana, El Seibo, Higuey) are acceptable and with the adequate investments [in tourism development] would provide an interesting tourism network. The vegetation is exuberant. The coconut trees right on the beach . . . convert the region into a tropical environment of great beauty. The water of the beaches is emerald [in color] with clean sand.[29]

In 1969, a group of American investors, Compañia de Desarollo Turístico, Residencial e Industrial, S.A. (CODETREISSA), headed by labor attorney and environmentalist Theodore Kheel, purchased thirty square miles of land near Macao. Other investors included George Meany, labor federation president, and John T. Dunlop, President Richard Nixon's director of the Cost of Living Council.[30] In 1969, the company hired twenty-four-year-old Dominican Frank Rainieri to locally manage the corporation's fledgling project. Raised in Santo Domingo and then educated in high school and college in the United States, Rainieri brought an expertise in business to a company intending to develop the region for beach tourism.[31] Rainieri set the evolution of Punta Cana's tourism infrastructure in motion in 1970 when he bulldozed a road from Higuey to Punta Cana at a capital investment of nearly $100,000. Electric generators were obtained, and a two thousand–foot landing strip was cleared near the present-day Corales residential area. Initially, Puntacana lived up to the "club" designation that it collectively assigned its ten cabanas capable of housing approximately forty tourists—or relatives of CODETREISSA investors. By 1974, Rainieri and Kheel realized that such a model would not be profitable.

Perhaps the most important external element of private stimulation of beach tourism in the Dominican Republic, as well as in other countries, was the arrival of Club Med. One of Theodore Kheel's fellow investors in CODETREISSA also held stock in Club Med and arranged a meeting between Kheel, Rainieri, and the president of Club Med.[32] By 1979, the Puntacana Club's ten cabanas of had been destroyed to make way for Club Med's Punta Cana Hotel. Club Med and CODETREISSA soon learned that the attraction of mass tourism required adequate transportation facilities. At the time, many of Club Med's guests made the drive from Santo Domingo's international airport to Punta Cana. Nevertheless, Arespacochaga y Felipe had noted that the easiest way to overcome the lack of an adequate highway infrastructure was through airport development at the country's principal tourism destinations. He added that any airport built in Macao should solely be a national airport, feeding off of international traffic from Santo Domingo.[33] The intense isolation of Punta Cana from the rest of the country, however, made international access via jet planes the preferred path of access to the region. At the time of Club Med's arrival in Punta Cana, the initial "airport" there consisted of a two thousand–foot runway located where the Corales residential area and golf course are now located. Rainieri secured a radio in order to communicate with incoming small planes, and the Dominican military sent representatives to oversee aviation. As Rainieri's daughter, Francesca, recalls, "They made the runway out of grass, but before the planes could land they had to make two flyovers so they could remove the cows."[34] The arrival of Club Med and its reliance on international tourists made seamless international access essential to tourism development. Pressed by CODETREISSA for assistance, the Dominican government contended that it did not have any money to build an airport at Punta Cana in the early 1980s. As a result, Frank Rainieri secured government permission to construct an airport in conjunction with Club Med at Punta Cana. The initial airport, opened in 1984, featured a five thousand–foot runway capable of handling small planes, mainly from Puerto Rico. This did not alleviate the transportation problem, as large jets could not land there, requiring passengers to make another connection in San Juan prior to arriving in Punta Cana. By 1986, in anticipation of handling jet planes, Grupo Puntacana (Rainieri and Kheel's corporate successor to CODETREISSA) extended the runway to seventy-five hundred feet and welcomed the first DC-9, leased by Club Med, in July of the same year.[35]

At about this time, Puntacana's evolving marketing strategy also shaped the scope of tourist flows to the region. Frank Rainieri recalls that by 1988, Grupo Puntacana initially looked at the most proximate market—the United States—as the target region for its new Puntacana Resort & Club (built adjacent to the earlier Club Med hotel). Despite having the proper business connections through Kheel, the plan did not materialize because, in Rainieri's words, "we didn't have the money to advertise in *The New York Times* every weekend and in *The Wall Street Journal*." As a result, Grupo Puntacana looked elsewhere for clients. "Punta Cana was an unknown destination," Rainieri recalled. "So instead we went to Europe where they sell package tours. Europeans travel in groups, with people from their professional societies and their community." The response was almost immediate. "For years [Europeans] were the backbone of development."[36]

Nevertheless, the growth of the Punta Cana International Airport was not driven solely by the business from Club Med and the new Puntacana Resort & Club. At the same time, Spanish hoteliers, led by the Barceló group, purchased beachfront properties some twenty miles to the north of Punta Cana at Bávaro Beach. Construction on the Barceló Bávaro Beach complex began in 1984, the first year of the Punta Cana International Airport, and was completed by 1985. In 1988, in anticipation of significant European air traffic, Grupo Puntacana expanded the runway to nine thousand feet. By 1990, Spanish hoteliers Riu and Sol Meliá had initiated construction of hotels in Bávaro. Thereafter the runway was expanded to approximately ten thousand feet, and an additional takeoff runway was added.[37] In 1996, Oscar de la Renta and Julio Iglesias, new partners with Kheel and Rainieri, assisted in the purchase of the remaining interest of the Punta Cana International Airport from Club Med. This transaction also facilitated the group's diversification into residential tourism. In 2005, the airport opened a new terminal and processed nearly three million arrivals and departures. At that point, the Punta Cana region had emerged from the Dominican periphery to become an improbable aviation center of cosmopolitan proportions. In that respect, Frank Rainieri has noted, "The DR is only two hours away from Miami, three

Figure 6. Punta Cana International Airport, Dominican Republic. Thatched storefronts inside of the airport suggest a strong link between environmental values, vacation experiences, and upscale consumer culture at the resort community. (Author's photo)

hours from New York. With good communication, that airport makes a difference. We have people from France, Spain, Italy, all over the U.S. Why? Because they jump in a plane from Paris to Punta Cana, Milan [to] Punta Cana, Rome to Punta Cana, Vancouver, and every major city and once they get here they are five minutes away from the airport. That opens the whole thing."[38]

Isolation also played a significant role in the evolution of Punta Cana's built environment. Rainieri has observed that limited funds prompted him to adopt architect Oscar Imbert's palm-topped terminal design for the first terminal at the Punta Cana International Airport. For Imbert, the belief in palm leaves as a legitimate tool for architecture stemmed from his study of Taino-inspired structures throughout the country. "The Indians were not stupid," he observed. "They were aware that the *cana* would stand up to hurricanes, to water." Imbert also took cues from nature to influence the architectural styles on the island. He noted:

We have a unique island and as an architect I feel really responsible to know the inhabitants of that spot. So if you see the plants and see how they sway and bend with the wind you can understand the intensity of the wind. But if you come in with a bulldozer and mow down the trees you'll never understand the wind. Similarly with termites: If you see termites in an area you know there can't be floods in the area because termites are very intelligent and choose dry land for their building nest.[39]

Nevertheless, shifts in market penetration often required design adaptations. The second terminal at the airport stands in stark contrast to the open environment of the palm-covered first terminal. Built as a glass-enclosed, air-conditioned structure, the second terminal caters to the tastes of North American customers, but offers a contrast in styles for discerning customers from all continents.

Imbert's architectural regionalism and attention to integrating local materials into Punta Cana's built identity are also evident in the architectural regulations of Grupo Puntacana. The impact of isolation on the built environment became an attractive factor for international tourists. More specifically, Punta Cana's geographic and political isolation contributed in large measure to the uniform presentation evident in the built environment in the community. With direct control of utilities, the fire department, security officers, and land sales, Grupo Puntacana opted for a uniform appearance, in contrast to the often-chaotic architectural evolution of competing tourist poles.

According to corporate regulations, all lands destined for residential uses at Puntacana properties must be carved out of a buffer zone comprised of the home's surrounding vegetative environment.[40] This process also implies that owners and contractors will respect the balance between the constructed and the natural environment. In order to avoid inordinate vertical construction that would block the views of surrounding property owners, Grupo Puntacana limits residential structures to two habitable floors. The company also discourages the use of bright lights on company grounds, while at the same time encouraging the use of soft lights to accentuate trees and other vegetative features. The emphasis on the natural aspects of Puntacana also extends to vehicle placement in subdivisions, with requirements that all automobiles and recreational vehicles ultimately be housed inside of a garage.[41]

Building regulations limit the impact of built structures not only by assigning size limitations but also by encouraging integration of all built facilities on each lot (except for one special structure, such as a gazebo) into one structure. This helps to maintain a less chaotic appearance and limits the amount of space dedicated to built structures. Furthermore, homeowners are enjoined to camouflage any mechanical structures, including air conditioners, as much as possible. "All exterior service equipment will be hidden from the sight of other houses, the street, and the golf course," the regulations stipulate, in order to preserve the balance between nature and the built environment.[42]

Grupo Puntacana's architectural requirements further reinforce a brand identity forged through isolation and a commitment to sustainable development. In keeping with efforts to preserve biodiversity, Grupo Puntacana requires architectural diversity within the context of corporate regulations. In reference to the volume and proportion of each home, for example, "the proportion of the structure to the area is of high importance to Puntacana Resort & Club. Lines of inclined roofs with variations in height and volume are suggested. Volumetric variation with the inclusion of elements of detail will result in an emotional composition from the natural level to the highest element of the town. The relationship of scale of each component of the building will be in relation to the general [scale of the community]."[43]

Landscaping and maintenance regulations for the natural buffer surrounding the home also stress commitment to local flora. Regional plants serve as the prominent feature of Punta Cana landscaping. One of their main purposes is to cover "service areas, vehicle entrances, guest parking, and all [other] elements that must be hidden" to preserve a sustainable image. Plants are also used to mark the transition between "the natural character of the area to the artificial structures of the house." In the hierarchy of design, "The bushes should initiate this progression and realize the transition to larger bushes closer to the house."[44]

The materials recommended for architectural design also reinforce local identity and a commitment to sustainable development, while discouraging methods and materials associated with mass construction. In the most general terms, "natural materials such as stone and wood function well with . . . [the] surroundings as well as materials of natural colors."[45] Recommended building materials included stone, stucco over masonry, and wood. Prohibited building materials included all plastics, imitation stone, block masonry, and plywood. Recommended colors included gray, taupe, and tan, while bright colors were discouraged except as a way to accent doors and windows. In an effort to integrate Grupo Puntacana's community into the broader Dominican context, regulations also "suggested colors inherent to Dominican architecture when these [colors] are used as accents." Architectural regulations for roofs suggested natural materials in neutral colors, while discouraging materials with an artificial appearance, "especially products of natural imitation like highly varnished tiles or white roofs." Grupo Puntacana also prohibited paved asphalt, asphalt shingles, asbestos cement shingles, and brilliantly painted metals.[46]

As noted, Grupo Puntacana's role as regional developer also laid the foundation for the entry of Spanish hotel chains to the Americas in the mid-1980s. While the Paris-based Club Med played the pioneering role in introducing the concept of "all-inclusive resorts" to the Americas, in places such as Guadeloupe, Cancún, and Punta Cana the Spanish hoteliers, including Sol Meliá, Barceló, Oasis, Occidental, Riu, and Iberostar, aggressively sought out opportunities to build mass tourism complexes and luxury resorts in the Caribbean. The majority of these Spanish hotel firms were based on the Balearic Island of Mallorca, which during the post–World War II era offered a paradigm for the development of mass tourism as an economic engine.[47]

Mallorca and the eastern Dominican Republic shared several important spatial-temporal similarities that appear to have contributed to the success of decentralized tourism and perhaps made the Punta Cana–Bávaro area an ideal point of entry and expansion for various Spanish hotel chains. First, both regions enjoyed relative anonymity on the geographic periphery of volatile conflicts during the twentieth century. In Spain, the Balearic Islands had enjoyed a tradition of tourism on the periphery since the nineteenth century. During the Spanish Civil War and, more important, during World II, Mallorca remained largely unscathed by national and global conflicts. This gave the Spanish islands a clear advantage following World War II in promoting mass tourism, as the rest of Europe awaited reconstruction. Similarly, the eastern Dominican Republic was largely ignored during the Trujillo dictatorship and its aftermath. This allowed CODETREISSA to consolidate its control over the Macao region relatively quickly prior to the arrival of the Spanish. One of the biggest differences between the two regions, however, concerns the promotion of tourism by their respective dictators. Francisco Franco's promotion of tourism in Spain lent cachet to the work of Mallorcan businessmen and their families in the vertical consolidation of tour-operating companies and hotels. In contrast, Trujillo's apathy toward the Macao region and tourism development in general allowed the Bávaro region to languish when Spanish hoteliers arrived in the mid-1980s to purchase parcels of land from private owners for hotel development.

Second, the organizational structure of hotel companies in Mallorca and Punta Cana–Bávaro revolved around family-operated businesses. While Spanish hoteliers Sol Meliá, Barceló, and Riu, for example, would introduce higher densities of tourist accommodations in Bávaro than Frank Rainieri and Grupo Puntacana allowed in Punta Cana, all groups shared a commitment to the continued legacy of complementary models of tourism in the Caribbean. As a result, similar organizational structures and commitment to tourism development contributed to the creation of hotel organizations on both sides of the Atlantic. In Punta Cana, a formalized Asociación Hotelera del Este embraced the concerns of all hoteliers in the Macao region who shared a commitment to marketing the destination as a unified region, and not as competing hotel interests. Less formally, Frank Rainieri and Grupo Puntacana regularly visited Spain to interact with the Spanish-based, and largely family-operated, hotel companies involved in the Macao region.

Finally, hotel developers in both regions created new modalities of hotel development in a rural setting. Many photos of Mallorca in the mid-twentieth century depict a densely populated (by residents and tourists) Palma de Mallorca, with its multistory hotels and crowded docks sharing space with its Gaudiesque cathedral. Nevertheless, Mallorca's dispersed shores and agrarian hinterland also gave rise to decentralized resort hotels and agro-tourism. In a similar vein, architect Oscar Imbert's inspired use of palm leaves and coral stone at Puntacana provided an alternative to beachfront, modernist hotels that dotted the Caribbean following World War II.

One of the important architectural links between the two regions is Mallorca-based Alvaro Sans. In the mid-1980s, about the same time that Spanish hoteliers were exploring methods of diversifying their interests away from a stagnating Spanish market, Sans became chief architect for Sol Meliá. In the Dominican Republic, and more particularly beginning in Punta Cana–Bávaro, Sans designed numerous low-density ecoresorts for Sol Meliá, Iberostar, and Princess. These hotels and touristic complexes included the Meliá Bávaro (770 rooms, 1990), Princess Bávaro (772 rooms, n.d.), Iberostar Bávaro (749 rooms, 1993), Iberostar Dominicana (347 rooms, 1995), Iberostar Punta Cana (342 rooms, 1997), Paradisius Punta Cana (448 rooms, 1996), Palma Real (Bávaro, four hotels, 630 villas, twenty-seven holes of golf, 1999), Meliá Tropical (Bávaro, 528 rooms, 1998), and Meliá Caribé (Bávaro, 528 rooms, 1999). Sans has noted the differences in designing hotels and urban tourism centers in the Caribbean and in the Mediterranean. He recommends that resort designs in the Caribbean should be open to the environment, as the climate varies less than in the Mediterranean, where designers should take greater extremes into account.[48] Accordingly, his hotel and urban tourism projects in the Punta Cana–Bávaro region largely consist of decentralized villas and dispersed blocks of rooms located amid natural settings of beaches, palm trees, and recreational facilities. In Bávaro,

Sans was also commissioned to design a public plaza, Plaza Bávaro, near the center of the largely unplanned development of hotels to the north of Punta Cana. Like the hotel chains for which he worked, Sans's influence took root in the Macao region and expanded throughout Latin America, in both urban and decentralized settings. Thereafter, his work expanded to Cancún, the Riviera Maya, Puerto Plata, Playa Conchal (Costa Rica), Puerto Rico, Cuba, and Belize.[49]

The Mallorcan-based Spanish hoteliers, led by the Barceló family, initiated the transformation of Bávaro in the mid-1980s, but had contemplated internationalization as a diversification strategy since the late 1970s. Initially, Gabriel Barceló pursued diversification through technology investments in the wake of the 1970s petroleum crises, but he was not satisfied with the results.[50] As a consequence, he turned his energies back to tourism, purchasing a tour agency, Turavia, which had offices in Latin America, including Mexico, Venezuela, Brazil, and Argentina. Following several minor investments in hotels in Mexico, Barceló identified the Bávaro Beach region as an ideal locale to build an ambitious tourism complex. According to Frank Elías Rainieri, Barceló made the decision to come after seeing "the airport, the presence of Club Med, and the beauty of the region."[51] As Spanish tourism scholar Marta María Vidal Suárez recounts, Barceló faced many of the same problems in developing Bávaro that CODETREISSA experienced in designing and maintaining Punta Cana. She writes: "At that time, Bávaro was a completely untouched area, without any type of infrastructure or development. Therefore, before construction of the hotel it was necessary to develop all of the necessary elements for the exploitation of a luxury tourist complex: construction of roads, energy plants, water treatment stations, etc. In all of these projects Barceló participated through its Construction Division."[52] Shortly thereafter, Sol Meliá announced its intentions to build the spacious Meliá Bávaro north of the Barceló resort complex. Drawn to the region initially by an offer from the Mexican government to invest in Cancún, Sol Meliá embraced the opportunity for private investment in the Dominican Republic. Princess, Riu, and Occidental would also follow, severely taxing the very limited public investment in infrastructure. In 1980, for example, there were 89 hotel rooms in the region, largely dominated by Club Med Punta Cana. By 1984, when Barceló announced his intention to build in Bávaro, there were 428 rooms. In 1985, with the opening of the Barceló Bávaro Beach complex, that number jumped to 1,028 rooms. In 1997, there were more than 10,000 rooms, and by 2005 there were nearly 23,000 rooms.[53]

From a sectoral perspective, Punta Cana–Bávaro boasted the highest concentration of hotel rooms in the country by 1993, with over 21,000 of the nation's 56,000 hotel rooms. By comparison, Boca Chica (6,261 rooms) and Puerto Plata (16,033 rooms), the latter of which had received significant government assistance in tourism development, stood in the shadows, particularly in the international market, of Punta Cana–Bávaro's international evolution. The Macao region also dominated national statistics regarding large hotels, with approximately two-thirds of the hotels with more than 500 rooms each. The Macao region boasted 11,914 of the 17,231 rooms in hotels with more than 500 rooms distributed throughout the Dominican Republic.[54] The advantages of private investment and an adequate air transportation infrastructure made Punta Cana–Bávaro one of the most important—and unique—tourist poles in the Caribbean. Geographic isolation contributed to a regional identity noted for self-sufficiency, as well as closer contact with the world outside of the Dominican Republic. Time will tell if the experiment of sustainable development and mass tourism in a single pole can continue to thrive in a mutually beneficial fashion.[55]

*   *   *

In early 2006, various participants in the evolution of Punta Cana shared their thoughts on its paradoxical condition: how isolation contributed to the evolution of an international resort community. They also commented on the complexities of regional development, with Punta Cana sharing the future with Bávaro, a city to the north built on mass tourism.

Francesca Rainieri, daughter of Frank and Haydee Rainieri, is in charge of hospitality and operations for the company. She remembers stories of her father. When he was unmarried and just out of the university, he came down to survey the location. Ten families lived where the resort is located today. The roads were so poor that they had never traveled to Higuey. The isolation of Punta Cana is reinforced in the story she tells of several members of the families living at Punta Cana jumping into the sea at the sight of her father's helicopter. In reflecting on her own experience there, she noted, "I have seen an immense change [in the area since my youth]. I began living here when I was a baby. Thus, I have many memories of my youth when Punta Cana was a completely different place than it is today."

Punta Cana's isolation also contributed to the Rainieri family's integration into the company and their commitment to Frank's vision. Francesca Rainieri notes that this is particularly true in regard to Haydee Rainieri, her mother. "Today my mother plays an equal part as my father [in Grupo Puntacana]. The vision has been of one, but the execution has been by two." In the early years, Haydee's decision to support Frank, and also integrate the children into Puntacana, contributed greatly to the family ethos of Grupo Puntacana. While living in Santo Domingo, Francesca recalled, Haydee and the children would drive four to five hours to Punta Cana to visit Frank. In the mid-1980s, Haydee took a more direct role in company operations, but as Francesca observed, "There have always been three voices in the project: my father, my mother, and Mr. Kheel."

In assessing the evolution of Punta Cana, Francesca argues that demand has played a significant role in the evolution of the company's master plan. She contends that Grupo Puntacana began not as a hotel company, but instead as a tourism development company, which contributed to the evolution of a conglomerate, instead of a dedicated hotel company. As a result, development tended to be more cyclical than linear, with infrastructure, hotels, and residential areas creating new streams of revenue and opportunity over time. Furthermore, development, within the bounds of the company's master plan, often produced new opportunities previously not considered. The company's decision to build a boutique hotel, Tortuga Bay, partly as a means of attracting interest for real estate sales, provides a strong case in point. Experts told Grupo Puntacana that a luxury boutique hotel would take approximately two years to build. The group subsequently decided to build the hotel in January 2005. Construction commenced in May 2005, and the string of villas was completed by December 2005 to meet market demands. At times, Francesca observed, "planning is not as important as the demand." However, she also noted that contingency—within the larger framework of a tourism development—often necessitates innovation. "Everything is well planned with the Master Plan," she noted, "but perhaps something happens and [you] need to build something that had not been planned. You cannot lose the moment."

In relation to the hybrid relationship between Punta Cana and Bávaro, Francesca characterized the relationship as one of interdependence through differing objectives. "The vision of what Puntacana is and what Puntacana wants to be is different from what the area of Bávaro . . . [wants] to be." She noted the amicable relationship between the hotels in the region, but stressed that the question of hotel density served as one of the most important differentiating factors in their approach to the industry. "There are different ways of seeing things," she pointed out. While Bávaro distinguished itself for high-volume, high-density hotels, the Puntacana Resort & Club has only 350 rooms and half a mile of beach. The residential areas spread fifteen hundred homes out over fifteen thousand acres. Despite these different objectives, Francesca observed, the Spaniards who owned hotels in Bávaro and Grupo Puntacana worked together to promote the area. "We have good relations with the Escarrers," she remarked. "Each time [Miguel] Fluxa comes, or [Gabriel] Escarrer, we meet together." She attributes the success of the Spanish, not only in Bávaro but also around the world, to their vertical integration and aggressive investments. "European [hoteliers] were visionaries and went out into the world, not just in the Caribbean, and they bought all over."[56]

Frank Elías Rainieri, son of Frank and Haydee, began working at the Puntacana Resort & Club as a young man at the reception desk, in the maintenance section, in the activities department, in the accounting department, and at the airport. Following graduate training in the United States, he returned to Grupo Puntacana and assumed duties as director of real estate, which included responsibility for residential sales, golf course operations, new parks, and new offices. In addition, his office manages a shopping center, an art gallery, and a bowling alley in the community of Puntacana Village. He confirms that real estate and golf course development had always been a part of Grupo Puntacana's master plan. The changes, as Francesca noted, were dictated by demand. Whereas a small marina had been planned in the first master plan in 1978, a larger marina with condominiums was actually built. Similarly, the airport, school, and residential areas are larger than initially planned. "Demand is what has changed the scale of the master plan and the actual resort," Frank Elías observed. "The master plan was always there with what would be there and where it would be."

Much as Conrad Hilton employed celebrities to promote his international hotels from the 1940s through the late 1960s, Frank Elías acknowledges the importance of Grupo Puntacana's celebrity partners, most notably Oscar de la Renta and Julio Iglesias, to the evolution of residential tourism at Puntacana. As he points out, they have accelerated the compression of distance between Grupo Puntacana and its potential real estate clients. "They are an important part of the plan," he commented, "because whenever someone is going to make an investment outside of their country and they see that there are notable people that have built homes there, the confidence that they have in making the purchase is much greater than if there was not someone of notoriety in the project. If they see that person, that they are already there, then they have greater confidence in the project than if these people were not there." He also noted the manner in which effective celebrity marketing compresses a marketing and development strategy. "The celebrities are able to attract people to come to the property and they come and enjoy it, and this moves the project to another level than if we were trying to do it by ourselves, step by step," he observed. "The period of time for achieving what we have achieved would be much longer than if we did it together with them."

While conscious of Puntacana's internal image in relation to community development and residential marketing, Frank Elías also recognizes the interdependence of the Punta Cana–Bávaro region. In contrasting Punta Cana and Bávaro, he asserted that Grupo Puntacana is a group of landholders with a master plan for all of the company's land. "We know where everything will go," he said. "Lamentably, the government has not done the same in the north. There has been [overdevelopment] in that area." Nevertheless, he also observed, "their success is our success. Their failure is our failure. We are not just Grupo Puntacana; we are a leader for this entire area, and we will encourage the planning of the entire area." Frank Elías expressed optimism that by 2012, collaboration with the government would provide planning for hotel and residential areas in the entire area.

For the new generation of Grupo Puntacana executives, Frank Elías has elaborated a business philosophy that encompasses sustainable development of the Punta Cana–Bávaro area. He emphasized that the company has always stressed its commitment to sustainable development, ecological preservation, low-density growth, and a focus on family-based tourism. "Without this concept," he avers, "no tourism pole can develop over the long haul." He continues, "Whenever we develop we always think in the long term, nothing in the short term. We have thirty-seven years and we want to have eighty more, if God permits." Such a philosophy also complements the family-based company structure of Grupo Puntacana that has emerged with the grooming of Frank Rainieri's children as the future of the company. In Frank Elías's mind, a private company with familial connections has a better chance of transmitting original values than a corporation. "We don't want to be a corporation," he bluntly stated. "They lose some of their values. Corporations are focused on every three months, and not on the long term. They have short-term goals. We are doing everything based on the long term. In a corporation expenses often do not matter; in a family business we measure every expense. We will continue with the vision and mission of Don Frank. This makes family companies better than corporations."[57]

Adolfo Ramírez, the chief development engineer for Grupo Puntacana, recalls the tremendous growth in the region during his ten years there. When he moved to Punta Cana in 1996, there were only eight thousand hotel rooms, a number that by 2006 had surpassed twenty thousand. In his estimation, one of the biggest changes in the region, given the explosion in hotel development, has been the rapid growth of adjacent areas that service the hotel districts with employees, such as Verón. When he arrived in Punta

Cana, there were probably fifteen to twenty homes; according to the 2002 census, the population of the sprawling community between Punta Cana and Bávaro had grown to fifteen thousand. Similarly, the lack of a service superstructure, including supermarkets, reinforced the sense of isolation. "Today it is still difficult," he noted, "but there is more support for tourism jobs." These challenges have shaped his approach to Puntacana's master plan, as well as his philosophy of urban development in Puntacana Village. In designing a community such as Puntacana Village, Ramírez emphasized that the goal is to deliver services efficiently. The creation of a school there was one important example. Given the paucity of state-run services, the school provided education for children living in Puntacana subdivisions and for those from the surrounding area, including Bávaro.

For Ramírez, the biggest problem created by geographic and political isolation over the years has been constant reliance on self-sufficiency. "If you were completing a project in the United States," he pointed out, "water and electricity would all be provided by the municipality or federal government. Here the government has not done a lot in thirty-seven years." However, he also noted that Puntacana's lack of federal assistance, unlike tourism destinations such as Puerto Plata, which the Dominican government developed with financial backing from the Inter-American Development Bank, has given Grupo Puntacana a greater degree of flexibility, as well as the opportunity to create a better quality tourism pole. As a result, he believes, Puntacana has been able to hone its talents in developing tourism. "The biggest thing that Puntacana needs from the government in this zone," he averred, "is not help with tourism, but help with the basic requirements of combating poverty in the area, [which is] something that the tourists do not want to see."

Ramírez also elaborated on Frank Rainieri's impact on planning, for both the resort and the region. "With the creation of Puntacana," he stated, "Frank gave the foundation for development in the region." Ramírez also asserted that Rainieri and Kheel's initial 1978 master plan laid out their vision for a unique, sustainable tourism development. While well-planned real estate developments and the expansion of the Ecological Foundation became a priority in the late 1990s, Ramírez observed that they had always been a part of the master plan. In addition, the marina, *lagunas*, and a golf course were also part of the original master plan. Ramírez also noted that this vision expanded to the regional level in the mid-1980s, when Grupo Puntacana and the Dominican government drew up architectural regulations for Bávaro, Macao, and Punta Cana. The plan dictated that no building in the region could be higher than the tallest coconut trees, which effectively limited hotels to four stories. This regulation was formulated in part to keep the region from becoming like competing mass tourism poles.

In differentiating between Punta Cana and Bávaro, Ramírez points out that Grupo Puntacana is a single entity that has pursued a policy of sustainable tourism, including providing basic services for the community such as garbage collection, water, and electricity. In contrast, Bávaro, developed by scores of unrelated hotel owners, lacks many of the basic services, including garbage collection, which might be expected from the state.[58] As a result, the individual hotels focus on the appearance of their hotels, yet the community that links them has been destroyed by what Garret Harden has termed "The Tragedy of the Commons," where a single resource or multiple resources are overexploited or neglected.

Punta Cana International Airport managers Francisco Alba and Walter Zemialkowski elaborated on the evolutionary process of operating an international airport on the periphery. In many senses, operating an international airport is the same anywhere in the world. Zemialkowski, airport assistant director, observed that all successful airports must deal with security, customer service, creating revenue, and safety. Teaching safety techniques "is a great challenge," he stated, "especially here in the Dominican Republic, because it is not always a part of their culture like it is in Europe and the United States." Another challenge for a rapidly expanding airport involves construction practices. Zemialkowski made it clear that the main challenge in the Dominican Republic is supervision, not skilled help. He observed that local construction companies and contractors tend to take on four or five construction jobs around the country and are always moving around. As a result, Punta Cana International Airport's second terminal was built only after an extensive period of planning. "When we built the terminal we built it in less than six months," he recalls. "The secret is that all of the supervisors of the contractors had to stay here in Puntacana while construction was going on. They couldn't just come here and kick off the project and then go back to Santo Domingo and come back in one week, two weeks, or a month and see how we were doing."

Alba and Zemialkowski also elaborated on the challenges and advantages of private airport development over state-managed or privatized airports. Despite the lack of public financial support, particularly for state-managed airports, international airports dependent on private investment allow owners and operators to control demand. "There is a large planning cycle, particularly in the federal government," Zemialkowski commented, that requires "all sorts of grants and permissions, [and] a lot of loopholes to satisfy [these] requirements." In contrast, with a private international airfield, there is a "tremendous efficiency factor. You meet with the Board of Directors, [they] take it to [their] Board of Directors and then you go and do it. It is a much more direct line." As a result, planning tends to be much more sensitive to sudden shifts in demand. "A lot of our time is spent on forecasting and on what I call just-in-time construction," Zemialkowski remarked. "You go and build what you need for the next couple of years."[59]

The Puntacana Ecological Foundation has also played a significant role in the evolution of Punta Cana's infrastructure and superstructure. Jake Kheel, the director of the foundation, noted the benefits of sustainable tourism as a founding principle of Puntacana's transformation from a state of national isolation to international integration. According to Kheel, conditions in the eastern Dominican Republic during the late 1960s shared some similarities with wartorn Iraq. "After the Trujillo dictatorship, land was pretty cheap," he observed, "sort of like [conditions] in Iraq right now with all of the instability." Despite the fact that his great uncle, Theodore Kheel, led a group of investors, almost on a whim, to purchase thirty square miles of land near Macao, the isolation helped members of the group to appreciate the region's beauty, even in 2006, as nearly fifty hotels with twenty-four thousand rooms and flights from as far away as Russia, Poland, and Canada descend on the region. "Because they started here thirty years ago," Jake Kheel asserted, "they have always had a vision for sustainable development." He believes that this singular approach has also differentiated Grupo Puntacana from its regional neighbors. Throughout the region, he sees differing developmental strategies as the catalyst not only for growth but also for competing visions of how the region is perceived by visitors. To the north, in the Bávaro region, for example, numerous hotel interests fueled intensive immigration to the region, which has ultimately manifested a serious lack of planning. In that region of Punta Cana–Bávaro, Kheel lamented, "It is almost as if you don't know which direction the ocean is in. It's on the eastern tip of the island, but because the roads are crisscrossed, each hotel built a different road for their hotel, and there is no real plan for the region there, no master plan, it is very chaotic. As soon as you get to Verón [coming from Punta Cana] you can really tell."

International isolation also posed challenges for the establishment of serious scientific investigation at Punta Cana, but has ultimately created a diverse research agenda and international interaction between Dominican and U.S. scholars. The Ecological Foundation was initially housed in an Imbertesque, palm-covered, coral stone building next to the Puntacana Resort & Club. In 2001, however, Theodore Kheel, Grupo Puntacana, and Cornell University built the foundation's current building away from the hotel, next to the corporate ranch. Labs were built to Cornell's specifications, classrooms for coursework and conferences were constructed, and a small library provided the context for conducting scientific research in the region. The general approach to research, however, has privileged local knowledge as much as that of visiting scholars and students. Kheel noted, "We bring in national students and professors, and they teach the [American] students. They come to a developing country and learn from the students of the developing country. You allow the local knowledge to be transferred, and they feel like they are the ones in charge of the project." This has facilitated a strong tradition of intellectual exchange between local and international scholars that probably would have never existed on the periphery without Theodore Kheel's and Frank Rainieri's long-term commitment to the environment.

Isolation not only helped to diversify Grupo Puntacana but also offered numerous opportunities for the Ecological Foundation to pursue sustainable development initiatives. Jake Kheel elaborated on the link between the company's diversification and the foundation's activities: "The company is so diverse; we have an airport, two electric companies, two hotels, water treatment facilities, a town with commercial businesses . . . two schools—one a bilingual school and the other a technical, skills [based] school for the tourism industry. We can adapt to any group [in reference to the universities that conduct research at the foundation] that comes to us because of the diversity of the company." Similarly, the company's diversity has also created opportunities for the foundation to focus on problems in the tourism industry that go beyond Puntacana and address sustainable approaches to the growth of tourism throughout the Caribbean basin.

Jake Kheel's initiative to improve sand retention on Puntacana's beaches is one of the best examples of this effort to prove the viability of sustainable practices in increasing the value of tourism receipts. One of the biggest problems for the company's hotels had been the erosion of beaches. In 2005, the Ecological Foundation made a presentation to the Grupo Puntacana's board of directors on the need to control erosion and received proposals from coastal engineering companies to use concrete partitions to stop erosion. There were questions as to whether such an approach would be successful and definite doubts regarding its sustainability. The foundation then brought in an oceanographer who had worked in Cuba and the Dominican Republic on beach erosion from a more holistic perspective. Diagnosing the problem as being much larger than simple beach erosion, he argued that mangroves, coral reefs, and sea grass beds were important elements in the creation of beaches. Accordingly, the foundation elected to address the interaction of mangroves, coral reefs, and the beach sand by using nearly

Figure 7. Mangroves, Punta Cana, Dominican Republic. Recently planted mangroves along resort beaches illustrate efforts to combat erosion with sustainable methods. (Author's photo)

five hundred concrete stabilization structures to block wave action on the beach, planting thousands of red mangroves, and using groins to encourage sand accretion. Kheel is hopeful that such an approach will demonstrate long-term solutions to regional problems. "If you can restore some of the hydrodynamics you can restore some of the fish populations, some of the existing habitats from before, and bring back some of the overall health of the system. . . . You don't have to do [invasive] interventions." Collaboration with firms constructing the various golf courses at Puntacana has also led to the preservation of trees and the use of salt-tolerant grasses that can be maintained with fewer pesticides. "Let's stop talking about not making golf courses," Kheel asserted, "and figure out how to make sustainable golf courses."[60] The search for sustainable solutions serves as an important reflection on the journey from isolation in regional tourism development to a leader in the most profitable sector of Dominican tourism.

The marketing forces behind Grupo Puntacana's success also lend insight into the move from isolation to an internationally respected tourism community. David Pearson, a pioneering sustainable tourism consultant, has known Frank Rainieri since nearly the inception of CODETREISSA. A gifted writer, Pearson began his career as a United Press International correspondent, but soon became involved with Charles Fraser in the development of

Sea Pines Plantation on Hilton Island. After starting his own consultancy firm, specializing in the marketing of upscale sustainable tourism projects, he began working in the early 1970s with Gulf and Western International's Casa de Campo project in La Romana, Dominican Republic. He recalls that one day in the early 1970s, while in La Romana: "Frank came down to Casa de Campo in a helicopter and he picked up Alvaro Carta and me. He took us over to Punta Cana where we got into a jeep and we were riding along the ocean on a dirt road with grass in the middle [of the road], avoiding flocks of chickens and pigs, and people were living in shanties. Frank said 'Someday I'm going to create a great resort here,' and we were all going 'right. . . .' This guy had a vision in 1970, 1971 and he made it happen."

Pearson formed the core of his marketing strategies for promoting Puntacana while working for Gulf and Western at Casa de Campo. In the immediate aftermath of the Juan Bosch revolution and the American intervention in the Dominican Republic in 1965, Pearson recalls, "The hard part was getting Americans to go down there because the image of the country was still one of revolution." Furthermore, security concerns scared off potential guests. "The hardest job we had," he remembers, "was to turn that image around and make it a country attractive to tourists." Pearson and his associates accomplished this by promoting Casa de Campo itself as the final destination, and not the Dominican Republic. "Anywhere we have had a resort in an area that is not popular or had some sort of strike against it in the public mind," he observed, "we sort of go around and over the name of the country and promote the destination itself." Pearson was forced to invent paradigms of marketing—particularly branding—for places, instead of products. "The modern concept of branding didn't exist," he quipped. "We thought that was a hot stick that you put on a cow. But our concept of branding is that you take everything in that you do, everything that you use before the public, you play up the name of the place and you play down the name of the country." For Casa de Campo, this involved positioning the name "Casa de Campo" on the top of brochures and placing the words "Dominican Republic" somewhere below. The same philosophy applied in promoting Puntacana as a resort destination to the "gringo" market.

In assessing his contributions at Puntacana, Pearson also addressed the reasons why there had been such a disjuncture between the need for governmental assistance in the region and the lack of such assistance. "The reason why," he notes, "is that there are no votes out there." In Pearson's estimation, the most valuable contribution of the Dominican government to Grupo Puntacana was former president Balaguer's legislation that simplified foreign ownership and promoted tax incentives for tourism development, including tax holidays and tax breaks. This made it possible for developers to build villas and hotels. Apart from these meager actions, Pearson and Grupo Puntacana forged their own idea, much as Pearson had done for Casa de Campo in the 1970s.

In assessing the evolution of the Puntacana Resort & Club's image, Pearson argues that it has been a double-edged sword. The airport, he avers, made the name famous well beyond the bounds of the resort itself, and as a result all of the hotels in the region, including those in Bávaro, have taken upon themselves the name to indicate the tourism pole where they are located. While Puntacana enjoyed ample international attention as a result of this exposure, the persistence of the all-inclusive model at many area hotels, as well as a focus on volume-oriented package programs, tended to affect the region's image, ultimately scaring off many well-heeled tourists who might have purchased real estate in the area. Pearson succinctly illustrated the conundrum: "On the one hand, we had the fame because of the name of the airport, but the implications of that fame were that you could take your family down there for a hundred dollars a day." As a result, Rainieri changed the resort hotel from an all-inclusive plan and decided to target tourists to whom he could sell property. Switching from all-inclusive plans to the European plan did not quite have the desired effect, as the hotel was set up to be a family-oriented property. So Rainieri created the Tortuga Bay boutique hotel in order to capture an affluent new clientele. As Pearson notes, with easy access to the golf course and clubhouses, the Tortuga Bay boutique hotel, among other features, lends itself to residential tourism.

Pearson also believes that the combination of sustainable tourism values and private funding for Puntacana has made the company and the community it has created unique. He points to the high-rise developments of Cancún and Puerto Vallarta, "one after another, strung along the beach, [where] money had to be the main driving force." Pearson argues that developers in the Dominican Republic (or elsewhere in the Caribbean where sustainable tourism practices are observed) are not morally superior, but instead were simply interested in different results.[61]

*   *   *

In retrospect, the UNESCO and OAS consultative reports prepared for the Dominican government in relation to tourism development shared a couple of important assumptions that were representative of the time when and place where they were written. First, both offered the Dominican government tourism development plans that would generate quick results for specific maladies in the national economy—namely, balance of payment debts and underemployment. The indispensable characteristic that would bring a quick return from tourism was significant government involvement in any plan. The private sector could contribute by partially financing elements of a plan or by investing in hotels, for example, but the state would play the primary role in developing a tourism infrastructure and hotel superstructure. Large low-interest loans from supranational organizations like the Inter-American Development Bank and the World Bank were becoming increasingly fashionable in the world of tourism development. These multimillion dollar loans accommodated large-scale tourism developments over short periods of time. That such loans often built tourism complexes beyond the true demand for a given tourism pole is common knowledge.

In contrast, on the far eastern plains of the Dominican Republic, amid coconut palms and fallen mahogany trees, Frank Rainieri, Theodore Kheel, and Grupo Puntacana challenged conventional wisdom in regard to the role that private capital should play in major tourism development. With resources limited to that invested by corporation members, the tourism pole of Punta Cana evolved at a much slower pace than Puerto Plata, Cancún, and Playa Dorado (Puerto Rico). The initial cabins were opened in 1971, followed by Club Med's hotel in 1982 and the Puntacana Resort & Club in 1988. The evolution of the private airport, which began as a grass landing strip near the beach, to an international airport with cutting-edge architecture and services tailored to the region's needs also played a central role in the growth of the region and the arrival of Spanish hoteliers.

Private capital in and of itself is not what made Punta Cana unique. Acapulco is probably the best example of unregulated private development in a tourism pole. The combination of a commitment to sustainable development and the cultivation of a regional identity forged in isolation from the rest of the country and governmental assistance made the tourist pole of Acapulco unique. Punta Cana and Bávaro share a similar future because of the airport that processes customers, but the region has cultivated a hybrid identity, with Grupo Puntacana operating according to precepts of sustainable development and Bávaro largely focused on all-inclusive mass tourism.

The spatial evolution of Punta Cana–Bávaro is unique in the annals of twentieth-century Caribbean tourism. In most cases, decentralized tourism poles that gained international stature after World War II depended on some sort of central urban area. At Dorado, Puerto Rico, for example, Laurance Rockefeller's and subsequently Hyatt Regency's Dorado Beach properties were integrated into the social and economic fabric of the community of Dorado, which had historical and economic traditions dating back

Figure 8. Bávaro, Dominican Republic. A lack of urban planning and infrastructure maintenance has plagued not only Bávaro but also many peripheral tourism poles throughout the world. (Author's photo)

to Spanish colonialism. Irénée Du Pont's development of Varadero, Cuba, benefited from the earlier establishment of a community on the western part of the peninsula by residents from Cardenas, Cuba, in the late nineteenth century. Finally, Cancún began from the ground up. However, the Mexican government realized that given the paucity of urban development in Quintana Roo, it would have to develop a significant urban center and residential area to service the tourism pole. Over time, Cancún's growth and expansion into the Riviera Maya, which took place almost as soon as it was born, transformed the decentralized urban area of Cancún into the metropolitan center of a sprawling tourism megacomplex.

In contrast, Irénée Punta Cana followed a wholly unique spatial and urban evolution. Initiated as a simple resort, Grupo Puntacana imperceptibly evolved into the center of a region that included Bávaro and Bayahibe due to the degree of isolation experienced during its history. What accounted for the centralization of the Punta Cana region (centered at Puntacana Village and the commercial area near the new boulevard to Bávaro)? Lack of public services, a nonexistent transportation infrastructure, and government neglect over a roughly thirty-year period created the crucible for Puntacana's improbable centralizing function for the region. The creation and evolution of the Punta Cana International Airport provided the appropriate infra-

Figure 9. Villa Puntacana, Dominican Republic. The residential community that borders Puntacana's planned communities and tourism developments demonstrates a measure of permanence, with a plaza flanked by cathedral and schools *(not pictured)*. (Author's photo)

structure to link all resort areas in the eastern area to Punta Cana. Finally, the creation of a quasi-public square at Puntacana Village flanked by a coral limestone church and a palm-roofed school symbolically established the heart of an international community in a region increasingly less isolated from the rest of the world and the Dominican Republic.

Epilogue

Observations from 135 Degrees

Historian Anthony Pagden has illustrated that during the fifteenth and six-teenth centuries, European explorers often appealed to their personal experience in the Americas to validate their authority on New World topics.[1] In historical methodology, however, appeals to documents as authoritative statements generally take precedence over the experiential knowledge of investigators. This creates an immense paradox for historians of tourism: the need to work in stuffy archives in order to establish the evolving reality of an activity best suited to sun, sand, and tropical landscapes. The preceding chapters have established a documentary basis for understanding the packaging of tourist poles in the Spanish Caribbean. This epilogue will integrate on-site observations from around the world, as if from a beach chair, or from a 135 degree angle, with a final comparative analysis of three of the major poles discussed in the book: Varadero, Punta Cana–Bávaro, and Cancún.

Havana/Varadero

When I traveled to Havana and Varadero in early 2004, it was clear that the fear engendered by the Helms-Burton Act (see chapter 8) had largely subsided. In Havana's Plaza San Francisco, under the imposing shadow of the Lonja de Comercio, the city's principal commercial building, the local Benetton store had shut its doors, not in preparation to leave the country, but instead for remodeling. On Obispo Street, the traditional pedestrian commercial artery of Old Havana since the eighteenth century, Cubans—as well as foreigners who spoke French, German, Dutch, Spanish, and distinctively British, Bahamian, and Irish strains of English—stopped to gawk at clothing stores covered with the names of European designers.

In Miramar, Havana's upscale suburban area and diplomatic core, the Miramar Trade Center stands surrounded by European hotels: the Habana Meliá (Spain), the glassy LTI Panorama (Germany), and the more subdued Novotel Miramar (France). Across the street from the Habana Meliá and kitty-corner to the Trade Center, the Galeria Comodoro, Cuba's finest shopping center, buzzed to a rock-and-roll beat and hosted upscale shoppers at its Mango (Spain), LaCoste (France), Façonnable (France), and Benetton (Italy) boutiques. Workers and shoppers alike took a moment to enjoy fresh French bread at the Pain de Paris bakery.

To the east of Havana, Varadero continued to welcome the world to its beaches. Instead of traveling overland from Havana, as most tourists had done during the 1950s, many Europeans, Canadians, and Latin Americans arrive on the peninsula via direct flights to the Varadero International Airport. The modest airport that has been carved out of the scrubby plain to the east of the city is a testament to the degree of Europeanization this once isolated part of Cuba has achieved. The Cuban Ministry of Tourism lists Canadians, Italians, Germans, the English, and Spaniards as the most frequent travelers to the island. An Air France office in Varadero shares building space with a Cuban snack bar on First Avenue. Russian tourists snap photos in front of Al Capone's old home near the eastern point of the peninsula. Germans and Italians stroll the beach, darkly tanned, in their Speedos, while Hungarians and Germans sit at a bar using English as their pidgin language to debate the merits of the best soccer players in Europe. Chinese tourists frolic in the water, taking pictures of each other, as the sun sets to the west of the peninsula. At the upper end of the peninsula, the Du Pont mansion shares San Bernardino Crag with its Spanish neighbors: Meliá las Américas, Meliá Varadero, Sol Palmeras, and the Iberostar Bella Costa. Miniature passenger trains run tourists to the Plaza Americas Shopping Center, where French and Canadian shoppers peruse Italian and Spanish designer clothing before munching on pizza, whose ingredients have been imported from Toronto by the Canadian chain Pizza Nova. This polyglot jungle provided a stark contrast to the more monolingual American beach haven to the west in Cancún, Mexico. And so does the flat, more horizontal skyline of Varadero, whose design has largely been left in the hands of Europeans and Cubans who have learned from the experiences of their Caribbean neighbors.

Punta Cana–Bávaro

In January 2006, I visited Punta Cana–Bávaro in the Dominican Republic and had an opportunity to see the struggle between sustainable tourism and unplanned mass tourism. On a Wednesday morning, I toured the Grupo Puntacana community and Bávaro, to the north. After touring the various Grupo Puntacana hotels, my guide and I went through the residential areas, including collections of homes in stunning Dominican architectural styles, inspired by architect Oscar Imbert's designs. The most impressive aspect of the entire community was its uniformity in maintaining ecological and landscaping standards. The sides of roads were well groomed. A sense of permanence also surrounded the built environment. The church at the center of Puntacana Village, built from coral limestone rocks, symbolically anchored the community. In contrast, after touring Grupo Puntacana's properties, we turned north, along a two-lane road that connects the Punta Cana International Airport to the resorts in Bávaro. The sides of the roads were overgrown and ragged. Large trucks, hotel buses, and cars jockeyed with mopeds, including one carrying a driver and passenger, the latter clutching a baby with one hand, on the long road to the north. Approaching Bávaro from the south, resort communities are situated to the right, where ecological conditions inside these communities are vastly different than the public spaces on the road. Almost like a broken record, my guide pointed out the ecological disconnection between the public and the private context. Trash amasses against the side of the road, or wanders, pushed here and there by the wind, across empty pieces of real estate. Signage sprouts up anywhere that it can be placed, creating a chaotic visual aesthetic. Plaza Bávaro, a public space created by Spaniard Alvaro Sans, does not appear to have been maintained as it was once created. As a result, very few people have made it the public space it deserves to be. To be sure, Bávaro is probably not much different than other decentralized tourist zones throughout the world. Yet the stark contrast between it and Punta Cana—connected by a thin ribbon of road and an airport—makes the difference that much more profound. As the twenty-first century progresses, it is to be hoped that these types of contrasts will force the industry to determine not only how much tourism the planet will sustain but also what conditions tourists will be willing to tolerate before demanding more sustainable resort communities.

Fethiye, Turkey

The Mediterranean coast of Turkey seems an odd place to learn about the evolution of resort development in the Caribbean, but it legitimates the global diffusion of architectural designs and development patterns. During a month-long visit to western Turkey, where I spent time doing fieldwork on Turkish tourism and consumer culture, we pulled into the Majesty All-Inclusive Resort outside the Mediterranean town of Fethiye. The cultural packaging of the resort was stunning for a researcher accustomed to the Spanish and native architectural paradigms of Caribbean resorts. The hotel itself, arranged over several acres, looked like an old Turkish village, with *çikma*, or extended Turkish balconies, projecting from the second-story facades of the hotel buildings. A Romanesque amphitheater—like so many historical Roman amphitheaters spread across the Turkish landscape—served as the stage for nightly shows. Other clues revealed the evolving stream of receptive tourists frequenting the hotel: jewelry shops catering to German guests and a beauty salon advertising its services in Russian.

I had a chance to meet the architect of many of the additions and alterations to the Majesty Resort, Muhammed Abu Albar, and he offered to take me around to see the all-inclusive resorts he had designed or updated in Fethiye. In tourism circles, Fethiye is best known for its cerulean lagoon, protected from the Mediterranean by an elongated sandbar. The majority of Fethiye's resorts are assembled around this lagoon, Ölüdeniz (literally, "The Dead Sea" in Turkish). My guide, a native of Saudi Arabia who had moved to Turkey, where he has designed and landscaped all-inclusive resorts for some time, took me to visit several of his projects that reflected his Mediterranean and Middle Eastern sensibilities. An elaborate water fountain in the swimming pool of one of his properties betrayed his Arabian heritage, while a stone facade, with a wooden *çikma* projecting from the second floor, towered over a pool and reception lodge at the Olive Tree Studio. These resorts reinforced the universal propensity to package hotels and resorts in local motifs and architectural patterns as a reflection of regional exoticism for international tourists.

Two additional stops on our tour demonstrated another surprising reality in relation to transcultural currents in resort design around the world. Muhammed informed me that during his early years in Fethiye, he had collaborated with an architect who had a fondness for Mexican- and Spanish-style architecture. At our first stop, he proudly showed me a dramatic open-air lobby, covered by an inverted wooden roof. Heavy, cast-iron light fixtures dangled in the summer breeze. Approximately eighteen months later, while visiting Punta Cana in the Dominican Republic, I felt as if I had returned to Fethiye as I stood under a Dominican-style porte cochere that was built in the same style.

Our next stop, the Club Belcekiz Beach Resort, revealed a Mexican-Mediterranean paradise improbably located in Turkey. Red Spanish tiles covered every structure, and cast-iron bars covered all of the hotel's large windows. White arches and black, cast-iron light fixtures hovered over the wooden floor in the lobby. Narrowly arched doors around the lobby's perimeter betrayed a hint of Moorish influence. Behind the lobby, a series of fountains, arched azaleas covering two walkways, and open-air patio spaces further added to this cross-cultural oasis. A blue-and-white tiled *hamam* (Turkish bath) and an expansive faux Roman amphitheater added Turkish influences to the property. Muhammed's interest in Mexican and Spanish architecture, based on his experience in Fethiye, confirmed the bidirectional flow of cultural influences between the Caribbean and the Mediterranean. The coming years will bring an even more intense globalization of resort design, as corporations and individual hotel owners look for elements to distinguish themselves from competitors. In many cases, these cross-cultural influences will reflect architectural preferences. In other cases, the convergence of resort packaging will stem from global trends in leisure (as can be seen in places such as Dubai). For example, resort hotels in Antalya and other Turkish resort towns have added soccer fields to their properties in order to attract European and Turkish teams to train and engage in "friendly" competition with other teams also spending off-months in Antalya. This same practice appears to be catching on in Mexico as well.

Cozumel/Riviera Maya/Cancún

In August 2006, I traveled to Cozumel and Calica, Mexico, eager to assess the lingering impacts of Hurricane Wilma as well as the prodigious growth of the tourist corridor south of Cancún from Playa Carmen to Tulum. My visit to Cozumel reiterated the physical fragility of many of many peripheral tourism poles, which are vulnerable, on a regular basis, to hurricanes and other forms of catastrophic weather. During October 2005, Hurricane Wilma unleashed its category-five devastation on Cozumel Island, compounding its impact by its apparent unwillingness to leave the island. Less than a year later, I boarded a tender ferry offshore Cozumel, and we made our way through the turquoise waters to the Puerto Maya cruise-ship dock. After stepping off of the ferry and looking to the right, back toward the anchored fleet of cruise ships, I first noticed part of the former pier, still dislocated, in large concrete chunks, against what remained of the pier. While the pier still required significant repair, the adjacent shopping center was open. Workers continued to repair thatched roofs in this postmodern Mexican shopping village, but all of the stores were open. A taxi ride up Rafael Melgar Boulevard, with an astute driver, revealed even more destruction that awaited repairs, including a naval building that was completely demolished. The long-term effects of Hurricane Wilma accounted for the severe drop in the numbers of tourists roaming the streets and main plaza. In the afternoon, we headed to Chankanaab National Park. While the main reception area—including a massive, covered pavilion—had been constructed since the hurricane, much of the park lay in ruins. Coral reefs, famous for their biodiversity and clarity, had been ripped from the bedrock, leaving an unusually dark appearance at the bottom of the sea near the shoreline. Faux statuary relics from a small museum still lay in shambles. Snarled trees dotted the park's entire landscape. Those elements of the park that generated the greatest revenue received the most immediate attention. A contemporary Mexican gift shop was functioning, as was the "dolphin experience." Scores of workers diligently worked on a new swimming pool near the shoreline. Cozumel's progress has been extraordinary, yet the devastating effects of natural disasters, which are compounded by instantaneous media coverage, repackage these one-time paradises in a way that knocks the developmental process back ever farther.

Playa del Carmen, and its adjacent cruise-ship port, Calica, represents the future of Mexican decentralized tourism. Having already surpassed the number of hotel rooms in Cancún, Playa del Carmen and resorts to the south bring together the improbable combination of once-sleepy resort coves and a four-lane freeway between Tulum and Cancún. The port of Calica sits as a future point for major tourism development between Cancún and Chetumal, the state capital of Quintana Roo to the south. Two pay phones, trinket vendors, and a handful of rental cars wait for the day when regional growth south of Playa del Carmen will justify further improvements to the infrastructure and superstructure. X'Caret, a cultural theme park based on Mayan culture and Yucatan landscapes, flanks Calica on its left, waiting for the boom as well. En route to the United States, I watched the shoreline as we sailed by Playa del Carmen and, eventually, Cancún. From Playa del Carmen until the southern reaches of Cancún, the most consistent features on the skyline are those of the infrastructure that links this tourism megalopolis. Electrical transformers stretch north and south, standing out against the skyline as a delicate lifeline, linking points south to Cancún. Miles off of

Cancún, as the sun faded in the sky, a boxlike relief of a major metropolitan city came into view. That was my last view of Cancún and the Riviera Maya. Time will only tell how far south that superstructure will reach, supplanting the spiderlike arms of the emerging infrastructure to the south.

*   *   *

By the turn of the twenty-first century, Cancún, Varadero, and Punta Cana–Bávaro continued to evolve as tourist destinations, but they also reflected the unique political, economic, and social circumstances of their origins. These unique patterns of packaging—reflecting historical realities as much as marketing programs—set these destinations apart in tourism history, as well as offer vital case studies for understanding the context (both policy and nonpolicy factors) within which tourism development takes place. In many ways, for example, Cancún has been the Mexican Mallorca. With clear goals to maximize hotel capacity and attract North American tourists, FONATUR created a model for mass tourism in the Americas. As chapter 7 illustrated, Cancún's own image and FONATUR's priorities there have evolved over time and will continue to do so as its creators seek a more affluent clientele. Furthermore, despite the environmental challenges associated with monumental growth, other Caribbean nations continue to look to Mexico as a model for tourism development as an economic engine. In Cuba, for example, hotel executives and top employees are often involved in training junkets to Cancún. Interviews with high-level Cuban authorities and hotel executives reveal the spell that Cancún and the Riviera Maya's sophisticated tourism infrastructure have cast on its Cuban neighbors.[2] Ultimately, Cancún is undergoing its own transformation, as the limits of growth make sustainable tourism increasingly attractive on its peripheries.[3]

In contrast, Varadero has probably changed less than Cancún during the past twenty years, but its built environment reflected improvements over the aesthetic perils of hotels catering to mass tourism. Part of the continuity exhibited in Varadero's offerings is a reflection of the substantial bureaucratic challenges that hotel franchises and developers face in dealing with the Cuban government. In Mexico, FONATUR serves as the primary conduit to hotel development in the agency's resort developments. In Cuba, however, a multitude of bureaucratic institutions determine whether a project is desirable. Paradoxically, Varadero's low-rise aesthetics have not translated into the triumph of sustainable tourism. Given Cuba's subcontinental dimensions, Varadero's role as the mass tourism capital of Cuba seems assured, while the keys, or *cayos*, have been tapped to host lower-density tourism. As chapter 8 suggested, the future of Cuban tourism, including in Varadero, will probably rest as much on what has already happened there with European investment as it will on what American corporations are dreaming of doing at present.

Finally, Punta Cana, the one locale where sustainable tourism preceded the development of mass tourism (twenty miles north at Bávaro), stands as a hybrid counterpart to Cancún to the west. On the one hand, the founding of Punta Cana signaled an alternative form of tourism to the mass tourism that had come to define Cancún and most of the Caribbean. On the other hand, however, nearby Bávaro, which shared a common airport with Punta Cana, served as the staging ground for the Mallorcan revolution in the Caribbean, beginning in 1984 with the arrival of Barceló. Tempered by the low-rise aesthetics of the region's existing resorts, Bávaro came to embody sprawling hotel communities on sandy beaches offering all-inclusive packages. In many ways, the future of Caribbean tourism rests on the outcome of this apparent paradox: the reconciliation of mass tourism with the urgent need for more sustainable tourism.

In retrospect, historical context provides us—simultaneously—with a localized and global understanding of similarities and differences in the nature of tourism development in the most prominent tourism poles in the Spanish Caribbean. In every case, geographic isolation enhanced the decentralized appeal of Cancún, Varadero, Punta Cana, and Dorado Beach. The advent of jet travel overcame the distance that would have made the locales inaccessible. Similarly, the vertical organization of Spanish tourism operators allowed Europeans to enter a field largely abandoned by American air carriers and hotels. Finally, local politics, particularly in the case of Varadero, created global repercussions as the U.S. government attempted to chasten Europeans for doing business with Cuba. In the end, these historical points of origin provide insight into the political, economic, and social idiosyncrasies and commonalities of Caribbean tourism poles. The ever-changing process of packaging resort destinations will continue to rely on those factors from the past, as much as they will be affected by conditions in the future.

Abbreviations

Organizations, Corporations, and Institutions

AUSCA	Auburn University Special Collections and Archives
CEDOC	Centro de Documentación, Secretaría de Turismo, Mexico City
CMR	Collection Office of Mssrs. Rockefeller
CNHC	Conrad N. Hilton Collection
CSD	Castro Speech Database: www.utexas.edu/la/cb/cuba/castro.html
EP	*El País* (Madrid, Spain)
FDHP	Floyd Hall Papers
FONATUR	Fondo Nacional de Fomento al Turismo
HHC	Hilton Hotel Collection
HHI	Hilton International
HHIN	Hilton International Newsletter
HIA	Hospitality Industry Archive
LN	Lexis Nexis Academic Universe Database: http://academic.lexisnexis.com
NYT	*New York Times*
RAC	Rockefeller Archive Center
RFA	Rockefeller Family Archive

RRI   RockResorts Incorporated
UH   University of Houston

Individuals

CMP   Carlos M. Passalacqua
FDH   Floyd D. Hall
FCR   Fidel Castro
LSR   Laurance S. Rockefeller

Notes

Introduction

1. FCR, "Castro Speech at the Inauguration of the Cienega de Zapata National Park."

2. Medina and Santamarina provide an excellent architectural description of the cabanas at Guamá and Playa Girón in *Turismo de naturaleza en Cuba*, 164–167, 178–180.

3. CEPAL, "Turismo."

4. See, for example, Villamil, "Impacto del turismo."

5. See Merrill, "Negotiating Cold War Paradise," 2.

6. This study is not an analysis of tourism development in the broader Caribbean. The analytical focus remains on the larger, Spanish-speaking Antilles islands and Mexico. These four political entities share a similar window for initiating serious tourism development, mainly between the late 1940s and 1970s.

7. Historian Lester Langley introduced me to the applicability of chaos theory to history.

8. Healy, as quoted in Wilkinson, *Tourism Policy*, 6.

9. The scholarship of the history of tourism development continues to grow, not only for the Caribbean but also throughout the world. In the Caribbean basin (including Florida), see Foglesong, *Married to the Mouse*. Foglesong examines the partnership between Disney and local and state governments in creating and operating Disney World. More recently, Mormino's *Land of Sunshine* explores the evolution of tourism development in the post–World War II era in Florida. One of the most elegant treatments of tourism development in the Caribbean is Schwartz's *Pleasure Island*. Schwartz illustrates the role that government and business decisions on the local level in Havana played in creating the image of a cultured and then more vulgar tourist pole in the first half of the twentieth century. Berger examines early Mexican state tourism promotion in *Pyramids by Day*.

10. Ioannides examines the evolution of centralized hotel and tourist zones in decentralized locations in the Mediterranean, citing Palma de Mallorca as one example, in "Tourism Development," 75–78. The metropolitan evolution of a peripheral tourism pole landed Cancún in an anthology focused on urban tourism. See Hiernaux-Nicolas, "Cancún Bliss," 124–142.

11. See Potter, *Room with a World View*, 8–57.

12. Soriano Frade offers an excellent narrative history of tourism development in Mallorca in his *Pequeña historia del turismo*.

13. Seguí Llinas, *Les Baleares*, 8.

14. I want to thank Francesca Rainieri and Frank Elías Rainieri, both of Grupo Puntacana, and Alberto Freitas, formerly with the company, for their input on why Spanish and other European-based companies have done so well in the Caribbean.

15. See Hayes, *Beauty, Health, and Permanence*.

16. Sans, *Alvaro Sans*.

17. FCR, "President Fidel Castro's Children's Day Speech."

18. Tewarie, "Development of a Sustainable Tourism," 41.

19. Wilkinson, *Tourism Policy*, 5.

Prologue

1. See Crystal, "Alexander Girard's Dream Village"; see also Gueft, "Inn of the Sun," 88–99.

2. Wilhelm, *John Wilhelm's Guide to Mexico*, 20.

3. The *Braniff Pages* catalog Calder's artistry.

4. Romero, *My Mexico City and Yours*, 140–143.

5. Willy, "Continental Hilton," 19.

Chapter 1. The Rockefellers

1. Rockefeller, "Memorandum on Post-War Planning."

2. Bottome, "Report Concerning the Construction and Operation of a Hotel in Caracas."

3. Ibid.

4. Abramovitz to Harrison and Fouilhoux, March 2, 1940.

5. Lane to Bottome, n.d.

6. Coles to Turnbull, January 12, 1945.

7. Coles to Turnbull, November 30, 1945.

8. Coles to Nelson A. Rockefeller, August 17, 1942.

9. Robbins to Nelson A. Rockefeller, March 1, 1940.

10. Coles to Turnbull, December 28, 1942.

11. Coles to Turnbull, June 24, 1946.

12. Coles to Turnbull, October 22, 1945.

13. Coles, "Notes on Venezuelan Revolution."

14. "A Is for Avila."

15. Winks, *Laurance S. Rockefeller*, 67, 68.

16. Ibid., 56.

17. "Resort Building in Undeveloped Areas," 102.

18. Winks, *Laurance S. Rockefeller*, 62.

19. Kaplan, "Rockefeller Offers U.S. a Virgin Island Park."

20. RRI, "Fact Sheet: Dorado Beach Hotel and Golf Club."

21. RRI, Press Release, August 2, 1954.

22. Fields, "Only Human."

23. RRI, "Fact Sheet: Caneel Bay Plantation."

24. RRI, "Fact Sheet: Dorado Beach Hotel and Golf Club."

25. Ibid.

26. RRI, "Fact Sheet: Caneel Bay Plantation."

27. RRI, "Fact Sheet: Dorado Beach Hotel and Golf Club."

28. Kennedy, "Puerto Rico," 299.

Chapter 2. Conrad Hilton

1. See Hilton, "Un Hotel Continental." Portions of this speech are also quoted in Hilton, *Be My Guest*, 266.

2. *Fortune Magazine* eds., *Changing American Market*, 200–213.

3. Romoli, *Colombia*, 209.

4. Houser, "Statement to the Committee on Foreign Affairs"; Pan American Airways, *Annual Report* (1946), 7, 9; Hilton, *Be My Guest*, 232–233. Wise discusses the rise of government-aided hotels around the world in "Global Hosts," 1, 9.

5. "Hotel Chain with Wings," 167.

6. Hilton, *Be My Guest*, 236.

7. Parker, "'TenSHUN!' Eyes South!"

8. "General Kincaid Stresses Tourist Opportunities," 71.

9. Strand, "Globalization," 10.

10. Hilton's management strategies have been the subject of numerous articles and books. Hilton discusses his innovations in *Be My Guest*, 259–260. See also *Hotel Management*, July 1947 (the issue was subtitled "The Inside Story of C. N. Hilton and His Hotels"); and Hughes, "Hilton's 'Private Statesmanship,'" 31–38.

11. See Strand, "Lessons of a Lifetime," 83–95.

12. Baird offers an in-depth discussion of Hilton International contracts in "Egypt's Modern Hotels," 67–114.

13. Meek, "Hotels of Latin America," February 1953, 37.

14. Baird, "From the Waldorf-Astoria to the Caribé Hotel," 26.

15. Baird, "Oral History Interview with Appendices of Curt Strand," 35

16. Ibid., 16.

17. Ibid., 7.

18. Baird, "Oral History with Udo Schlentrich," 7.

19. Ibid., 8.

20. Meek, "Hotels of Latin America," March 1953, 28.

21. "Monthly Master List."

22. Radio Reports, Inc., "Caribé Hilton Hotel [Is] Very Beautiful."

23. *Hilton Hotel International News* (*HHIN*), November 1960, December 1960, March 1961, July 1961, December 1961, February 1961.

24. See Wharton, *Building the Cold War*. Contemporary newspaper articles examined the phenomenon of the new, modern hotels. See Louchheim, "New Design Proves Worth in Hotels," 1; and Friedlander, "Warm West Indies." The Caribé Hilton particularly merited attention for its architectural achievements. See "Bold New Design for San Juan Hotel"; "1950s Hotel Accommodations"; Shellaby, "Puerto Rico's New Hotel Epitomizes Island Quest"; "'Custom Built' Room Temperatures"; and "Spectacular Luxury in the Caribbean."

25. Baird, "From the Waldorf-Astoria to the Caribé Hotel," 36–37.

26. Ibid.

27. Beard, "Art of Dining Out," 7.

28. Baird, "Oral History with Udo Schlentrich," 3.

29. Bradshaw, "View from the Tall Glass Oasis," 128.

30. "Hotel Furnishings Go by Air Freight"; "Big Air Freight Movement."

31. "1950s Hotel Accommodations," 39.

32. Ibid., 40.

33. Romero, *My Mexico City and Yours*, 59–60.

34. "Habana Hilton," *Hotel Industry*.

35. "Habana Hilton," *Hotel Bulletin*, 18.

36. Hamilton to Hilton, August 9, 1951.

37. Strand, "Globalization," 9.

38. Willy, "Continental Hilton," 46–47.

39. Ibid., 48.

40. "Tavern Talk."

41. HHI, "Minutes of Special Meeting."

42. Welton Becket and Associates, "Havana Hilton—Artwork."

43. Baird, "Oral History Interview of Sid Wilner," 33.

44. Hilton, "Hotels International," 2.

45. Bradshaw, "View from a Tall Glass Oasis," 126–127.

46. Hilton, "Hotels International," 6.

47. Houser, "How Hotels and Travel Contribute to International Understanding," 37.

48. Joseph, "Around the World," 8–9.

49. This limited survey suggests that the international patronage of Hilton International hotels was significant. Conrad Hilton notes in *Be My Guest* that during April 1957, "men from thirty-eight countries [stayed at the Istanbul Hilton], three behind the Iron Curtain, had been guests there. Thirty-five per cent came from the United States but there were visitors from Bulgaria, China, Pakistan, all over Europe, Thailand, Trinidad, India. And I found myself hoping that they had found time at least to drink a cup of coffee together" (266).

50. *HHIN*, November 1960, 5; December 1960, 3 and 5; February 1961, 3 and 5.

Chapter 3. Cathedrals of Chaos

1. *HHIN*, November 1960, 4.

2. Ibid., February 1961, 4.

3. Ibid., October–November 1961, 7.

4. Bolton, "How a Man, Hotel Took the 'Quake."

5. Romero, *My Mexico City and Yours*, 60.

6. Baird, "Oral History Interview with Appendices of Curt Strand," 36.

7. Baird discussion with Rodolfo Casparius in ibid., 36. Former Mexican president Miguel Alemán Valdés (1946–1952) not only served as landowner for Hilton properties in Mexico but also transformed Mexican tourism in the mid-twentieth century, particularly with his development of Acapulco. See Romero, *Miguel Alemán Valdés*.

8. Casparius, a Hilton International labor counselor, wrote a very detailed account of the efforts of the Hilton staff to cater not only to the guests at the hotel but also to the revolutionaries who took up lodging on the premises. See Elminger to Hilton, January 7, 1959.

9. Habana Hilton, "Emergency Staff Meeting."

10. Baird, "Oral History Interview of Sid Wilner," 14.

11. HHI, "Castro Assures Welcome to American Tourists." The memo also includes a hand-signed copy of Castro's statement.

12. Battelle, "Smile Behind the Beards," 25.

13. Caverly to Hilton, February 1, 1959.

14. Elminger to Hilton, July 27, 1959.

15. Radio Reports, Inc., "Paar Tells of Visit to Cuba."

16. Caverly to Hilton, February 11, 1959. Caverly, one month removed from his initial visit with Castro, criticized Castro for his inability to take responsibility for running the country. "Castro himself has become unapproachable," he noted to Hilton.

17. Ibid.

18. Baird, "Oral History Interview of Sid Wilner," 15, my emphasis.

19. Hilton to Elminger, November 21, 1959.

20. Elminger to Hilton, November 23, 1959.

21. See Lefever and Baird, "Expropriation of the Habana Hilton," 14–20.

22. See FCR, "Castro Speech to the Food Industry Workers," 5–20; see also FCR, "Castro Speaks to Hotel Workers Union."

23. Caverly, "Reservations for the Havana Hilton Hotel"; Joseph to General Managers, "Habana Hilton Materials."

24. See Loving, "Hilton International," for a discussion of Hilton's growth under TWA.

25. Meek, "Hotels of Latin America," February 1953, 38.

26. Casparius, *Turismo*, 193, 194.

27. See Barron Hilton, "Foreword," in Hilton, *Be My Guest*, 6–8.

Chapter 4. Dorado Beach

1. Weber to FDH, September 29, 1967.
2. FDH to Weber, October 3, 1967.
3. Weber to FDH, October 6, 1967.
4. See Maldonado, *Teodoro Moscoso.*
5. LSR, "Speech at the Opening of Dorado Beach Hotel," 10.
6. Canino Salgado, *Dorado, Puerto Rico*, 103–134.
7. Whitman to Schutt, January 19, 1953.
8. LSR, "Speech at the Opening of Dorado Beach Hotel," 2–3.
9. Schutt to LSR, May 29, 1953.
10. LSR to Schutt, June 23, 1953. In a later letter to Brunner, Rockefeller noted that Schutt's plans were "too pretentious and too expensive to execute by Ted Moscoso."
11. LSR to Moscoso, July 30, 1953.
12. Rodríguez to LSR, August 11, 1953.
13. Jennen to LSR, August 19, 1953.
14. LSR, "Speech at the Opening of the Dorado Beach Hotel," 3.
15. Boyer to CMP, December 1, 1953.
16. See Canino Salgado, *Dorado, Puerto Rico*, 205.
17. CMP to LSR, December 29, 1953.
18. Ibid., 3.
19. Ibid., 5–6.
20. Jennen to LSR, January 5, 1954.
21. Goldstone to LSR, January 11, 1954.
22. LSR to CMP, January 18, 1954.
23. CMP to LSR, January 27, 1954.
24. CMP to LSR, March 4, 1954.
25. LSR to CMP, March 11, 1954.
26. CMP to LSR, March 11, 1954.
27. Moscoso to LSR, March 9, 1954.
28. LSR to CMP, March 12, 1954.
29. CMP to LSR, March 16, 1954.
30. LSR to CMP, March 25, 1954.
31. "Study of a New Deal."
32. Boyer to LSR, June 3, 1954.
33. LSR to CMP, August 6, 1954.
34. CMP to LSR, August 19, 1954.
35. CMP to LSR, October 6, 1954.
36. Moscoso to LSR, December 29, 1954.
37. See Boyer to LSR, February 28, 1955.
38. LSR to CMP, December 1955.
39. CMP to LSR, January 20, 1956.
40. LSR to CMP, February 6, 1957.

41. LSR to CMP, February 28, 1957.

42. Villamil, "Planning, Tourism, and the Environment," 2–3.

43. All quotes from the inauguration are from LSR, "Speech at the Opening of Dorado Beach Hotel."

Chapter 5. A Second Marriage

1. LSR, "Speech at the Opening of Dorado Beach Hotel."

2. See "Dorado Beach Hotel" and "Dorado Beach Hotel, Recalculated Operating Results."

3. Stone and Webster, "Appraisal of Property."

4. Eastern Airlines, "Response to 'Appraisal of Property.'"

5. "Memorandum of Agreement between Laurance S. Rockefeller and Eastern Airlines."

6. LSR and Cole to FDH, December 1, 1958.

7. RRI, "Five Year Financial Projection."

8. A copy of the master plan and an acreage breakdown per type of structure are contained in FDHP, RG 488, Series 4, Box 51, Folder 3, "RockResorts, Dorado Beach—Trip, 1969," AUSCA.

9. Harris, Kerr, Forster, and Company, "Economic Study of a Proposed Resort Hotel," 11.

10. Ibid., 6.

11. Ibid., 30.

12. Ibid., 13.

13. Ibid., 11–12.

14. Ibid., 19.

15. Ibid., 23, 33.

16. Dorado Beach Hotel Corporation, "Minutes of Meeting of the Board of Directors," September 18, 1969.

17. Dorado Beach Hotel Corporation, "Dorado Beach/Brenas Beach Hotels," February 3, 1970.

18. Dorado Beach Development Inc., "Minutes of Meeting of the Board of Directors." Neiman Marcus later declined to participate in the proposed deal.

19. Coleman of Eastern Airlines outlines the need to infuse approximately $10 million into the Cerromar Hotel in his letter to Simons, "Capital Contributions—Cerromar Hotel and Related Projects."

20. The star-studded grand opening is discussed by Gonzales in "Nuevo hotel atraerá más convenciones a PR," 10. The guests at the grand opening, as well as the activities for those attending, are outlined in "VIP List." Other events of notoriety, such as the 1972 Miss USA Pageant and the 1972 Miss Universe Pageant, were also calculated to bring publicity and prestige to the hotel, but backfired. During the 1972 Miss USA Pageant, for example, bombs planted by extremist political factions exploded outside of the hotel during the event.

21. See RRI, "Minutes of the Meeting of the Board of Directors," July 14, 1969.

22. RRI, "Meeting of the Board of Directors," November 10, 1969.

23. RRI, "Minutes of the Meeting of the Board of Directors," April 14, 1970.

24. Coleman to Howard, "Hotel Operations—Profits and Cash Flows," August 11, 1970.

25. Howard to FDH, "Hotel Operations—Profits and Cash Flows."

26. Holtzman to FDH, January 5, 1970.

27. RRI, "Recap of 536 Questionnaires."

28. Hucks, "Recommendations on a Master Plan for Excess Dorado Properties," 11.

29. Ibid., 12.

30. Ibid., 13–14.

31. Description of the condominiums has been adapted from Dorado Beach Estates, Inc., *Villa Dorado Resort Condominiums*; and Holtzman, "Impact of Resort Hotels on Real Estate."

32. Dorado Beach Estates, Inc., "Minutes of Meeting of the Board of Directors," March 14, 1972.

33. Simons to FDH, "Cerromar and Villa Dorado Projects."

34. Coleman to Glass, "Villa Dorado Condominium Project."

35. Simons to FDH, "Dorado Properties."

36. Simons to FDH, "Hotel Status Report."

37. Simons to FDH, "Profit Plan Review—Hotels."

38. Squire to Cramer, March 16, 1973.

39. Dorado Beach Development, Inc., "Agenda for Meeting of the Board of Directors," August 28, 1974.

40. Dorado Beach Estates, Inc., "Minutes of Meeting of the Board of Directors," February 19, 1975, 36.

41. Dorado Beach Development, Inc., "Summer Marketing Report."

42. Simons to FDH, "L. S. Rockefeller Visit with Governor Colón."

43. RRI, "Minutes of the Meeting of the Board of Directors," October 6, 1975.

44. Dorado Beach Corporation, "Agenda for Meeting of the Board of Directors," November 24, 1975.

45. *NYT*, January 1, 1975. p. 36

46. Dorado Beach Corporation, "Agenda for Meeting of the Board of Directors," November 24, 1975.

47. "Can Frank Borman Make Eastern Take Off?"

48. Loercher, "Dorado Beach in Summer."

49. Bell, "Problems Facing the Hotel Industry," 4.

50. Ibid., 3, 4–5.

51. Ibid., 1.

52. Ibid., 3.

Chapter 6. Destination Cuba!

1. *I Am Cuba.*

2. Pérez, *On Becoming Cuban*; Schwartz, *Pleasure Island*; Cirules, *Empire of Havana*; Villalba Garrido, *Cuba y el turismo*.

3. Truslow, *Report on Cuba*.

4. Ibid., 766.

5. Ibid., 767.

6. Ibid., 768.

7. Ibid., 769.

8. Ibid., 768.

9. Ibid., 770.

10. Ibid., 771.

11. Ibid., 772.

12. Ibid., 498

13. Ibid., 776.

14. Cirules, *Empire of Havana*, 153.

15. Ibid., 154.

16. Villalba Garrido, *Cuba y el turismo*, 52.

17. Maribona, *Turismo y ciudadania*; Maribona, *Turismo en Cuba*.

18. Villalba Garrido, *Cuba y el turismo*, 57

19. Ibid., 57–58.

20. Ibid., 58.

21. Maribona, *Turismo y ciudadania*, 85–86.

22. Maribona, *Turismo en Cuba*, 210.

23. Ibid., 66.

24. Maribona, *Turismo y ciudadania*, 137.

25. Ibid.

26. Ibid., 81.

27. Ibid., 82.

28. Maribona, *Turismo en Cuba*, 92.

29. Ibid., 93.

30. Ibid., 94.

31. Pérez, *On Becoming Cuban*, 492.

32. Ibid., 483.

33. FCR, "4 Hour TV Appearance."

34. "Acomete Cuba plan de turismo."

35. "Dedican 20 millones de pesos."

36. FCR, "Castro in Interview Attacks Eisenhower."

37. FCR, "President Fidel Castro's Children's Day Speech."

38. INIT, *El sol de Cuba*.

39. Ibid., 4.

40. Ibid., 15.

41. Republic of Cuba, "Constitución política de la República de Cuba," Chapter 6, Article 43.

42. Varela, "Tropicollage."

43. For an overview of restoration efforts in Havana, see Rodríguez Alomá and Ochoa, *Desafío de una utopia*.

44. Author's e-mail communication with anonymous Cuban tourism official, February 19, 2004.

45. Maribona, *Turismo en Cuba*, 13.

Chapter 7. Visions of Cancún

1. Gann, *In an Unknown Land*, 148–153.

2. Martin and Martin, *Standard Guide to Mexico*, 307.

3. Barbachano Gómez Rul, "Hechos biográficos complementarios."

4. Consejo Nacional de Turismo, *Incorporación del turismo del caribé al sureste de México*, 12–13.

5. Ibid., 26.

6. Ibid., 33.

7. Ibid., 27.

8. Ibid., 68.

9. Ibid., 70.

10. Ibid., 106.

11. Ibid., 152, 153.

12. Ibid., 154.

13. Ibid., 161. With reference to the golf course, the Consejo Nacional de Turismo report observed, "In the United States there are six million persons that play golf, which constitutes an attraction in that country. In Europe they are building large golf courses and in Mexico their construction should be encouraged, [and this will be] a motive to stimulate foreign tourists to visit us" (168).

14. Ward, "'This Great Show Window.'"

15. Consejo Nacional de Turismo, *Incorporación del turismo del caribé al sureste de México*, 166, 167.

16. Ibid., 170, 171.

17. Booz, Allen, y Thompson, *Estudio general del desarrollo del turismo en México*, xx.

18. Ibid., 173.

19. Ibid., 179.

20. Ibid., 174, 176.

21. Ibid., 179.

22. Ortiz Mena, *El desarrollo estabilizador*, 221–225.

23. Fondo de Promoción de Infraestructura Turística, "Proyecto de desarrollo turístico en Cancún," 4, 8.

24. Ibid., 6–7.

25. Ibid., 10–11.

26. Ibid., 14.

27. Ibid., 16.

28. Ibid.

29. Banco Interamericano de Desarrollo, "México," 91.

30. Ibid., 72–73.

31. Ibid., 77.

32. Secretaría de Asentamientos Humanos y Obras Públicas, "Bases para la formulación del programa de dotación de infraestructura para centros turísticos."

33. FONATUR, *Cancún*, 26.

34. Ibid., 51.

35. Ibid., 52, 54, 55.

36. Ibid., 56.

37. Ibid., 62.

38. Ibid., 74.

39. Ibid., 70.

40. Ibid., 73, 75, 97, 98–99, 100, 102.

41. FONATUR, "Quintana Roo, Cancún," ix, 20, 47.

42. Ibid., 78.

43. Ibid., 81.

44. Ibid., 98.

45. Ibid., 103.

46. Ibid., 105.

47. Ibid., 106.

48. Ibid., 94.

49. Ibid., 97.

50. Ibid., 126, 129, 130.

51. Ibid., 133.

52. Dirección Adjunta de Desarrollo, "Centros Integralmente Planeados," 2.

53. Ibid., 2–5.

54. Ibid., 6–13.

55. "Reunión de evaluación de los efectos del huracán Emily."

56. Cobar, *Cancún está de pie*.

57. "Reunión que encabezó el Presidente Vicente Fox con empresarios hoteleros de Quintana Roo."

58. Ibid.

59. Cobar, *Cancún está de pie*, 154–155, 157.

60. Cobar, e-mail.

61. *El Universal* (Mexico City), "Cancún busca recuperar las pérdidas provocadas por el huracán Wilma."

Chapter 8. A Means of Last Resort

1. Blanco to Gomez, April 1898.

2. FCR, "Mass Rally at Girón Victory Square."

3. Ibid.

4. For a definitive overview of Escarrer's life, see Uriol Alvarez, *Sol Meliá*.

5. Molina, "Questions for Historians"; Cánaves, author's e-mail interview.

6. *La Provincia*, "El Grupo Martiñon."

7. Vincent, "Fidel Castro."

8. EFE, "Cuba-España: Presidente Autonomia Balear visita Varadero."

9. EFE, "Presidente Autonomia Balear se reunión [*sic*] seis horas con Castro"; EFE, "Presidente communidad Canaria se entrevistó con Fidel Castro."

10. Cánaves, author's e-mail interview.

11. FCR, "Castro Discusses Tourism Plans, Medical Issues."

12. FCR, "Castro Speaks at Partnership Hotel Inauguration."

13. FCR, "Fidel Castro Speaks at Hotel Opening 14 December."

14. Ibid.

15. "Nature in Harmony with Tourism Development."

16. FCR, "Castro, Delegates Comment at Havana PCC Meeting."

17. Ibid.

18. Ibid.

19. Ibid.

20. Morley to Aronson, "Cuba's Declining Trade Prospects."

21. Pisani, "Cuban Trade Caught in Battle for Florida Vote."

22. Rodríguez Parrilla, "Measure to Eliminate International Terrorism."

23. See Roy, *Cuba, the United States, and the Helms-Burton Doctrine.*

24. Vincent, "La Helms-Burton amenaza."

25. "Spanish Companies in Crossfire of U.S.-Cuba Battle."

26. *EP,* "La lista negra."

27. Ibid.

28. Vincent, "Sol Meliá ampliará inversiones en Cuba."

29. "U.S. Won't Punish Spanish Group."

30. Administración del Senado, "Informe sobre las relaciones con Cuba."

31. The United States established a Registry of Claims at the same time in order to facilitate the due process of reclamations by Cuban exiles.

32. Martínez, "Castro denuncia que EE.UU."

33. Gonzales and Manzano, "Presiones y intereses."

34. *EP,* "EEUU aplica la ley Helms Burton a Club Med y a la alemana LTE."

35. Vincent, "La Helms-Burton amenaza."

36. Arrieta, "Los hoteleros."

37. Radio Havana, *BBC Summary of World Broadcasts.*

38. The governor of the Balearic Islands, Francesc Antich Oliver, vowed to "do what is necessary to not leave these businesses without support that operate 'outside of Spain.'" EFE, "Empresas-Meliá."

39. Cortes Generales, "Diario de sesiones del congreso de los diputados, comisiones."

40. Ibid.

41. Ibid.

42. Helms to Pickering, November 16, 2000.

43. Cano, "Negocios, sí."

Chapter 9. Punta Cana

1. See Morales Troncoso, "El turismo en el caribe," 114.

2. Ibid.

3. *Fodor's 1960 Guide to the Caribbean, Bahamas, and Bermuda* showered praises

on the "new" Santo Domingo. "The new Ciudad Trujillo is in its way as impressive as the old. Its tone is set by the Avenida George Washington, a magnificent palm-lined boulevard, punctuated by the Trujillo-Hull Monument and the white obelisk that reminds every visitor of the Washington Monument in the U.S. capital." Despite a multitude of activities in the city, including botanical gardens, a zoo, and other cultural amenities, decentralized tourism remained largely off limits. "Excursions outside of Ciudad Trujillo are currently somewhat circumscribed by the government's security program," the guide noted (333–334).

4. There are several important historical works related to the evolution of Dominican tourism. See, for example, Miolan, *Turismo*; Miolan, *Datos para la historia del turismo de la República Dominicana*; Llado, *Turismo y desarrollo*; and Jiménez, *El turismo en la República Dominicana*.

5. H. Zinder and Associates, *Outlook for Tourism in the Dominican Republic*.

6. Arespacochaga y Felipe, *Desarrollo turístico regional de Cartagena*.

7. Arespacochaga y Felipe, *República Dominicana*.

8. H. Zinder and Associates, *Outlook for Tourism in the Dominican Republic*, 7.

9. Ibid., 8.

10. Ibid., 11.

11. Ibid., 20.

12. Ibid., 36–37.

13. Ibid., 60.

14. Ibid., 63.

15. Ibid., 61.

16. Ibid., 62, 64.

17. Ibid., 70.

18. Ibid., 71–72, 73.

19. Ibid., 75–76.

20. Ibid., 78–79.

21. Ibid., 87.

22. Ibid., 88.

23. Arespacochaga y Felipe, *República Dominicana*, 20, 21.

24. Ibid., 53.

25. Ibid., 55.

26. Ibid. INFRATUR discusses its early development accomplishments at Boca Chica and Puerto Plata in "La experiencia del fondo," 171–182.

27. Pearson, author's interview.

28. Arespacochaga y Felipe, *República Dominicana*, 56.

29. Ibid., 57.

30. "Dunlop and Meany Own Shares."

31. For an excellent contemporary overview of Rainieri and Grupo Puntacana, see Gupta and Gupta, *Natural Way of Business*.

32. Frank Elías Rainieri, author's interview.

33. Arespacochaga y Felipe, *República Dominicana*, 45–46.

34. Francesca Rainieri, author's interview.

35. Gupta and Gupta, *Natural Way of Business*, 18.

36. Ibid., 30, 31.

37. Alba and Zemialkowski, author's interview.

38. Gupta and Gupta, *Natural Way of Business*, 26.

39. Ibid., 36, 38.

40. Grupo Puntacana, "Reglamentos protectores de Punta Cana Resort," 16.

41. Ibid., 18, 19, 21, 22.

42. Ibid., 28, 29.

43. Ibid., 24.

44. Ibid., 36.

45. Ibid., 24.

46. Ibid., 24, 25.

47. Soriano Frade provides an excellent history of tourism development in the Baleares in *Pequeña historia del turismo en las Baleares*; Ana Belén Ramón Rodriguez explores the financial aspects of Spain's internationalization of hotel services in her doctoral thesis, "La internacionalización de la industria hotelera española." Journalistic accounts of the expansion of Mallorcan hotel firms into Latin America abound, particularly in the Spanish press. See, for example, *Expansión* (Madrid), "Baleares."

48. Sans, author's e-mail interview.

49. Sans, *Alvaro Sans*.

50. See Barceló, "Empresas Barceló."

51. Frank Elías Rainieri, author's interview.

52. Vidal Suárez, "Desarrollo y expansión internacional."

53. Asociación Nacional de Hoteles y Restaurantes, "Oferta habitacional en la zona de Bávaro–Punta Cana."

54. Asociación Nacional de Hoteles y Restaurantes, *Estadísticas selecionadas del sector turismo*, 35.

55. On at least one occasion, Gabriel Escarrer, CEO of Sol Meliá, warned about the decline of infrastructure and environmental conditions in the Dominican Republic due to uncontrolled growth. This has been a common complaint in the Bávaro sector of Punta Cana–Bávaro. See *Expansión* (Madrid), "Gabriel Escarrer."

56. Francesca Rainieri, author's interview.

57. Frank Elías Rainieri, author's interview.

58. Ramírez, author's interview.

59. Alba and Zemialkowski, author's interview.

60. Kheel, author's interview.

61. Pearson, author's interview.

Epilogue.

1. Pagden, *European Encounters with the New World*, 51–52.

2. Interviews conducted by the author with Cuban tourism and hotel officials, February 2004.

3. See FONATUR, *30 años de inversión*.

Bibliography

Abramovitz, Max, to Wallace Harrison and André Fouilhoux. Letter, March 2, 1940. Collection Office of Mssrs. Rockefeller (CMR), RG III 2C, Series Business Interests (BI), Box 110, Folder 820, Rockefeller Archive Center (RAC), Pocantico Hills, N.Y.

"Acomete Cuba plan de turismo por 200 millones de dolares." *Diario de la Marina*, September 10, 1959. Caribbean Newspaper Imaging Project, George A. Smathers Libraries, University of Florida, Gainesville.

Administración del Senado (Spain). "Informe sobre las relaciones con Cuba. Boletín oficial de las cortes generales, Senado, VI legislatura." Serie I: *Boletín General*, March 17, 1997. www.senado.es/boletines/I0169.html, accessed April 19, 2007.

"A Is for Avila." *Caracas Daily Journal*, March 25, 1966. CMR, RG III 2C, Series BI, Box 109, Folder 818, RAC.

Alba, Francisco, and Walter Zemialkowski. Interview by author, January 23, 2006

Apostolopoulos, Yorghos, and Dennis J. Gayle, eds. *Island Tourism and Sustainable Development: Caribbean, Pacific, and Mediterranean Experiences.* Westport, Conn.: Praeger, 2002.

Arespacochaga y Felipe, A. *Desarrollo turístico regional de Cartagena: Colómbia.* Paris: UNESCO, 1968.

———. *República Dominicana: Desarrollo turístico.* Paris: UNESCO, 1968.

Arrieta, Olatz. "Los hoteleros de EE UU premian a Sol Meliá y el Gobierno investiga sus inversions en Cuba." *Ideal*, November 10, 1999. http://www.cubanet.org/CNews/y99/nov99/10o19.htm, accessed April 19, 2007.

Asociación Nacional de Hoteles y Restaurantes. "Oferta habitacional en establecimientos de alojamiento turístco según los numeros de habitaciones, año 2003." *Estadísticas selecionadas del sector turismo del año 2003*, 35.

———. "Oferta habitacional en la zona de Bávaro–Punta Cana, años 1980–2005 (no incluye Bayahibe)."

Baird, Cathleen D. "Egypt's Modern Hotels: From the Historic Shepherd's to the Nile Hilton." Master's thesis, University of Houston.

———. "From the Waldorf-Astoria to the Caribé Hotel and Back: An Oral History Interview with Frank G. Wangeman, 'Hotelman Extraordinaire.'" Parts 1 and 2: October 21, 1992, and December 6, 1993; April 27–28, 1994. HIA, UH.

———. "An Oral History Interview of Sid Wilner." August 1, 1994. HIA, UH.

———. "An Oral History Interview with Appendices of Curt Strand, President, retired, Hilton International Hotels." Parts 1 and 2: October 21, 1992, and December 6, 1993. HIA, UH.

———. "Oral History with Udo Schlentrich." December 23, 1993. HIA, UH.

Banco Interamericano de Desarrollo. "México: Préstamo a Nacional Financiera, S.A. proyecto de infraestructura turística en Cancún." June 14, 1971. CEDOC.

Barbachano Gómez Rul, Fernando. "Hechos biográficos complementarios." http://fernandobarbachano.com, accessed April 19, 2007.

Barceló, Gabriel. "Empresas Barceló: De Felanitx al mundo." Speech to the Fundaciaó Cátedra Iberoamericana, Universitat de les Illes Balears, April 21, 2002. www.uib.es/catedra_iberoamericana/pdf/barcelo_cast.pdf, accessed April 21, 2007.

Battelle, Phyllis. "Smile Behind the Beards." *New York Journal-American*, January 12, 1959, 25. HHC, CNHC, Box 10, Folder 12, HIA, UH.

Beard, James. "The Art of Dining Out." [In the paid advertisement entitled "Come Enter the Wonderful World of Hilton Hotels."] *NYT*, May 25, 1958.

Bell, Charles A. "The Problems Facing the Hotel Industry in the Caribbean: A Summary of Remarks Offered to the Panel of Problems of Financing and Refinancing Hotels at the Caribbean Tourism Conference." January 9–11, 1975. FDHP, RG 488, Series 4, Box 51, Folder 6, AUSCA.

Berger, Dina. *Pyramids by Day, Martinis by Night: The Development and Promotion of Mexico's Tourism Industry, 1928–1946*. New York: Palgrave MacMillan, 2006.

"Big Air Freight Movement: $700,000 Worth of Furniture Shipped to New Puerto Rican Hotel on Planes." *New York Sun*, November 7, 1949. HIA, UH.

Blanco, Ramón, Capitán General de Cuba, to Máximo Gomez. Letter, April 1898. Exhibit in the Palacio de los Capitanes Generales, Havana.

"Bold New Design for San Juan Hotel: New Hotel That Will Soon Welcome Visitors to Puerto Rico." *NYT*, October 23, 1949. HIA, UH.

Bolton, Whitney. "How a Man, Hotel Took the 'Quake." *Morning Telegraph*, August 6, 1957. HIA, UH.

Booz, Allen, and Thompson, S.A. de C.V. *Estudio general del desarrollo del turismo en México*. Mexico City: Impulsora de Empresas Turísticas, S.A. de C.V., 1968.

Bottome, Robert. "Report Concerning the Construction and Operation of a Hotel in Caracas, Venezuela." September 19, 1939. Nelson A. Rockefeller Collection, RG 2C, Series BI, Box 109, RAC.

———, to Nelson A. Rockefeller. Letter, May 1940. CMR, RG III 2C, Series BI, Box 110, Folder 823, RAC.

Boyer, Allston, to CMP. Letter, December 1, 1953. RFC, RG 2, Series AE: LSR, Box 9, Folder "Livingston—Dorado Financing—PRIDCO," RAC.

———, to LSR. Letter, June 3, 1954. RFC, RG 2, Series AE: LSR, Box 9, Folder "Livingston—Dorado Financing—PRIDCO," RAC.

———, to LSR. Letter, February 28, 1955. RFC, RG 2, Series AE: LSR, Box 9, Folder "Livingston—Dorado Financing—PRIDCO," RAC.

Bradshaw, George. "The View from a Tall Glass Oasis: The Subliminal Pleasures of Hilton Hotels." *Vogue*, July 1965, 82, 126–128.

Braniff Pages. www.braniffpages.com, accessed April 23, 2007.

Cánaves, Gabriel. Author's e-mail interview. March 4, 2004.

"Can Frank Borman Make Eastern Take Off?" *Business Week*, December 22, 1975. LN.

Canino Salgado, Marcelino J. *Dorado, Puerto Rico: Historia, cultura, biografías, y lecturas*. Dominican Republic: Editora Corripio, C. por A., 1993.

Cano, Antonio. "Negocios, sí; en Cuba, también." *EP*, February 8, 1996.

"The Caribé Hilton: An Object Lesson in What You Can Do with $7,000,000." *Interiors*, April 1950, 74–87.

Casparius, Rodolfo. *Turismo, La Opción!* Mexico City, 1982.

Castro, Fidel. "Castro, Delegates Comment at Havana PCC Meeting," Tele-Rebelde Network Transcript, November 17, 1993. CSD.

———. "Castro Discusses Camping in Pinar del Rio Province." Cubavision Network Transcript, May 17, 1996. CSD.

———. "Castro Discusses Tourism Plans, Medical Issues." Tele-Rebelde Network Transcript, September 26, 1988. CSD.

———. "Castro in Interview Attacks Eisenhower." Radio Centro (Havana) Transcript, April 23, 1960. CSD.

———. "Castro Speaks at Hotel Opening 14 December." Tele-Rebelde Network Transcript, December 14, 1991. CSD.

———. "Castro Speaks at Partnership Hotel Inauguration." *Havana Cuba Vision*, Transcript, May 10, 1990. CSD.

———. "Castro Speaks to Hotel Workers Union." Radio Progreso Transcript, June 16, 1960. CSD.

———. "Castro Speech at the Inauguration of the Cienega de Zapata National Park." *Revolución*, July 28, 1961. CSD.

———. "Castro Speech to the Food Industry Workers." *Obra Revolucionaria*, no. 9 (June 16, 1960): 5–20. CSD.

———. "4 Hour TV Appearance." Telegram, Havana Embassy to Secretary of State, no. 1004. February 20, 1959. CSD.

———. "Mass Rally at Girón Victory Square." Havana Domestic Service. June 30, 1988. CSD.

———. "President Fidel Castro's Children's Day Speech." Havana Domestic Service. July 19, 1981. CSD.

Caverly, Robert. "Reservations for the Havana Hilton Hotel." June 22, 1960. HHC, CNHC, Box 10, Folder 10, HIA, UH.

———, to Conrad N. Hilton. Letter, February 1, 1959. HHC, CNHC, Box 10, Folder 12, HIA, UH.

———, to Conrad N. Hilton. Letter, February 11, 1959. HHC, CNHC, Box 10, Folder 12, HIA, UH.

CEPAL. "Turismo: Resolución del 13 de junio de 1949." Santiago: CEPAL, 1949.

Cirules, Enrique. *The Empire of Havana*. Trans. Douglas Edward LaPrade. Havana: Editorial Jose Martí, 2003.

Clancy, Michael. *Exporting Paradise: Tourism and Development in Mexico*. Amsterdam: Pergamon, 2001.

Cobar, David. *Cancún está de pie: De la destrucción a la recuperación luego del huracán Wilma*. Cancún: David Cobar, 2006.

———, to the author. E-mail, August 1, 2006.

Coleman, Gerald A., to C. J. Simons. Letter, "Capital Contributions—Cerromar Hotel and Related Projects," April 15, 1971. FDHP, RG 488, Series 4, Box 49, Folder 5, AUSCA.

———, to C. L. Glass. Letter, "Villa Dorado Condominium Project." FDHP, RG 488, Series 4, Box 51, Folder 5, AUSCA.

———, to W. R. Howard. Letter, "Hotel Operations—Profits and Cash Flows." August 11, 1970. FDHP, RG 488, Series 4, Box 52, Folder 18, AUSCA.

Coles, William F. "Notes on Venezuelan Revolution, October 18–20, 1945." CMR, RG III 2C, Series BI, Box 110, Folder 832, RAC.

———, to Barton P. Turnbull (BPT). Letter, December 28, 1942. CMR, RG III 2C, Series BI, Box 109, Folder 818, RAC.

———, to BPT. Letter, January 12, 1945. CMR, RG III 2C, Series BI, Box 110, Folder 832, RAC.

———, to BPT. Letter, October 22, 1945. CMR, RG III 2C, Series BI, Box 110, Folder 832, RAC.

———, to BPT. Letter, November 30, 1945. CMR, RG III 2C, Series BI, Box 110, Folder 832, RAC.

———, to BPT. Letter, June 24, 1946. CMR, RG III 2C, Series BI, Box 110, Folder 832, RAC.

———, to Nelson A. Rockefeller. Letter, August 17, 1942. CMR, RG III 2C, Series BI, Box 109, Folder 818, RAC.

Consejo Nacional de Turismo. *Incorporación del turismo del caribé al sureste de México: Ensayo económico-turístico de mercado*. Mexico: Consejo Nacional de Turismo, 1965.

Cortes Generales (Spain). "Diario de sesiones del congreso de los diputados, comisiones," 1999, VI legislature, no. 754, Asuntos Exteriores, session 58, Sr. D. Francisco Javier Rupérez Rubio (president). www.senado.es/boletines/CO0754.html, accessed April 19, 2007.

Crystal, Jeff. "Alexander Girard's Dream Village: La Fonda del Sol, New York (1961–1971)." http://www.lafondadelsol.net/wst_page7.html, accessed April 23, 2007.

"Cuba's Economy 'On the Verge of Collapse." *Toronto Star*, March 31, 1993. LN.

"'Custom Built' Room Temperatures." *Hotel Bulletin*, September 1949. HIA, UH.

"Dedican 20 millones de pesos más a obras en el sur del Oriente." *Diaro de la Marina*, September 23, 1959. Caribbean Newspaper Imaging Project, George A Smathers Libraries, University of Florida.

Dirección Adjunta de Desarrollo, "Centros Integralmente Planeados: Revisión planes maestros; Cancun/Ixtapa/Los Cabos/Loreto; Resumenes ejecutivos." Internal Report. Mexico City: FONATUR, 1997. CEDOC.

Dorado Beach Corporation. "Agenda for Meeting of the Board of Directors." November 24, 1975. FDHP, RG 488, Series 4, Box 47, Folder 4, AUSCA.

Dorado Beach Development, Inc. "Agenda for Meeting of the Board of Directors." August 28, 1974. FDHP, RG 488, Series 4, Box 46, Folder 10, AUSCA.

———. "Minutes of Meeting of the Board of Directors." May 27, 1970. FDHP, RG 488, Series 4, Box 52, Folder 10, AUSCA.

———. "Summer Marketing Report: Cerromar Beach Hotel." FDHP, RG 488, Series 4, Box 46, Folder 8, AUSCA.

Dorado Beach Estates, Inc. "Minutes of Meeting of the Board of Directors." February 19, 1975. FDHP, RG 488, Series 4, Box 46, Folder 12, AUSCA.

———. "Minutes of Meeting of the Board of Directors." March 14, 1972. FDHP, RG 488, Series 4, Box 45, Folder 5, AUSCA.

———. *Villa Dorado Resort Condominiums, Prospectus.* 1970. FDHP, RG 488, Series 4, Box 49, Folder 8, AUSCA.

"Dorado Beach Hotel." FDHP, RG 488, Series 4, Box 50, Folder 16, AUSCA.

"Dorado Beach Hotel, Recalculated Operating Results." FDHP, RG 488, Series 4, Box 50, Folder 16, AUSCA.

Dorado Beach Hotel Corporation. "Dorado Beach/Brenas Beach Hotels." February 3, 1970. FDHP, RG 488, Series 4, Box 49, Folder 7, AUSCA.

———. "Minutes of Meeting of the Board of Directors." September 18, 1969. FDHP, RG 488, Series 4, Box 52, Folder 7, AUSCA.

"Dunlop and Meany Own Shares in Resort Project." *NYT*, January 13, 1973.

Eastern Airlines. "Response to 'Appraisal of Property.'" FDHP, RG 488, Series 4, Box 50, Folder 15, AUSCA.

EFE Spanish Newswire. "Cuba-España: Presidente Autonomía Balear se reunión [*sic*] seis horas con Castro." February 6, 2000. LN.

———. "Cuba-España: Presidente Autonomía Balear visita Varadero." February 5, 2000. LN.

———. "Cuba-España: Presidente communidad Canaria se entrevistó con Fidel Castro." May 14, 2000. LN.

———. "Empresas-Meliá: Sol Meliá 'desconoce' ultimatum y recuerda apoyos España y EU." October 30, 1999. LN.

Elminger, Arthur M., to Conrad N. Hilton. Letter, January 7, 1959. HHC, CNHC, Box 10, HIA, UH.

———, to Conrad N. Hilton. Letter, July 27, 1959. HHC, CNHC, Box 10, HIA, UH.

———, to Conrad N. Hilton. Letter, November 23, 1959. HHC, CNHC, Box 10, Folder 2, HIA, UH.

El País (EP). "EEUU aplica la ley Helms Burton a Club Med y a la alemana LTE." September 10, 1999. www.elpais.es, accessed March 1, 2004.

———. "El encanto de las playas de Varadero." August 12, 1994. www.elpais.es, accessed March 1, 2004.

———. "La lista negra de EE UU incluirá al grupo Sol por sus hotels en Cuba." May 22, 1996. LN.

El Universal (Mexico City). "Cancún busca recuperar las pérdidas provocadas por el huracán Wilma; Despega Cancún luego de Wilma." July 7, 2006. LN.

Expansión (Madrid). "Baleares. El prestigio empresarial de una región; las companías más activas." November 19, 2003.

———. "El presidente de la cadena, Gabriel Escarrer, destaca el desequilibrio en calidad y precio; Sol Meliá advierte sobre la perdida de atractivo de República Dominicana." June 26, 2001. LN

Fields, Sidney. "Only Human: Laurance S. Rockefeller: Plan for a Paradise." *Mirror* (New York), December 12, 1954. RFA, RG 13, Box 19, Folder "Dorado," RAC.

Fodor, Eugene, ed. *Fodor's 1960 Guide to the Caribbean, Bahamas, and Bermuda.* New York: David McKay, 1960.

Foglesong, Richard E. *Married to the Mouse: Walt Disney World and Orlando.* New Haven, Conn.: Yale University Press, 2001.

Fondo de Promoción de Infraestructura Turística. "Proyecto de desarrollo turístico en Cancún, Q. R." Mexico City: Banco de México, 1971. CEDOC.

Fondo Nacional de Fomento al Turismo (FONATUR). *Cancún.* Mexico City: FONATUR, 1982. CEDOC

———. "Quintana Roo, Cancún. Planeación a corto y mediano plazo del desarrollo turístico." Mexico City: FONATUR, 1987. CEDOC

———. *30 años de inversión con buen destino.* Mexico City: FONATUR, 2004.

Fortune Magazine, eds. *The Changing American Market.* Garden City, N.Y.: Hanover House, 1955.

Friedlander, Paul J. C. "Warm West Indies: The Stepping Stones to South America Enjoy New and Deserved Popularity." *NYT*, January 15, 1950. HHC, CNHC, Box 5, HIA, UH.

Gann, Thomas. *In an Unknown Land.* Freeport, N.Y.: Books for Libraries Press, 1924.

"General Kincaid Stresses Tourist Opportunities in Caribbean Due to Packed European Hotels." *Hotel Monthly*, November 1949. HIA, UH.

Goldstone, Harmon H., to LSR. Letter, January 11, 1954. RFC, RG 2, Series AE: LSR, Box 9, Folder "Livingston—Dorado Financing—PRIDCO," RAC.

Gonzales, G., and G. Manzano. "Presiones y intereses." *Cinco Días*, August 13, 1999.

Gonzales, Mario. "Nuevo hotel atraerá más convenciones a PR." *El Diario–La Prensa [Puerto Rico]*, 10. January 16, 1972. FDHP, RG 488, Series 4, Box 49, Folder 6, AUSCA.

Grupo Puntacana. "Reglamentos protectores de Punta Cana Resort." Punta Cana, n.d.

Gueft, Olga. "The Inn of the Sun: Even the Salt Shakers Smile in Alexander Girard's Dream Village of Glittering Suns and Amiable Puppets, the Most Deceptively Childlike of New York's Restaurants." *Interiors*, 1961, 88–99.

Gupta, Kathleen, and Udayan Gupta. *A Natural Way of Business: Grupo Punta Cana, an Unusual Partnership in Sustainable Tourism*. Calgary: Gondolier, 2006.

Habana Hilton. "Emergency Staff Meeting." January 5, 1959. HHC, CNHC, Box 10, Folder 8, HIA, UH.

"The Habana Hilton." *Hotel Bulletin*, n.d. HIA, UH.

"The Habana Hilton: Latest Addition to Cuba's Booming Hotel Industry." *Hotel Industry*, March 1958, 18–19.

Hall, Floyd D. (FDH) to Paul S. Weber. Letter, October 3, 1967. FDHP, RG 488, Series 4, Box 50, Folder 15, AUSCA.

Hamilton, Robert M., to Conrad Hilton. Letter, August 9, 1951. HHC, CNHC, Box 5, HIA, UH.

Hancock, Ralph. *Puerto Rico: A Success Story*. Princeton, N.J.: D. Van Nostrand, 1960.

Harris, Kerr, Forster, and Company. "Economic Study of a Proposed Resort Hotel to Be Located near Dorado, Puerto Rico." FDHP, RG 488, Series 4, Box 51, Folder 2, AUSCA.

Hayes, Samuel P. *Beauty, Health, and Permanence: Environmental Politics in the United States, 1955–1985*. Cambridge: Cambridge University Press, 1989.

Helms, Jesse, to Honorable Thomas Pickering. Letter, November 16, 2000. www.cubatraderpublications.com/Helmsletter/index.htm, accessed December 15,2003.

"Helms Demands Helms-Burton Sanctions against Spanish Hotel Chain." November 21, 2000. www.cubatraderpublications.com/story5/, accessed December 15, 2003.

Hiernaux-Nicolas, Daniel. "Cancun Bliss." In *The Tourist City*, ed. Dennis R. Judd and Susan S. Fainstein, 124–139. New Haven, Conn.: Yale University Press, 1999.

Hilton, Conrad N. *Be My Guest*. New York: Fireside Book, 1994.

———. "Hotels International." Speech, Ithaca, N.Y., April 21, 1954. HIA, UH.

———, to Arthur Elminger. Letter, November 21, 1959. HHC, CNHC, Box 10, Folder 2, HIA, UH.

———. "Un Hotel Continental para la unidad continental." HHC, CNHC, Speeches, HIA, UH.

Hilton International (HHI). "Castro Assures Welcome to American Tourists." January 13, 1959. HHC, CNHC, Box 10, Folder 8, HIA, UH.

———. *Hilton Hotel International News* (*HHIN*). November 1960–February 1961, October–November 1961. HHC, CNHC, HIA, UH.

———. "Minutes of Special Meeting of Board of Directors, Hilton Hotels International, Inc." September 16, 1952. HHC, CNHC, Box 10, Folder 2, HIA, UH.

Holtzman, Richard. "The Impact of Resort Hotels on Real Estate." *RockResorts News*, July 1969, 2. FDHP, RG 488, Series 4, Box 48, Folder 27, AUSCA.

———, to FDH. Letter, January 5, 1970. FDHP, RG 488, Series 4, Box 49, Folder 8, AUSCA.

"Hotel Chain with Wings." *Business Week*, March 28, 1953, 167–169.

"Hotel Furnishings Go by Air Freight," *NYT*, November 7, 1949. HIA, UH.

Hotel Management. July 1947.

Houser, John W. "How Hotels and Travel Contribute to International Understanding." *Hotel Monthly*, February 1958, 37.

———. "Statement to the Committee on Foreign Affairs, U.S. House of Representatives." March 3, 1954. Document 43B, in T. Farrell, "Hilton Hotels International Development Binder," HHC, CNHC, HIA, UH.

Howard, William R., to FDH. Letter, "Hotel Operations—Profits and Cash Flows." August 26, 1970. FDHP, RG 488, Series 4, Box 52, Folder 18, AUSCA.

Hucks, Lew. "Recommendations on a Master Plan for Excess Dorado Properties." In C. J. Simons to FDH. Letter, "Dorado Master Plan," December 14, 1972. FDHP, RG 488, Series 4, Box 51, Folder 1, AUSCA.

Hughes, Lawrence M. "Hilton's 'Private Statesmanship' Shapes World-Wide Hotel Empire." *Sales Management*, October 19, 1956. HIA, UH.

H. Zinder and Associates. *The Outlook for Tourism in the Dominican Republic.* Washington, D.C.: Organization of American States, 1968.

I Am Cuba. DVD. Directed by Mikhail Kalatozov. Chatsworth, Calif.: Image Entertainment, 1999.

INFRATUR. "La experiencia del fondo para el desarollo de la infraestructura turística (INFRATUR)." In *El turismo y su financiación en España, Caribe, y Centro America*, Asociación Latínoamericana de Instituciones Financieras de Desarrollo, Banco Hipotecario de España, Madrid, Banco Central de la República Dominicana, Instituo de Crédito Oficial (España), 171–182. Madrid: I.C.O., 1977.

Instituto Nacional de la Indústria Turística (INIT). *El sol de Cuba: Panorama turístico.* Havana: INIT, n.d.

Ioannides, Dimitri. "Tourism Development in Mediterranean Islands: Opportunities and Constraints." In *Island Tourism and Sustainable Development: Caribbean, Pacific, and Mediterranean Experiences*, ed. Yorghos Apostolopoulos and Dennis J. Gayle, 67–89. Westport, Conn.: Praeger, 2002.

Jennen, Joseph, to LSR. Letter, August 19, 1953. RFC, RG 2, Series AE: LSR, Box 9, Folder "Livingston—Dorado Financing—PRIDCO," RAC.

———, to LSR. Letter, January 5, 1954. RFC, RG 2 Series AE: LSR, Box 9, Folder "Livingston—Dorado Financing—PRIDCO," RAC.

Jiménez, Felucho. *El turismo en la República Dominicana: Conferencias.* Santo Domingo: Amigo del Hogar, 1999.

Joseph, John, to General Managers, "Habana Hilton Materials." July 26, 1960. HHC, CNHC, Box 10, Folder 10, HIA, UH.

Joseph, Richard. "Around the World." In "Come Enter the Wonderful World of Hilton Hotels." *NYT*, May 25, 1959. HIA, UH.

Kaplan, Morison. "L. S. Rockefeller Offers U.S. a Virgin Island Park." *NYT*, November 19, 1954. RFA, RG 13, Box 19, Folder "Caneel Bay Plantation," RAC.

Kennedy, William J. "Puerto Rico: Destination: El Dorado." In *Fodor's Guide to the*

Caribbean, Bahamas, and Bermuda, ed. Eugene Fodor, 285–322. New York: David McKay, 1967.

Kheel, Jake. Author's interview, January 21, 2006.

Lane, Charles, to Robert Bottome. Letter, n.d. CMR, RG II, Series BI, Box 110, Folder 821, RAC.

Lefever, Michael M., and Cathleen D. Baird. "The Expropriation of the Habana Hilton: A Timely Reminder." *International Journal of Hospitality Management* 9, no. 1 (1990): 14–20.

Llado, Juan A. *Turismo y desarrollo: El despegue de la industria sin chimineas en la República Dominicana*. Santo Domingo: [s.n.], 2002.

Loercher, Diana. "Dorado Beach in Summer." *Christian Science Monitor*, June 15, 1982. LN.

Louchheim, Aline B. "New Design Proves Worth in Hotels: Modern Buildings Save Operators Money, Give Guests More Comfort." *NYT*, June 11, 1950. HIA, UH.

Loving, Rush, Jr. "Hilton International Has 75 Palatial Profit Centers." *Fortune*, August 28, 1978, 71–74.

Maldonado, A. W. *Teodoro Moscoso and Puerto Rico's Operation Bootstrap*. Gainesville: University Press of Florida, 1997.

Maribona, Armando. *Turismo en Cuba*. Havana: Editorial "Lex," 1959.

———. *Turismo y ciudadania*. Havana Editorial Alrededor de América, 1943.

Martí, Fernando. *Cancún, fantasía de banqueros: La construcción de una ciudad turística a partir de cero: Una narración periodística*. [Mexico]: F. Marti, 1985.

———. *Cancún: Paradise Invented*. Mexico City: Impresora Formal, S.A. de C.V., 1998.

Martin, Lawrence, and Sylvia Martin. *The Standard Guide to Mexico and the Caribbean*. New York: Funk and Wagnalls, 1958–1959.

Martínez, Sixto. "Castro denuncia que EE.UU. trata de sabotear la IX Cumbre Iberoamericana." *La Estrella Digital*, March 11, 1999. www.fut.es/~mpgp/amigos 266.htm, accessed April 19, 2007.

Medina, Norman, and Jorge Santamarina. *Turismo de naturaleza en Cuba*. Colombia: Ediciones UNION, 2004.

Meek, Howard B. "The Hotels of Latin America." *Hotel Monthly*, February 1953, 34–42.

———. "The Hotels of Latin America." *Hotel Monthly*, March 1953, 28–37.

"Memorandum of Agreement between Laurance S. Rockefeller and Eastern Airlines, Inc." October 30, 1967. FDHP, RG 488, Series 4, Box 50, Folder 16, AUSCA.

Merrill, Dennis. "Negotiating Cold War Paradise: U.S. Tourism, Economic Planning, and Cultural Modernity in Twentieth Century Puerto Rico." *Diplomatic History* 25, no. 2 (Spring 2001): 179–214.

Miolan, Angel. *Datos para la historia del turismo de la República Dominicana*. Santo Domingo: Editora de Colores, S.A., 1998.

———. *Turismo: Nuestra industria sin chimeneas*, 3rd ed., expanded. Santo Domingo: Editorial Letras de Quisqueya, C. por A., 1994.

Molina, Christina. "Questions for Historians." Office of the Director of Communications, Sol Meliá Corporate Headquarters, Palma de Mallorca, April 4, 2004.

"Monthly Master List, 1950–1951, the Caribé Hilton Hotel." HHC, CNHC, HIA, UH.

Morales Troncoso, Pedro. "El turismo en el caribé y en la República Dominicana." In *El turismo y su financiación en España, Caribé, y Centro America*, Asociación Latínoamericana de Institucionces Financieras de Desarrollo, Banco Hipotecario de España, Madrid, Banco Central de la República Dominicana, Institituo de Crédito Oficial (España), 114. Madrid: I.C.O., 1977.

Morley, Robert B., to Mr. Aronson. Letter, "Cuba's Declining Trade Prospects," January 24, 1990. www.foia.state.gov/documents/foiadocs/6e85.PDF, accessed April 19, 2007.

Mormino, Gary R. *Land of Sunshine, State of Dreams*. Gainesville: University Press of Florida, 2005.

Moscoso, Teodoro, to LSR. Letter, March 9, 1954. RFC, RG 2, Series AE: LSR, Box 9, Folder "Livingston—Dorado Financing—PRIDCO," RAC.

———, to LSR. Letter, December 29, 1954. RFC, RG 2, Series AE: LSR, Box 9, Folder "Livingston—Dorado Financing—PRIDCO," RAC.

"Nature in Harmony with Tourism Development." June 26, 2001. http://www.dr1.com/news/2001/dnews062601.shtml, accessed April 20, 2007.

"News of Hotels and Hotelmen." *International Hotel Review*, August 1949. HIA, UH.

Nichols, Elizabeth, ed. *RockReports*. December 1968. FDHP, RG 488, Box 48, Folder 27, AUSCA.

"1950s Hotel Accommodations at the Crossroads of the Nation: How a Great New Hotel, the Caribé Hilton, Was Created in San Juan, Puerto Rico, with New Luxury for Guests and New Ideas for Alert-Minded Hotel Men." *Hotel Monthly*, February 1950, 27–40.

Ortiz Mena, Antonio. *El desarrollo estabilizador: Reflexiones sobre una época*. Mexico City: El Colegio de México, Fondo de Cultura Económica, 1998.

Pagden, Anthony. *European Encounters with the New World*. New Haven, Conn.: Yale University Press, 1993.

Pan American Airways. *Annual Report*. 1946.

Parker, Mary. "'TenSHUN! Eyes South!" *Mademoiselle*, January 1950, 21, 40.

Passalacqua, Carlos M. (CMP) to LSR. Letter, December 29, 1953. RFC, RG 2, Series AE: LSR, Box 9, Folder "Livingston—Dorado Financing—PRIDCO," RAC.

———, to LSR. Letter, January 27, 1954. RFC, RG 2 Series AE: LSR, Box 9, Folder "Livingston—Dorado Financing—PRIDCO," RAC.

———, to LSR. Letter, March 4, 1954. RFC, RG 2, Series AE: LSR, Box 9, Folder "Livingston—Dorado Financing–PRIDCO," RAC.

———, to LSR. Letter, March 11, 1954. RFC, RG 2, Series AE: LSR, Box 9, Folder "Livingston—Dorado Financing—PRIDCO," RAC.

———, to LSR. Letter, March 16, 1954. RFC, RG 2, Series AE: LSR, Box 9, Folder "Livingston—Dorado Financing—PRIDCO," RAC.

———, to LSR. Letter, August 19, 1954. RFC, RG 2, Series AE: LSR, Box 9, Folder "Livingston—Dorado Financing—PRIDCO," RAC.

———, to LSR. Letter, October 6, 1954. RFC, RG 2, Series AE: LSR, Box 9, Folder "Livingston—Dorado Financing—PRIDCO," RAC.

———, to LSR. Letter. December 21, 1954. RFC, RG 2, Series AE: LSR, Box 9, Folder "Livingston—Dorado Financing—PRIDCO," RAC.

———, to LSR. Letter, January 20, 1956. RFC, RG 2, Series AE: LSR, Box 9, Folder "Livingston—Dorado Financing—PRIDCO," RAC.

Pearson, David. Author's interview, February 8, 2006.

Pérez, Louis A., Jr. *On Becoming Cuban: Identity, Nationality, and Culture.* New York: ECCO Press, 1999.

Pisani, Elizabeth. "Cuban Trade Caught in Battle for Florida Vote: A New Law Aimed at Winning Support from an Exile Community." *Financial Times*, October 27, 1992. LN.

Potter, James E. *A Room with a World View: 50 Years of Inter-Continental Hotels and Its People, 1946–1996.* London: Weidenfeld and Nicholson, 1996.

La Provincia: Diario de las Palmas. "El Grupo Martiñon incia a final de año las obras de tres nuevos hotels en Cuba." February 17, 2000. www.cubanet.org, accessed April 10, 2004.

Radio Havana. *BBC Summary of World Broadcasts.* December 4, 1999. CSD.

Radio Reports, Inc. "Caribé Hilton Hotel [Is] Very Beautiful." January 19, 1950. WOR Radio (New York). HHC, CNHC, Box 5, HIA, UH.

———. "Paar Tells of Visit to Cuba." October 12, 1959, *The Jack Paar Show*, 11:15 p.m., WRCA-TV (N.Y.) and NBC-TV Network. HHC, CNHC, Box 10, Folder 3, HIA, UH.

Rainieri, Francesca. Author's interview, January 23, 2006.

Rainieri, Frank Elías. Author's interview, January 26, 2006.

Ramírez, Adolfo. Author's interview, January 24, 2006.

Ramón Rodríguez, Ana Belén. "La internacionalización de la industria hotelera española." Ph.D. diss., Universidad de Alicante, España, 2000. http://www.eumed.net/tesis/abrr/005035_1.pdf, accessed April 25, 2007.

Reich, Cary. *The Life of Nelson A. Rockefeller: Worlds to Conquer, 1908–1958.* New York: Doubleday, 1996.

Republic of Cuba. "Constitución política de la república de Cuba de 1976." http://pdba.georgetown.edu/Constitutions/Cuba/cuba2002.html, accessed April 19, 2007.

"Resort Building in Undeveloped Areas: RockResort Company." *Cornell Hotel and Restaurant Administration Quarterly* 7, no. 4 (1967): 102–109.

"Reunión de evaluación de los efectos del huracán Emily." Benito Juarez Municipality, Quintana Roo, July 18, 2005. www.presidencia.gob.mx, accessed May 29, 2006.

"Reunión que encabezó el Presidente Vicente Fox con empresarios hoteleros de Quintana Roo." Primera parte, Hotel Le Meredien, Cancún, Quintana Roo, Mexico, October 27, 2005. http://fox.presidencia.gob.mx/actividades/orden/?contenido=21574, accessed April 19, 2007.

Rivas, Darlene. *Missionary Capitalist: Nelson Rockefeller in Venezuela.* Chapel Hill: University of North Carolina Press, 2002.

Robbins, Edward, to Nelson A. Rockefeller. Letter, March 1, 1940. CMR, Series BI, Box 110, Folder 824, RAC.

Rockefeller, L. S. (LSR). "Speech at the Opening of Dorado Beach Hotel." Dorado, Puerto Rico, December 2, 1958. RFC, RG 2, Series AE: LSR, Box 9, Folder "New Hotel Opening," RAC.

———, to Burton A. Schutt. Letter, June 23, 1953. RFC, RG 2, Series AE: LSR, Box 9, Folder, "New Hotel Construction, Livingston," RAC.

———, to Carl B. Brunner. Letter, July 30, 1953. RFC, RG 2, Series AE: LSR, Box 9, Folder, "New Hotel Construction, Livingston," RAC.

———, to CMP. Letter, January 18, 1954. RFC, RG 2, Series AE: LSR, Box 9, Folder "Livingston—Dorado Financing—PRIDCO," RAC.

———, to CMP. Letter, March 11, 1954. RFC, RG 2, Series AE: LSR, Box 9, Folder "Livingston—Dorado Financing—PRIDCO," RAC.

———, to CMP. Letter, March 12, 1954. RFC, RG 2, Series AE: LSR, Box 9, Folder "Livingston—Dorado Financing—PRIDCO," RAC.

———, to CMP. Letter, March 25, 1954. RFC, RG 2, Series AE: LSR, Box 9, Folder "Livingston—Dorado Financing—PRIDCO," RAC.

———, to CMP. Letter, August 6, 1954. RFC, RG 2, Series AE: LSR, Box 9, Folder "Livingston—Dorado Financing—PRIDCO," RAC.

———, to CMP. Letter, December 1955. RFC, RG 2, Series AE: LSR, Box 9, Folder "Livingston—Dorado Financing—PRIDCO," RAC.

———, to CMP. Letter, February 6, 1957. RFC, RG 2, Series AE: LSR, Box 9, Folder "Livingston—Dorado Financing—PRIDCO," RAC.

———, to CMP. Letter, February 28, 1957. RFC, RG 2, Series AE: LSR, Box 9, Folder "Livingston—Dorado Financing—PRIDCO," RAC.

———, to Teodoro Moscoso. Letter, July 30, 1953. RFC, RG 2, Series AE: LSR, Box 9, Folder, "New Hotel Construction, Livingston," RAC.

Rockefeller, L. S., and Todd Cole, to FDH. Telegram, December 1, 1958. FDHP, RG 488, Series 4, Box 50, Folder 15, AUSCA.

Rockefeller, Nelson A. "Memorandum on Post-War Planning for the Hemisphere." RFA, RG 4, Series O, Box 8, Folder 63, RAC.

RockResorts Incorporated (RRI). "Fact Sheet: Caneel Bay Plantation." RFA, RG 13, Box 19, Folder "Caneel Bay Plantation," RAC.

———. "Fact Sheet: Dorado Beach Hotel and Golf Club, Dorado, Puerto Rico." RFA, RG 13, Box 19, Folder "Dorado," RAC.

———. "Five Year Financial Projection." FDHP, RG 488, Series 4, Box 48, Folder 26, AUSCA.

———. "Meeting of the Board of Directors." November 10, 1969. FDHP, RG 488, Series 4, Box 48, Folder 5, AUSCA.

———. "Minutes of the Meeting of the Board of Directors." July 14, 1969. FDHP, RG 488, Series 4, Box 48, Folder 4, AUSCA.

———. "Minutes of the Meeting of the Board of Directors." April 14, 1970. FDHP, RG 488, Series 4, Box 48, Folder 8, AUSCA.

————. "Minutes of the Meeting of the Board of Directors." October 6, 1975. FDHP, RG 488, Series 4, Box 48, Folder 22, AUSCA.

————. Press Release, August 2, 1954. RFA, RG 13, Box 19, Folder "Dorado," RAC.

————. "Recap of 536 Questionnaires Received through 3/9/70." FDHP, RG 488, Series 4, Box 52, Folder 9, AUSCA.

Rodríguez, Guillermo, to LSR. Letter, August 11, 1953. RFC, RG 2, Series AE: LSR, Box 9, Folder "Livingston—Dorado Financing—PRIDCO," RAC.

Rodríguez Alomá, Patricia, and Alina Ochoa. *Desafío de una utopia: Una estrategia integral para la gestión de salvaguarda de la Habana vieja.* Navarra, Spain: Colegio Oficial de Arquitectos Vasco Navarro, 1999.

Rodríguez Parrilla, Bruno. "Measure to Eliminate International Terrorism." General Assembly, Fifty-sixth Session, Agenda Item 166, Security Council, October 29, 2001. www.un.org/documents/ga/docs/56/a56521.pdf, accessed April 19, 2007.

Romero, Manuel. *Miguel Alemán Valdés (1905–1983) Arquitecto del turismo de Mexico.* Sociedad Mexicana de Geografía y Estadística, 1993.

Romero, Pepe. *My Mexico City and Yours.* Dolphin Books, 1962.

Romoli, Kathleen. *Colombia: Gateway to South America.* Garden City, N.J.: Doubleday, 1946.

Roy, Joaquin. *Cuba, the United States, and the Helms-Burton Doctrine: International Reactions.* Gainesville: University Press of Florida, 2000.

Sans, Alvaro. *Alvaro Sans: Arquitectura hotelera.* Palma de Mallorca, n.d.

————. Author's e-mail interview, March 15, 2004.

Schutt, Burton A., to LSR. Letter, May 29, 1953. RFC, RG 2, Series AE: LSR, Box 9, Folder "New Hotel Construction, Livingston," RAC.

Schwartz, Rosalie. *Pleasure Island: Tourism and Temptation in Cuba.* Lincoln: University of Nebraska Press, 1997.

Secretaría de Asentamientos Humanos y Obras Públicas (Mexico). "Bases para la formulación del programa de dotación de infraestructura para centros turísticos." May 1979. CEDOC.

Seguí Llinas, Miguel. *Les Baleares: Un laboratoire du tourisme Mediterranee.* Sophia Antipolis, France: Plan Bleu Centre d'Activités Régionales, 2004. http://www.planbleu.org/publications/baleares.pdf, accessed April 19, 2007.

Shacochis, Bob. "In Deepest Gringolandia: Mexico: The Third World as Tourist Theme Park." *Harper's Magazine*, July 1989, 42–50.

Shellaby, Robert K. "Puerto Rico's New Hotel Epitomizes Island Quest." *Christian Science Monitor*, December 29, 1949. HIA, UH.

Simons, C. J., to FDH. Letter, "Cerromar and Villa Dorado Projects," November 19, 1971. FDHP, RG 488, Series 4, Box 49, Folder 5, AUSCA.

————, to FDH. Letter, "Dorado Properties," July 7, 1972. FDHP, RG 488, Series 4, Box 50, Folder 14, AUSCA.

————, to FDH. Letter, "Hotel Status Report," September 1973. FDHP, RG 488, Series 4, Box 52, Folder 18, AUSCA.

————, to FDH. Letter, "L. S. Rockefeller Visit with Governor Colón," February 21, 1975. FDHP, RG 488, Series 4, Box 51, Folder 6, AUSCA.

————, to FDH. Letter, "Profit Plan Review—Hotels," November 1, 1973. FDHP, RG 488, Series 4, Box 48, Folder 28, AUSCA.

Soriano Frade, Francisco. *Pequeña historia del turismo en las Baleares*. Palma de Mallorca: Los Iconos de Ferón, 1996.

"Spanish Companies in Crossfire of U.S.-Cuba Battle." *NYT*, July 20, 1996.

"Spectacular Luxury in the Caribbean—The Caribé Hilton Hotel at San Juan, Puerto Rico." *Architectural Forum*, March 1950, 98.

Squire, John B., to Charles W. Cramer Jr. Letter, March 16, 1973. FDHP, RG 488, Series 4, Box 49, Folder 5, AUSCA.

Stone and Webster Engineering Corporation. "Appraisal of Property, Dorado Beach Properties, Dorado, Puerto Rico." May 1967. FDHP, RG 488, Series 4, Box 50, Folder 15, AUSCA.

Strand, Curt. "The Globalization of the Hotel Industry." Speech transcript, Conrad N. Hilton College of Hotel and Restaurant, University of Houston, October 4, 1994. HIA, UH.

————. "Lessons of a Lifetime: The Development of Hilton International." *Cornell Hotel and Restaurant Administration Quarterly* 37, no. 3 (July 1996): 83–95.

"Study of a New Deal—Dorado Project: 'Preliminary Discussions with Mr. Jennen—May 19, 1954.'" RFC, RG 2, Series AE: LSR, Box 9, Folder "Livingston—Dorado Financing—PRIDCO," RAC.

"Tavern Talk: Hilton Art Consultant." March 1950. HHC, CNHC, Box 5, HIA, UH.

Tewarie, Bhoendradatt. "The Development of a Sustainable Tourism Sector in the Caribbean." In *Island Tourism and Sustainable Development: Caribbean, Pacific, and Mediterranean Experiences*, ed. Yorghos Apostolopoulos and Dennis J. Gayle, 35–48. Westport, Conn.: Praeger, 2002.

Truslow, Francis Adams. *Report on Cuba: Findings and Recommendations of an Economic and Technical Mission Organized by the International Bank for Reconstruction and Development in Collaboration with the Government of Cuba in 1950*. Baltimore: Johns Hopkins University Press, 1951.

Uriol Alvarez, Ester. *Sol Meliá: El viajero universal*. Madrid: Piramide Ediciones SA, 2004.

"U.S. Won't Punish Spanish Group 'For Now.'" *Miami Herald*, October 8, 1996.

Varela, Carlos. "Tropicollage." Sound recording. *Jalisco Park* (1989). www.carlosva rela.com/lirica/47_tropicollage.asp, accessed April 20, 2007.

Vidal Suárez, Marta Maria. "Desarrollo y expansión internacional de una empresa turística: La experiencia del grupo 'Barceló.'" www.cepade.es/Ademas/revista25/art4.pdf, accessed August 24, 2006.

Villalba Garrido, Evaristo. *Cuba y el turismo*. Havana: Editorial de Ciencias Sociales, 1993.

Villamil, José J. "Impacto del turismo: La experiencia del caribé." CEPAL/PNUMA report for the Estilos de Desarrollo y Medio Ambiente en America Latina Project. September 1979. CEPAL Library, Santiago, Chile.

————. "Planning, Tourism, and the Environment: The Puerto Rican Experience."

December 2, 1985, for the Economic Commission for Latin America and the Caribbean: Subregional Headquarters for the Caribbean, United Nations Environment Program. CEPAL Library, Santiago, Chile.

Vincent, Mauricio. "Array." *EP*, June 3, 2002. www.elpais.es, accessed March 1, 2004.

———. "La bendición de Fidel Castro," *EP*, October 2, 1998. www.elpais.es, accessed March 1, 2004.

———. "La Helms-Burton amenaza otra vez a Sol Meliá las reclamaciones de antiguos propietarios ponen en jaque a la práctica totalidad del sector turístico en Cuba." *EP*, November 7, 1999. www.elpais.es, accessed March 1, 2004.

———. "Sol Meliá ampliará inversions en Cuba pese a la ley Helms-Burton." *EP*, May 24, 1996. www.elpais.es, accessed March 1, 2004.

———. "Sol Meliá y la herencia de los Duponts." *EP*, July 17, 1996. www.elpais.es, accessed March 1, 2004.

"VIP List." FDHP, RG 488, Series 4, Box 49, Box 6, "RockResorts, Dorado Beach, Cerromar Opening," AUSCA.

Ward, Evan. "A Means of Last Resort: The European Transformation of the Cuban Hotel Industry and the American Response, 1987–2004." In *The Business of Tourism: Place, Faith, and History*, ed. Philip Scranton and Janet F. Davidson, 213–238. Philadelphia: University of Pennsylvania Press, 2007.

———. "Delayed Gratification: The Evolution of Turkish Tourism Policy, 1955–2005." *Insight Turkey* 8, no. 1 (January–March 2006): 156–167.

———. "International Basic Economy Corporation and the Transformation of Consumer Culture in the Americas 1946–1980." *Rockefeller Archives Center Research Reports*, 2004, 1.

———. "'This Great Show Window': Consumerism Transforms the United States-Mexico Borderlands, 1960–1970." Unpublished manuscript. William P. Clements Center for Southwestern Studies Symposium Series, "A Tale of Two Borderlands, 1960–1975," Southern Methodist University, April 1, 2006.

Weber, Paul S., to FDH. Letter, September 29, 1967. FDHP, RG 488, Series 4, Box 50, Folder 15, AUSCA.

———, to FDH. Letter, October 6, 1967. FDHP, RG 488, Series 4, Box 50, Folder 15, AUSCA.

Welton Becket and Associates. "Havana Hilton—Artwork." April 29, 1959. HHC, CNHC, Box 10, Folder 2, HIA, UH.

Wharton, Annabel Jane. *Building the Cold War: Hilton International Hotels and Modern Architecture*. Chicago: University of Chicago Press, 2001.

Whitman, Frederick Crocker, to Burton Schutt. Letter, January 19, 1953. RFC, RG 2, Series AE: LSR, Box 9, Folder "New Hotel Construction, Livingston," RAC.

Wilhelm, John. *John Wilhelm's Guide to Mexico*, 3rd ed. New York: McGraw-Hill: 1966.

Wilkinson, Paul F. *Tourism Policy and Planning: Case Studies from the Commonwealth Caribbean*, 19–42, 49–53. Elmsford, N.Y.: Cognizant Communication, 1997.

Willy, J. Knight. "Continental Hilton." *Hotel Monthly*, March 1957.

Winks, Robin W. *Laurance S. Rockefeller: Catalyst for Conservation*. Washington, D.C.: Island Press, 1997.

Wise, T. A. "Global Hosts: U.S. Hotelkeepers Are Stepping up Invasion of Foreign Cities." *Wall Street Journal*, January 19, 1954.

Index

Evan R. Ward is director of International Programs at the University of North Alabama in Florence. As associate professor, he also teaches history courses on Latin America, tourism, and consumer culture.

DATE DUE
